PRAISE FOR
Simon Kuper's *SOCCER AGAINST THE ENEMY*

WINNER OF THE WILLIAM HILLS SPORTS BOOK OF THE
YEAR AWARD.

Voted best book on soccer ever by *Four Four Two* magazine

Voted as one of the TOP 50 books on sport by the *Observer* newspaper

"The best from the last few years."
—Nick Hornby, author *Fever Pitch* and *About A Boy*

"It probably won't be long before Americans discover the decade's worth of
smart British books about the culture, political history and sociology of the
game, like Simon Kuper's *Soccer Against the Enemy*."
—*New York Times Book Review*

"An inspiration."
—Franklin Foer, author *How Soccer Explains the World*

"*How Soccer Explains the World* is a good and largely interesting read, but
based on the failings that I found within its pages, I find it hard to recommend. A better choice for an interested reader would be Simon Kuper's
Soccer Against the Enemy."
—Roger Holland, *Pop Matters*

"If you like [soccer] read it. If you don't like [soccer] read it."
—*The Times* (London)

"Highly entertaining."
—*Financial Times*

"A terrific book."
—*The Guardian*

ALSO BY
SiMON KUPER

Ajax, the Dutch, the War

SOCCER AGAINST THE ENEMY

How the World's Most Popular Sport Starts and Stops Wars,
Fuels Revolutions, and Keeps Dictators in Power

SiMON KUPER

NATION BOOKS
NEW YORK

SOCCER AGAINST THE ENEMY
*How the World's Most Popular Sport Starts and Stops Wars, Fuels Revolutions,
and Keeps Dictators in Power*

First published by The Orion Publishing Group, London.

Published by
Nation Books
An Imprint of Avalon Publishing Group, Inc.
245 West 17th Street, 11th Floor
New York, NY 10011

AVALON
publishing group incorporated

Nation Books is a co-publishing venture of the Nation Institute and Avalon
Publishing Group Incorporated.

Library of Congress Cataloging-in-Publication Data

ISBN-10: 1-56025-878-0
ISBN-13: 978-1-56025-878-0

9 8 7 6 5 4 3 2

Book design by Maria E. Torres

Printed in the United States of America
Distributed by Publishers Group West

To my family,
and to the memory of Petra van Rhede

CONTENTS

ACKNOWLEDGMENTS

THIS BOOK COULD ONLY have been written thanks to conversations with hundreds of people around the world. Many others acted as interpreters (some paid, others not) or as contacts. Some simply helped me buy train tickets—an act of mercy in Russia. I thank all the people I met and have quoted in the text, and also:

- in England, Debbie Ashton and Francisco Panizza; at Amnesty International, Henry Atmore, Rachel Baxter, Joe Boyle, Nancy Branko, Jordi Busquet, Rachel Cooke, Shilpa Deshmukh, Gillian Harling, Matt Mellor, Simon Pennington, Celso Pinto, Keir Radnedge, Gavin Rees, Katrine Sawyer, and Simon Veksner
- in Scotland, Raymond Boyle, Mark Dingwall, Gerry Dunbar, Jimmy Johnstone, Mark Leishman, and John Scott
- in Northern Ireland, Thomas "D.J." McCormick and his family, and John McNair
- in Ireland, John Lenihan, and Marina and Pauline Millington-Ward
- in Holland, Willem Baars, Rutger, and Jan Maarten Slagter, the staffs of *Nieuwe Revu* and *Vrij Nederland*
- in Germany, the Klopfleisch family, and the Hertha BSC fan club
- in the Baltics, the Norwegian Information Office in Vilnius and Markus Luik
- in Russia, Julia Artemova, Ana Borodatova, Vladimir Shinkaryov, Mark Rice-Oxley, Carey Scott, Sasha, and Irina
- in Ukraine, Peter Lavrenjuk

- in the Czech Republic, Václav Hubinger, Karel Novotny, Jan Tobias, and the Press and Information Center for Foreign Journalists
- in Hungary, Krisztina Fenyö and Gabor Vargyas
- in Italy, the Herrera family, Isabelle Grenier, and Virginie
- in Spain, Elisabet Almeda, Salvador Giner, and Nuria
- in Cameroon, the staff at the British Embassy
- in South Africa, all my relatives, Raymond Hack, Doctor Khumalo, Steve Komphela, and Krish Naidoo
- in Botswana, the Masire family
- in the USA, Michelle Akers-Stahl, Joy Bifeld, Sue Carpenter, Julie Faudi, Duncan Irving, Leo Kuper, Dean Linke, Celestin Monga, John Polis, Michael Whitney, Mike Woitalla, Ade, Ruth Aguilera, Andres Cavelier, Chris Cowles, Frank dell'Apa, Gus Martins, Meghan Oates, Derek Rae, Kristen Upchurch and Bea Vidacs
- in Argentina, Rafael Bloom, Estela de Carlotto, Peter Hamilton, Fabian Lupi, Nathaniel C. Nash, Daniel and Pablo Rodriguez Sierra, and Eric Weil
- and in Brazil, Ricardo Benzaquem, Cunca Bocayuva Cunha, Marcio Moreira Alves, Adam Reid, and Herbert de Souza.

I also want to thank Peter Gordon and Nick Lord of Yorkshire Television. In 1990 they produced a marvelous TV series on soccer around the world called *The Greatest Game*, and they let me take what I wanted from their enormous files of facts and interviews. I took a lot.

I owe a particular debt to Bill Massey and Caroline Oakley, my editors at Orion.

PREFACE TO THE U.S. EDITION

I HAVE NEVER MANAGED to stop writing about soccer. After finishing this book in 1993, I had intended to devote my journalistic life to important subjects like economics. Those whom the gods want to punish, they give what they ask for: I soon became currency correspondent of the *Financial Times*, writing a daily report on the doings of the dollar, yen, and Deutschmark. After two years, tedium forced me to quit, and I became a "world football" columnist at the *Observer* newspaper.

Over the years I drifted back to the *Financial Times*, where I now sometimes get to write about important things, like the British Conservative Party or the vote for "Greatest Belgian," but I can't leave soccer alone. My weekly sports column in the newspaper often reads like an update of *Football* (and now *Soccer) Against the Enemy.*

Recently I have written about Silvio Berlusconi, prime minister of Italy and owner of AC Milan; about the bid of his former player George Weah, to become president of Liberia; and about the night out I had in Rotterdam with a German and a Dutch player from the 1974 World Cup final, which showed me that the two countries are patching up old rifts. The new chapter in this edition, "Global Game, Global Jihad," is partly taken from my *Financial Times* and *Observer* columns, though some of it came from an article in *The New York Times Magazine*.

Soccer matters as much today as when I first made the journey that became this book, but it now matters in different ways. For a start, the world when I left England, as a twenty-two year old, by ferry in July 1992, with a typewriter in my backpack, was a much bigger place. Before the Internet, it was hard to find out much about Ukraine or Cameroon, say, without going there.

Because these countries were so isolated, they were much more different from one another than they are today. Certainly their soccer cultures were more distinctive then. When I travel around the world watching soccer now, I notice the same things repeated everywhere: the face-painted fans, the Manchester United shirts, and, increasingly, an identical style of play. The Dutch, English, Americans, and Cameroonians are all converging on the same kind of soccer.

In Europe, soccer no longer sets tribe against tribe the way it used to. When I wrote this book, soccer stadiums were still the place to uncover western Europe's suppressed ethnic, religious, regional, and class tensions.

Then in Glasgow in 1999 I met a Celtic fan who taught me that things were changing. When "Catholic" Celtic played their "Protestant" rivals, the Rangers, this man shouted outrageous abuse at the "Prods." He had even named his second son for every member of the 1967 European Cup-winning Celtic team ("the subs wouldn't fit on the birth certificate," he grumbled). It sounded like the usual story—except that this man was married to a Protestant. While his wife was recovering in hospital, he had sneaked to the town hall to name his child. When she found out, she kicked a door down in frustration.

He showed me a picture of his son at two days old, dressed in the Celtic home shirt, in the arms of his older brother who was wearing the Celtic away shirt. "Put it this way," said the father triumphantly, "the boy will never play for Rangers."

To this man, who had no problem with Protestants, Celtic vs. Rangers was no longer about religion. Nor is it to many other Celtic or Rangers fans: almost half of Glaswegians who marry do so across religious divides. Few go to church any longer. In other words, though Celtic and Rangers fans still shout sectarian slogans at soccer matches, they usually no longer mean them.

And this is becoming true all over Western Europe. When I wrote this book, soccer conflicts in Europe still reflected religious or class or regional passions. Just as FC Barcelona used to stand for Catalan nationalism, the Milan-Inter derby match once set the city's migrant working classes against the local middle classes, while the Dutch in 1988 still carried around a war trauma about Germans. But today, these passions are weaker. Europeans are ceasing to believe in God, class divides have narrowed, and it is hard to be quite so fanatical about your region now that countries like Spain are decentralized democracies and regions like Catalonia could choose independence if they really wanted.

So when Barcelona fans wave Catalan flags, or Glaswegian fans sing sectarian songs, they are simply using traditional symbols to express a soccer rivalry. For that Glaswegian father, his feelings for Celtic were stronger than any sectarian sentiment he brought to the game. What you hear in European soccer stadiums today is no longer the reflection of other passions. Rather, soccer has become a cause in itself.

Outside Europe, however, the tribal divides survive. The rule of thumb is that the less free a country is, the more soccer matters, and it therefore matters very much indeed in North Africa, the Middle East, and the Gulf. The new chapter at the end of this book describes the game's appeal to Osama bin Laden and the rest of the region.

In the U.S. over the last twelve years, soccer has continued its onward march. When I wrote this book, I still had to convince my British readers that Americans played soccer; now probably more Americans do so regularly than western Europeans. At first glance, though, the U.S. would still seem to be immune to the social resonances of soccer, given that the game struggles even to make the papers here. The average Major League Soccer match draws only 15,000 people, and no American player is a household name.

"Small" soccer thrives in the U.S. without "big" soccer. This looks like a paradox. Indeed, some proponents of the American game fear the situation is unsustainable, and that grassroots soccer will die unless the MLS takes off. In fact, however, soccer has succeeded as a suburban kids' game in the U.S. precisely because there is no big American pro league. Soccer appeals to many suburbanites because it is free of certain aspects of modern America: it is not violent, not male dominated, and not peopled by scary characters. Instead of Charles Barkley and Allen Iverson, the MLS features lots of white college boys drawing modest salaries. The league's minimum wage is $28,000, which is rather different from the NBA. Nobody in the MLS has shot his limo driver yet.

Soccer in America has come to be seen as a protective white mother's heaven, suitable for children of both genders. The U.S. is the only country where the women's national soccer team is better known than the men's. In many American towns (or "communities," in the current euphemism), soccer is seen as more appropriate for kids than for adults.

All this has helped soccer in the U.S. become shorthand for happy prosperous families. It has accordingly received the blessing of the advertising industry. A typical ad, which once might have taken baseball as a symbol of family values, now features a beaming child kicking a ball, with a text that begins: "While Jessica takes an afternoon off to focus on scoring goals, her parents' financial advisor at Merrill Lynch focuses on meeting her family's goals." Oscar Goodman, the veteran mob attorney who was elected mayor of Las Vegas in 1999, ran a television campaign ad that showed pictures of his four children and ended with a shot of him and his wife Carolyn, above the caption: "We never missed a soccer game."

Perhaps the greatest change in global soccer since I wrote this book has been the rise of the women's game. Banned by the English Football Association for much of the twentieth century, women's soccer is now reportedly the fastest growing sport in the world, with 30 million players. Yet except for brief flurries in the U.S. during women's World Cups, few people follow it. WUSA, the American women's pro soccer league, closed in 2003 due to lack of interest.

It's a paradox: women play soccer, but not even many women want to watch them doing so. Generally, few men or women follow women's sport. In western newspapers, the sports pages are the *de facto* "men's pages": studies consistently show that more than 90 percent of the space on them is devoted to men.

When women's sport does get covered, it's usually in one of three ways. Most commonly, it's written about as a beauty pageant: the so-called "Kournikova syndrome." Then there is a genre of serious "boosterish" articles, which run something like this: "Women's soccer has always been ignored. But Jane Smith is a brilliant striker and works just as hard as the men although she earns no money." This kind of propaganda is boring to both sexes. Otherwise, women athletes attract attention only when they compete against men, as when the Mexican player Maribel Dominguez tried to join a men's professional team.

It may be that a male journalistic establishment doesn't give female sports a chance; that people would follow women's soccer if only the biased media covered it. However, Kathryn Jay, sports historian at Barnard College in New York, believes that few readers want more coverage of women's sports. "Many women readers are more interested in men's sports than in women's sports," she told me. "Sports for generations were a way to understand masculine identity, to become a man. Women's sports never made it onto the landscape, except maybe tennis and golf." Only now is this starting to change, Jay says.

Even now, whereas men often look to athletes as role models, role models for women tend to be actresses. Just as men follow the antics of sports stars, many women track the lives of Jennifer Aniston or Madonna and subconsciously try to learn from their ups and downs. It seems that sport without role models loses much of its appeal.

* * *

Though the U.S. remains a strange bird in the world of soccer, it has at least joined one new international trend: the rise of the sports politician. When I finished writing this book in September 1993, the type barely existed. But six months later, the Italian television magnate Silvio Berlusconi became the world's first prime minister to emerge from soccer.

In 1986 Berlusconi had taken over AC Milan, then still recovering from a bribery scandal. He turned it into a wealthy organized and modern team, which in May 1989 won the European Cup.

Even on that night of triumph, anyone could see that the man's ambitions extended further. I once listened to Frank Rijkaard, a Dutchman then playing for Milan, describe the banquet that followed that first European trophy. All Milan's players, directors, and hangers-on were already sitting at their tables when the doors of the hall opened and Berlusconi walked in. Practically everyone rose from their seats to applaud, and as *il presidente* strode beaming from table to table, people jumped forward to grasp his hand.

But as Berlusconi approached the table of his three great Dutch soccer players, he stopped smiling: the Dutch had remained seated. As Rijkaard tells it, Marco van Basten kept eating, while Ruud Gullit kept talking. The Dutch just don't do deference. Poor Berlusconi didn't know how to react. It was several agonizing seconds before Rijkaard took pity on him and half-rose to shake his hand. The president's face had been saved.

This was the psychological profile of a man who wanted to lead a country. In 1993 Berlusconi founded *Forza Italia*, a political party named after a soccer chant. Part of his pitch to voters was that he would transform the country as he had AC Milan. Italy, recovering from its own bribery scandal, the "Tangentopoli" affair, longed to be organized, rich, and respected in Europe. Berlusconi became prime minister for seven months, returned to the job in 2001, and as I write, is about to become the first postwar Italian prime minister to serve out his full term.

In matters of sport, George W. Bush is an American Berlusconi. Bush had ended the 1980s as nothing but the middle-aged son of the American president. After a mediocre college career, he avoided the Vietnam War, failed to get elected to Congress, failed in the oil business, and generally drank a lot. In 1989 he reportedly confided to a friend: "You know I could run for governor [of Texas] but I'm basically a media creation. I've never done anything."

Then Bush and some friends bought the Texas Rangers baseball club. He became managing director, a largely honorary post that involved long hours in the stands handing out signed baseball cards of himself. The Rangers began winning, Bush became a well-known Texan, and in 1994 he ran for governor on something of a "baseball ticket." Asked in the campaign about his career, he tended to talk about baseball. There was not much else to say. Crucially, too, the game helped him seem a regular guy. "I'm not out of touch," he said during the campaign. "I've worked with working people every day at my ballpark." He was duly elected governor, and proceeded from there.

Other American sports politicians include Jesse Ventura, the wrestler turned governor of Minnesota, Jack Kemp, the quarterback who made it to Republican candidate for vice president in 1996, and lately Arnold Schwarzenegger.

The Pakistani cricketer-turned-politician Imran Khan, brandishing a *Newsweek* article about a Koran being flushed down the toilet in the Guantanamo Bay prison camp, unleashed anti-American riots in several Muslim countries in May 2005. But in most of the world, soccer politicians do best. Mauricio Macri, president of the Boca Juniors club, has become one of Argentina's leading politicians. In November 2005, George Weah made it to the final runoff in the Liberian presidential elections, where he lost to Ellen Johnson-Sirleaf. Expect more soccer stars to follow.

The reason is that traditional political parties are in decline in many countries. At the same time, more countries are electing their leaders: there have never been so many democracies. Elected leaders are therefore increasingly emerging from outside parties. To emerge as a leader it helps to be rich, famous, and yet be regarded as a man of the people.

There are several ways of achieving this. The impeached former Philippine president Joseph Estrada did it by acting, Bulgaria's former prime minister by being the country's King Simeon II, but the surest path, increasingly, is through sport. This is because the growing number of TV seats around the world shows ever more sport—and most of all soccer. In this era of what might be called cable-ocracy, games are the new political campaigns. We are going to see more Berlusconis. I will keep watching.

CHAPTER 1

CHASING SOCCER AROUND THE WORLD

NO ONE KNOWS HOW many soccer fans there are. World Cup USA 1994, Inc., put out a booklet claiming that the TV audience for the Italian World Cup was 25.6 billion (five times the world's population), and that 31 billion are expected to watch the American World Cup.

These figures may be meaningless. For any recent World Cup final, you can find viewing figures that disagree by billions, and the same booklet claims that Striker, the World Cup's canine mascot, will have been seen one trillion times by the end of 1994. One trillion precisely? Are they sure?

But for certain, as the booklet states, "soccer is the most popular sport in the world." They say in Naples that when a man has money, he first buys himself something to eat, then goes to the soccer match, and then sees if he has anything left to find a place to live. The Brazilians say that even the smallest village has a church and a soccer field—"well, not always a church, but certainly a soccer field." More people in the world go to church than to soccer matches, but otherwise there is no public pursuit to match the game. This book is about its place in the world.

When a game matters to billions of people it ceases to be just a game. Soccer is never just soccer: it helps make wars and revolutions, and it fascinates mafias and dictators. I began writing this book with vague thoughts about how this works. I knew that when

Celtic play the Rangers in Glasgow, Ulster grows tenser, and that over half the Dutch population took to the streets to celebrate when Holland beat Germany in 1988. I had read that the Brazilian team gave the military government a few more years in power by winning the 1970 World Cup (this turned out to be nonsense), and that the Nigerian–Biafran war ceased for a day to allow Pelé, then visiting the country, to play a match. We have all heard of the Soccer War between El Salvador and Honduras.

My first question, then, was how soccer affects the life of a country. My second was how the life of a country affects its soccer. What, in other words, makes Brazil play like Brazil, England like England, Holland like Holland? Michel Platini told *L'Equipe*, "A soccer team represents a way of being, a culture." Is that so?

I began this book as an outsider to the world of professional soccer. I had lived and played and watched the game in Holland, England, Germany and the USA, and had written about it in magazines, but I had never sat in a press box or spoken to a professional soccer player. For this book, I traveled around the world watching games and talking to soccer managers, politicians, mafiosi, journalists, and other fans, sometimes even to the odd player. The big names scared me. Interviewing Roger Milla, for instance, I could barely look up from my list of prepared questions. Slowly I grew less starstruck and now, ten months on from the Maracaña, sitting at home in London, I almost miss the soccer life.

I traveled for nine months, visiting 22 countries, from Ukraine to Cameroon to Argentina to Scotland. It was a disorientating time. There are now several languages in which I can more or less say, "I am an English journalist," but in Lithuanian and Estonian I never progressed as far as that. I relied a lot on friends, and on interpreters when I could afford them.

Then there was the moving about. Once, I flew home from Los Angeles, spent 48 hours in London, flew to Buenos Aires, from there to Rio, returned to London a month later, spent another 48 hours there, flew to Dublin, took a bus up to Ulster, and then the ferry to Glasgow. I arrived in Scotland a week after flying out of Rio, and five days later I was home again. My small budget—£5,000 for the whole year—made the trip even more complex than the itinerary suggests.

Traveling the world, missing the English winter, and watching soccer was sometimes bearable, but I never lived in luxury. All right: I did in the old USSR, where anyone with Western money is a millionaire who can take taxis, but as soon as I returned to the West I was back in youth hostels. Not that I minded, of course, but I worried what people in soccer would think. Soccer directors, managers, and players are rich, and they respect wealth in others. They were always asking me which hotel I was staying in, and wondering whether my jacket was ripped across the seam because I liked it that way. Josef Chovanec of Sparta Prague asked me for £300 for an interview. They all have expensive hairstyles—which is why they need to earn so much money—and hanging around them, I tended to feel unclean.

But wherever I went I was told, "Soccer and politics! You've come to the right place here." Soccer turned out to matter rather more than I had thought. I found a soccer club that exports nuclear materials and gold, and another that is setting up its own university. Mussolini and Franco understood the game's significance, and so do Silvio Berlusconi, Nelson Mandela, and President Paul Biya of Cameroon. Because of soccer, Nikolai Starostin was sent to the Soviet gulags, but it was soccer that saved his life there. He was amazed, he writes, that these "camp bosses, arbiters of the life and death of thousands upon thousands of human beings . . . were so benevolent to anything concerning soccer. Their unbridled power over human lives was nothing compared to the power of soccer over them." Enough has been written about soccer hooligans. Other fans are much more dangerous.

CHAPTER 2

SOCCER iS WAR

THINGS MAY CHANGE WHEN Serbia first plays Croatia, but for the moment the greatest grudge match in European soccer is Holland vs. Germany.

It all began in Hamburg, on a summer night in 1988, when the Dutch beat the Germans 2–1 in the semifinal of the European Championships. Back in Holland, the staid nation surprised itself: nine million Dutchmen, over 60 percent of the population, came out onto the streets to celebrate. Though a Tuesday night, it was the largest public gathering since the Liberation. "It feels as though we've won the war at last," a former Resistance fighter said on TV.

Ger Blok, a 58-year-old Dutchman, heard the news in Tegucicalpa, where he was managing the Honduran national team. He responded by running through the streets carrying a Dutch flag. "Hysterical, intensely happy," he said. "The next day I was ashamed of my laughable behavior."

In the Leidseplein square, Amsterdammers threw bicycles (their own?) into the air and shouted, "Hurray, we've got our bikes back!" The Germans, in the biggest bicycle theft in history, had confiscated all Dutch bicycles during the Occupation.

"When Holland scores I dance through the room," said Professor Dr L. de Jong, a small gray man who has spent the last 45 years writing the official history of the Netherlands in World War II in umpteen volumes. "I'm crazy about soccer," he revealed. "And

4

what these boys have done! Of course it's got to do with the war. Strange that people deny that."

Willem van Hanegem, who had played for Holland against Germany in the World Cup final of 1974, told the magazine *Vrij Nederland*: "In general I can't say that Germans are my best friends. Beckenbauer was OK. He seemed arrogant, but that was just because of his style of play. Everything was easy for him." "What's wrong with them?" asked the journalist. "Well, they've got the wrong ancestors, of course," answered Van Hanegem. The Dutch word *fout*, meaning "wrong," also has the specific meaning of "wrong in the war." "That's not their fault," said the journalist, who was playing the devil's advocate. "Maybe not," Van Hanegem replied, "but the fact remains." He had lost his father and two brothers to a wartime bomb, while *Vrij Nederland*, which means "Free Holland," had started life as an underground newspaper in World War II. "A shame the Japs don't play soccer," it lamented, largely in jest.

It turned out that Hamburg had purged frustrations all over the world. At the press conference after the match, 150 foreign journalists gave the Dutch manager Michels a standing ovation. A reporter for the Dutch newspaper *De Telegraaf* (wrong in the war) wrote that an Israeli journalist in the press box had told him he was supporting Holland, and had added, "You understand why."

Professional soccer players are always polite about their opponents, because they know that they will run into them again somewhere. But the Dutch were not polite about the Germans. Ronald Koeman was furious that they had offered no congratulations after the match. He said that Olaf Thon, with whom he had swapped shirts, was the only nice guy among them. Rinus Michels, the Dutch manager and the man who coined the phrase "Soccer is war," admitted to "an extra feeling of satisfaction for reasons which I don't want to sum up now." Coming out of the tunnel for the second half to jeers from the German crowd, he had raised a dignified middle finger. Arnold Mühren said that beating Germany meant the same as Ireland beating England, but that was weak indeed.

A few months later, a Dutch book of poetry appeared under the title, *Holland–Germany Soccer Poetry*. Some of the poems are by professional poets, and others by professional soccer players.

> the Germans wanted to be world champions
> Ever since I can remember
> and before that
> the Germans wanted to be world champions

wrote A.J. Heerma van Voss. The Rotterdam poet Jules Deelder, in a work called *21–6–88*, finished with these lines on Van Basten's goal:

> Rose cheering from their graves.
> Those who fell
> Rose cheering from their graves.

Hans Boskamp wrote:

> And then there was that unbelievably beautiful
> Dumb generalizations about a people
> Or a nation, I despise.
> A sense of proportion is very
> Dear to me.

> Sweet revenge, I thought, does not exist
> Or lasts only briefly
> And then there was that unbelievably beautiful
> Tuesday evening in Hamburg.

The poems by players are mixed in quality. The worst are by Arnold Mühren, Johan Neeskens, and Wim Suurbier. Jan Wouters' effort is the most sophisticated: blank verse with enjambements in cliché-free language. Ruud Gullit's poem, two lines long and untranslatable, is the best by any player, and one of the best in the whole collection. Johnny Rep's poem ends with:

> That new shirt is only really worth
> P.S.
> That new shirt is only really worth
> Wiping your bum with.

The poet is referring to Holland's foul, tiger-striped shirts, but also to the admission Ronald Koeman made after the match: that he had used the German shirt given him by his friend Thon as toilet paper. Almost all the poems make reference to the war.

It is tempting to think that Van Basten (who refuses to speak German in interviews) unleashed the hidden traumas of 43 postwar years by scoring in Hamburg, but he did not. The war has less to do than one might think with European soccer's greatest rivalry. Before Hamburg, few Dutchmen felt strongly about Germans.

Certainly there was distaste. I lived in Holland for ten years, in Leiden near the North Sea, and I could see that our German tourists were not greatly popular. "How do the Germans celebrate the invasion of Europe?" "By doing it again every summer." But I also remember that when England played West Germany in 1982 most of the teenage boys in my class wanted Germany to win. Jaap de Groot's poem in *Holland–Germany* recalls that not only he but the whole world mourned the German defeat in the World Cup final of 1966. Even the World Cup final of 1974 passed off calmly, though the war was then still quite fresh. Van Hanegem did leave the field in tears, and the match meant more to him than just any old World

Cup final, but the mood of 1988 was absent. In 1974, the players of both teams seemed of a kind. Beckenbauer and Johan Cruyff, the two captains, were friends, and Rep and Paul Breitner thwarted the FIFA ruling against shirt-swapping on the pitch by trading jackets and ties at the post-match banquet. Jan Jongbloed, the elderly Dutch keeper, wrote in his diary afterwards: "A short disappointment which slowly passed into a being-satisfied-with-silver."

The euphoria after Hamburg took even the Dutch by surprise. The national transformation that occurred that day (June 21st, to be precise) is best observed in Jongbloed, who said on the day before the match that any feelings between Dutch and Germans had evaporated. The day after, on behalf of the 1974 team, he sent the 1988 team a telegram that read: "We have been released from our suffering." After Hamburg, whenever Holland met Germany the Dutch erupted.

It seems that on the evening of Hamburg, Dutch views of Germans changed for the worse. The evidence supports this. In 1993, the Netherlands Institute of International Relations "Clingendael" produced a report on Dutch teenagers' attitudes to Germans. Asked to rank EC countries in order of affection, the teenagers placed Germany bottom. (The Republic of Ireland finished second last, probably because the Dutch think that that is where the sectarian murders are. Britain came third last. Spain was the most popular nation after Holland, with Luxembourg in third place.) The report showed that Dutch teenagers hate Germans far more than most adult Dutchmen do. Only those who lived through the Occupation are as antagonistic. "There is reason for concern," the report concluded. A change had taken place, and its cause lay in soccer itself.

In his poem "How Deeply It Runs," Erik van Muiswinkel wonders how to explain good and evil to his daughter:

Look, darling, look at the TV:

Adam, Eve, apple?

Hitler, Florence Nightingale?

I don't know, I'm agnostic.

And preferably amoral.

Good and Evil

Look, darling, look at the TV:

Orange, Gullit, White.

White, Matthäus, Black.

The German players were evil and the Dutch were good. Or: the Germans were German and the Dutch were Dutch.

This had become plain long before kickoff. *Bild*, Germany's answer to the *Sun*, placed a reporter in the Dutch hotel to dig out undermining gossip. In 1974, before Holland and Germany met in the World Cup final, *Bild* had run a story about goings-on in the Dutch camp, under the headline, "Cruyff, Champagne and Naked Girls." Cruyff was distraught, Germany won the final, and the Dutch captain decided to skip the 1978 World Cup. In 1988, to keep out of *Bild*'s way, the Dutch barely left their hotel rooms. Even so, there was no peace to be had. Dutch FA officials had blithely agreed to a German request for the two teams to swap hotels, and so the Dutch had ended up in the noisy Intercontinental Hotel in the center of town.

At 1 A.M. on the night before the match, a German journalist rang Gullit, the Dutch captain, in his room to ask which club he had played for before joining AC Milan. Later that night the phone rang again, and, as Gullit reported, "someone made a ridiculous remark." Then a German journalist knocked at his door.

The next day, as the two sides inspected the pitch before the match, the Dutch players noticed their opponents sneaking awed glances at Gullit. When the German fullback Andy Brehme, who knew Gullit slightly, went up to talk to him, the other Germans gaped at their teammate. "They're definitely worse than us," said Ronald Koeman. But he added gloomily, "It's when you have to play them that it gets difficult." We (my sympathies were not with the Germans) shared his foreboding.

In the first half, Holland played some of the best soccer seen in Europe that decade. They treated the Germans as if they were Luxembourgeois, but failed to score. The Germans came out for the second half with a new tactic: kicking Dutchmen. The Dutch retaliated and the match grew even tenser. Then Jürgen Klinsmann fell over Frank Rijkaard's legs—it would flatter the clumsy Klinsmann to say that he dove—and Ion Igna, the Rumanian referee, gave a penalty. "Were the Rumanians wrong in the War?" a reporter from *Het Parool* found himself wondering. (They were.) Matthäus, grey, po-faced and a diver, scored. Germany 1–0 up thanks to a lucky penalty, taken by their most German player: we had seen it all before.

But minutes later, Marco van Basten collapsed in the German box and Igna gave a penalty. UEFA should have spotted the referee's deficient powers of observation before, for when they had mistakenly given him and his linesmen plane tickets for Stuttgart instead of Hamburg, the trio dutifully flew to the wrong city. They reached Hamburg only just in time to distort the game.

Then in the 87th minute, in the phase of a match when Germany typically score the winning goal, Van Basten scored. "Justice," as Gullit said, had unexpectedly been done. Don Howe had a heart attack watching the match, at which point I do not know.

Holland vs. Germany, good vs. evil. Our shirts were bright, if unfortunately striped; the Germans wore black and white. We had several players of color, including our captain, and our fans wore Gullit-hats with rasta hair; their players were all white and their fans made monkey noises. Our players were funny and natural; *A Thousand Years of German Humor* is the shortest book in the world, and

Rudi Völler had that absurd perm. Our players were individuals; the Germans could barely be told apart by their numbers. They dived. Two days after the match, a German journalist confronted Ronald Koeman with a statement he had purportedly made about hatred of the German people. "I never said that," responded Koeman. "It's about players in the German team who constantly ask the referee to give yellow cards, who provoke, roll on the ground for nothing— that irritates us." But in a way the journalist was right: these were ancient German customs Koeman was insulting.

The two teams, in short, summed up the way the Dutch wanted to see themselves and the way they saw the Germans. We were like Ruud Gullit and they were like Lothar Matthäus. There were obvious flaws in this notion, and so, to make it fit, the Dutch briefly forgot their own discipline, their own staidness, and their own intolerance of Turks and Moroccans and Surinamese like Gullit. "We should really explain to the Germans that we hate all foreigners," suggested *Vrij Nederland*, but no one did. The Germans were evil and we were good.

The contrast was perfect in 1988, which is why Holland vs. Germany never used to be a grudge match: never before had our players been so much more noble than theirs. True, in 1974 Holland was the best team in the world. ("I liked very much what my chauffeur said. He said, 'The best team didn't win.' the Dutch Prince Bernhard, a German who fought in the Dutch Resistance, told Cruyff after the final.) True, even then the Dutch were individuals. But the Germans of 1974 had charm too: Hamburg, by contrast, was World War II all over again.

Germany occupied Holland for five years in the war, and as the Dutch tell it, they were all in the Resistance. Naturally then, on the night of Hamburg the decades seemed to fall away. The Germans even still wore eagles on their chests. The Dutch players were the Resistance, and the Germans the Wehrmacht—these comparisons are absurd, but they occurred to most Dutchmen. It was Gullit who noted after Hamburg that though the Dutch had played as dirtily as the Germans, the stern Dutch press had for once made no complaints. (Never before had Dutch journalists been seen hugging players and sobbing, "Thank you.") The fouls were sanctioned, even blessed, because they were acts of Resistance. Here is *Vrij Nederland* interviewing the full-back Berry van Aerle:

> "In the match against Germany, you pulled the injured Völler's hair."
>
> "Did I pull his hair? I can't remember that. I patted him on the head. I didn't pull his hair."
>
> "No?"
>
> "No. I patted him on the head and he got angry. I don't know why either. He reacted quite strangely, suddenly jumped up to chase after me, but when Ronald stopped him he fell again and started rolling about. I thought that was strange behavior."

Both the journalist and Van Aerle knew what really happened, but a Resistance fighter never discusses his heroics. He hints at them, using irony, which Germans cannot understand. As Van Basten said of the Dutch penalty: "Kohler brought me off balance, after which the referee pointed to the spot. And then I just had to bow to his judgment." The Dutch journalists laughed.

But *Wehrmacht* against Resistance was not the only metaphor for the match. Hamburg was also a reversal of the invasion: an orange-clad Dutch army drove its cars into Germany and defeated the inhabitants. (In the era of regular England vs. Scotland games, the Scots would come down and conquer London for the day.) The Germans, typically, had allotted the Dutch just 6,000 tickets, but even so the Volkspark stadium was full of Dutchmen. "It would have been better to have played in Germany," commented Frank Mill, the German striker, in what was really quite a good joke, for a German. People in Holland sang:

In 1940 they came
In 1940 they came
In 1988 we came,
Holadiay,
Holadio.

Hamburg was not only the Resistance we never quite offered but also the battle we never quite won. It reminded us of the war in yet another way: briefly, after Hamburg, all Dutchmen, from captain of the national team to fan to prime minister, were equal. The players set the tone. After the match they danced the conga and sang, "We're Going to Munich," a fan's song, and "We're Not Going Home Yet," a popular drinking song, while at the Intercontinental, Prince Johan-Friso, the queen's second son, joined in for, *"O wat zijn die Duitsers stil,"* the Dutch version of "Can you hear the Germans sing?" Gullit said he would have liked to have been with the crowds on the Leidseplein square in Amsterdam: "After all, you can hardly have a proper party in Germany." He coined the noun *bobo* to describe a useless official in a blazer, and the word has passed into the language. Every day now, people in Holland call each other *bobo*.

As we were egalitarian, the Germans had to be arrogant. "The way those guys treat you, a colleague, is unacceptable. If they meet you in a corridor one meter wide they can't even summon the decency to greet you," complained Hans van Breukelen, the Dutch goalkeeper.

True to type, the Germans completely (but completely) missed the moral of the match. Even Beckenbauer, the good German, who boarded the Dutch bus after the match to congratulate his opponents, called the defeat "undeserved." (He then weakened his argument by adding, "But on the other hand Holland played so well that I can hardly detract from their success.") Matthäus thought the referee should have added on more stoppage time. Völler said weirdly:

"The Dutchmen have been praised into heaven as though they came from another planet." (Not from another planet! From another country.) Only *Bild* got it right: *"Holland Super,"* said their headline.

The two nations next played each other in Munich, in October 1988. The German players (newspaper readers to a man) met and decided not to exchange shirts after the match. In Rotterdam, in April 1989, a banner in the stadium likened Matthäus to Adolf Hitler.

Holland and Germany qualified for Italy, and met there in the second round. They always meet at World Cups and European Championships, or at least they do when Holland manages to qualify. In Milan, the Germans won 2–1, but that was the least of it. Rijkaard fouled Völler, who dived; the referee showed Rijkaard the yellow card, which meant that he would be suspended for the next match; Rijkaard spat at Völler, ran after him, and spat again. The whole world, the Netherlands apart, was disgusted. Both players were sent off, Völler for obscure reasons. There were riots along the Dutch–German border.

The spitting has been badly misinterpreted. People outside Holland seem to think that Rijkaard is a temperamental character, a kind of Dutch Paul Ince or Diego Maradona. In truth, he is one of the mildest soccer players around. So why did he spit?

Some of the Dutch players claim that Völler made racist remarks to him. Certainly, TV pictures show Völler shouting at Rijkaard after the initial foul. Völler claims he was asking, "Why did you foul me?," and just conceivably he was. But the main flaw in the German-as-Nazi theory is that Rijkaard disputes it: he insists Völler said nothing racist. Perhaps he is protecting Völler, or defusing the row. (Rijkaard, unlike many Dutch players, does not enjoy rows.) Perhaps he is telling the truth, and the Dutch players who accuse Völler are being hysterical. The Dutch press probed the spitting until Rijkaard said: "Looking back, it's really quite funny, isn't it?"

This was sacrilege. Here was the nation, trying to prove that Germans are racist and the Dutch good, and then Rijkaard goes and turns the whole thing into a joke! It turned out that he really meant it when he said he did not hate Germans. And the same is true of most Dutch West Indians.

Gullit, beyond all doubt, hates Germans. But then Gullit has a Dutch mother and a Dutch West Indian father, only found out that he was black when he was ten years old, and once caused a furor among Dutch West Indians by saying that he feels Dutch. Rijkaard is different. His father and Gullit's father came to Holland together, to play professional soccer, but Herman Rijkaard married a Dutch West Indian woman and Frank Rijkaard always knew he was black. Like Rijkaard, Stanley Menzo, Holland's third goalkeeper in 1990, born in Paramaribo, Suriname, said he could live with the German victory. "What bothered me most," Menzo added, "is that Aron Winter, Rijkaard and later Gullit too were whistled at a couple of times when they had the ball. On the other hand, I heard Dutchmen shouting all sorts of things at Germans. It's all absurd, but I'm powerless to stop it." The Dutch West Indians are out of this game. They spent the war in the Dutch West Indies, and Dutch patriotism is more likely to worry than enthuse them. When Rijkaard spat the general hysteria had plainly got to him, but he regretted it later. For him spitting was not Resistance, just plain bad manners.

All the same, the incident made the next Holland vs. Germany a bit tenser. The teams met on June 18, 1992, in Gothenburg, at the European Championships, and Ronald Koeman said it was the devil who had brought the two together again.

This time, Matthäus, the arch-German, was out injured. *De Telegraaf* complained that his stand-in, Andy Moller, was an unsatisfactory stand-in symbol, for "how can a true Dutchman decently hate a German who has even been rejected by his own country?" The Dutch fans managed somehow. It hardly mattered who played for

Germany. As Van Aerle said before the match: "Riedle, Doll, Klinsmann, what's the difference? They're all dangerous. All Germans are dangerous." And, he meant, they are all the same. Ten million Dutchmen watched the match, a new Dutch TV record, and the Ullevi stadium was packed with Dutchmen.

German fans were less interested. Holland vs. Germany had become special to them too, but not that special. After all, Holland was not the only country Hitler had invaded. The Dutch hysteria rather bewilders the Germans. It seems to them just another kind of racism, which, I suppose, it is. "What can my little daughter do about the fact that some people in the past hurt Jews?" *Bild* writer and former soccer manager Udo Lattek asked *Vrij Nederland*. Völler blamed the rivalry on "outsiders." "I've got nothing against Dutchmen," he insisted, missing the point again. "I've been to Amsterdam as a schoolboy." Beckenbauer said, "Matches against Holland have cost me years of my life. But I wouldn't have missed them for anything. Those matches always breathed soccer of class, emotion, and unprecedented tension. Soccer in its pure form." To Beckenbauer, the match is just a great derby: it's what soccer's all about. To the Dutch, it is a darker affair.

In Gothenburg, as the Dutch team were leaving the changing-room, Michels stopped them and said: "Gentlemen, what I'm going to say now I have never said before. You will score three goals today, our midfield players will score two, and the Germans will score either one or two. I wish you a pleasant match."

Rijkaard, playing in midfield, scored after two minutes, and two Germans threw a small fragmentation bomb into a Dutch nightclub, wounding three people who for some reason were not watching the match. The nightclub stands in the Dutch town of Kerkrade, on a street called the Nieuwstraat that starts in Holland and ends in Germany.

Then the Dutch lefthalf Rob Witschge scored from a free kick, his shot skidding under Riedle in the German wall, who jumped upwards and sideways. "You make plans for free kicks," Michels said later, "but you never know whether the players will stick to them. Fortunately, the Germans did." Klinsmann scored for Germany, and then Dennis Bergkamp, playing upfront for Holland, made it 3–1. With a couple of minutes to go, Michels and his assistant Dick Advocaat tried to bring on Peter Bosz for Wouters. Wouters refused to leave the pitch, and so did several other Dutch players. In the end the coaches had to take off meek young Bergkamp. "Dennis, we're giving the fans a chance to clap you," said Advocaat. Bosz had had to promise his brother not to swap his shirt with a German. The score stayed 3–1, as Michels had said it would. Holland vs. Germany activates supernatural powers.

After the match, at the border by Enschede, and in the Nieuwstraat in Kerkrade, Dutchmen and Germans pelted each other with beer glasses and stones. Five hundred citizens of Enschede crossed the border and started taking apart the German town of Gronau. It was as close to war as things get in the EC. Holland's highbrow daily, the *NRC Handelsblad*, complained that the young fans "were using an indignation to which they had no right, and that borrowed moment of indignation has to justify a moment of tasteless bad behavior"—but in fact World War II was not the issue. War, Resistance, and *Wehrmacht* were just words with which to say that our players were quintessentially Dutch and theirs typically German.

Thanks to the Scots, who beat the former Soviet Union 3–0, both Germany and Holland progressed to the semifinals. Holland had to play Denmark, and Germany Sweden, but both sides expected to reach the final. "I've always said we'd meet Germany twice in this tournament," Michels told the press. "The next time it will be difficult again."

Michels' nicknames are The Sphinx, The General, and The Bull. He is, then, no Ally MacLeod, hardly given to hubris, and yet he forgot that Holland had to beat Denmark in the semifinal first. So did everyone else in Holland. Several charter flights to the semifinal were annulled, as fans saved for the final against Germany. Against Denmark, whole sections of the stands stayed empty. Naturally the Dutch lost. They were just too arrogant. Peter Schmeichel, the Danish keeper, noted with rage that they barely bothered to slap hands when Bergkamp scored their first goal. After the game they were distraught: Germany had beaten Sweden to reach the final. "We've saved the Germans' skin. They're already world champions and now they'll get our title. This will give me sleepless nights," said Van Breukelen.

The Germans lost the final, and in Copenhagen, the Danish players and the crowd sang, *"Auf Wiedersehen, Deutschland."* They had been occupied too.

Holland vs. Germany will lose its edge soon. For a few years from 1988, Holland had the most glorious players in Europe and Germany some of the dullest. As Gullit, Rijkaard, Van Basten, Wouters and Ronald Koeman retire from international soccer, Germany will start to beat Holland easily. Perhaps our players will even cease to be better human beings than theirs. When that happens the Dutch will give up on Holland vs. Germany, and the Clingendael Institute will no longer need to worry.

CHAPTER 3

THE SOCCER DISSIDENT

I MOVED TO BERLIN in September 1990, ten months after the Wall fell. The city then had two big clubs, FC Berlin in the East and Hertha BSC in the West, and Helmut Klopfleisch had already moved from East to West.

FC Berlin had been called Dynamo Berlin. Before the Wall fell, they had played in the Jahn Stadium, ten minutes' walk from my first flat in East Berlin. The neighborhood, the Prenzlauer Berg, was one of the few in Berlin to have survived the Allied bombs, and was long since decrepit. The last repairmen had called in the 1920s, and in May 1945 the Red Army had had to fight for every street. My building was one of the few without bullet holes, but to make up for that, the window of the front door, a fine example of 1920s art deco, was broken in four places. The wind blew in—the peculiar air in Berlin means it always feels ten degrees colder than it is—and provided relief against the stench of cat urine.

On the landings you could listen to the noises from each flat: the arguments, the coffee being poured, and the coal shovelled. The tenants were usually all home: four of the seven breadwinners in the building were no longer winning bread, and the neighbor, once some species of bureaucrat, had become a cleaning woman. "If it was up to me they'd rebuild the Wall tomorrow," she liked to say. She had yet to lose the habit of calling East Berlin "Berlin."

Apart from mass unemployment, neo-Nazi graffiti, and the odd

19

Rumanian beggar with polio, East Berlin still looked like a Communist capital, and it always seemed to be November. The city is built in khaki, light brown, and endless shades of grey, and no joy is provided by the statues of stern socialist workers, which resemble nothing so much as the statues of Aryans they replaced. In the center of town Marx and Engels survive in stone: Marx sitting, Engels standing. Lenin would presumably be lying down. "Next time it will work out better," someone had scrawled on the front of the statue, and on the back: "We are sorry." It was an exciting time to be in Berlin. As an Eastern student magazine grumbled: "Hardly anything is as it used to be and, on the other hand, no one knows what it will become. The only thing that's certain is that it will change."

No one knew what Dynamo would become, but they had already changed their name and left the Jahn Stadium, where they could no longer afford the rent. The ground was the smartest building in the Prenzlauer Berg. It lay just yards from the old Wall, and whenever I passed it on my way West to make a phone call I marvelled. Its towering floodlights, twice the height of the stands and quite as gray, gave the ground the feel of a prison camp, which on matchdays it had been. To prevent escapes, soldiers had occupied the stand nearest the border during games. Crowds were small.

Dynamo was popularly known as the "Eleven *Schweine*." They were the least loved club in Europe, but they were also the most successful: between 1979 and 1988, they won the East German title ten times in a row.

Dynamo had been founded after the war with the expressed aim of keeping the East German league title in the capital. The club president until the revolution of 1989 was Erich Mielke, the feared octogenarian chief of the East German secret police, the Stasi. Mielke was known as Erich the Elder to distinguish him from Erich Honecker, leader of the GDR, who was Erich the Younger. (Honecker was only in his seventies.) Mielke loved his club and made all the best players in the GDR play for it. (One was Thomas Doll, now with Gazza at Lazio.) He also talked to referees, and Dynamo won lots of matches with penalties in the 95th minute.

In East Berlin, Union were the workers' club that Dynamo always aspired to be. The club's braver fans would intersperse their chants of "Iron Union" with *"Deutschland, Deutschland,"* and when Union met Dynamo, the ground would be full, with everyone supporting Union. Dynamo always won, and ten minutes from the end the crowd would leave the stadium.

Dynamo's players was by no means over the moon at winning the league every year, but most of the time they kept their mouths shut. A couple of years before the Wall fell, the club's striker Andreas Thom was allowed to give an interview to the West German magazine *Stern.* "A lot of people flee the GDR because they do not like life here," Thom confessed, concluding timidly: "I believe this is a very unusual country."

He was still banned from talking to the Western press when the Wall fell. When it did, he and his colleagues immediately joined Bundesliga clubs. Jürgen Bogs, the manager with ten league titles, stayed at Dynamo, but seemed unable to work his old magic.

By the time I arrived in the city, FC Berlin was playing at the tiny Sportforum ground. (I tried to find it one night and failed.) They were by then drawing crowds of just 1,000, so many of whom were hooligans that it was possible to speak of a lunatic majority. These sons of Communist officials and Stasi agents ranked marginally below Colombian drug dealers and Serb ethnic cleansers as the nastiest people on Earth. Because of their contacts, they could travel to the West even in the old days: once, a large group followed Dynamo to Monaco. After the Wall fell, they bizarrely began to combine Communism with neo-Nazism: their favorite chants were "Sieg Heil" and "We love Mielke." FC Berlin despaired. The club hired a PR company to whiten their name, but were swiftly relegated to the Berlin amateur league. In five years' time, perhaps sooner, two lines in a local paper will announce that FC Berlin (East German champions 1979–1988) have folded.

West Berlin had Hertha. Champions of Germany in 1930 and 1931, they were what the Germans call a Tradition Club, and they had once been the team of all Berlin. But on the night of August 13, 1961, the Wall went up, and half of Hertha's players and fans found themselves sealed up in East Berlin. The club began to buy the wrong players, suffered bribery scandals, missed a teenage winger named Pierre Littbarski who was playing around the corner, and in the mid-Eighties even descended to the Berlin amateur league. They were playing in the German second division when the Wall came down, and hordes of tearful East Berliners in 1950s' Hertha shirts descended on the Olympic Stadium. Perhaps Hertha's greatest Eastern fan was Helmut Klopfleisch.

Anyone who thinks that soccer has nothing to do with politics should speak to Klopfleisch. He is a large, blond, moon-faced man who was expelled from the GDR for supporting the wrong teams. I met him towards the end of my time in Berlin. It was 1991, he had left East Berlin two years before, and the GDR was no longer even a place on the map, but he could not stop himself talking about Communism. "I can't sleep at night anymore, my wife can't sleep at night, because the criminals who ran that country are still free." It was a theme he returned to every few minutes, quite involuntarily, as his wife to-and-froed with coffee and cake.

I have two sources of information on Klopfleisch's extraordinary life: he is one, and the other is the bulging file that Mielke's Stasi kept on him. The new German state has let the victims of the Stasi read their own files. Famous East German novelists have published theirs; Klopfleisch has posted me photocopies of his. It is a credit to the Stasi that their account of his life tallies in every detail with his.

Klopfleisch, both sources agree, was born in East Berlin in

1948, and lived there until 1989. He worked as an electrician in a People's Company, and later as a window cleaner in a rare private firm. "We were little people because they kept us little," he told me. He explained that he had changed jobs because in the People's Company "they told you what to think all the time."

He likes to talk, or as the Stasi put it, he has "an emotional manner that is founded in his character." The file warns: "K. has a good mental grasp and is able to recognize connections." (Had the Stasi not always used his initial, the file would read a little less like Kafka.)

On politics, the file says: "From his comments it is clear that he informs himself from Western electronic mass media. K. glorifies the Bundesliga. In K's opinion sport and politics have nothing to do with one another." This was not a view the Stasi shared. When the West German bureaucrat handed Klopfleisch his file, she told him: "It's all about soccer!"

"The leisure interests of the K. family are largely limited to soccer and their weekend plot of land at . . ." the Stasi reports. Klopfleisch elaborated to me: "The best times in East Germany were in our summer house. It was outside Berlin, quiet, nobody around, no Communist propaganda, and we'd sit there on a summer's evening watching Western soccer and we'd be happy. When we were in our summer house it felt like being in the West. It was our Little California. Then, when we left the GDR, they took it away from us." He has been trying for five years now to get it back.

"K. calls himself a fanatical supporter of the West Berlin soccer club 'Hertha BSC,' " the file says. When he was born, three years after the war, Hertha had already moved from the east of the city to the west. But the Wall had yet to be built, and so as a boy Klopfleisch went to Hertha's home games. The Wall went up when he was 13. "It was a mad, German thing to do. You wouldn't build a Wall across the center of London, would you?" He had to wait 28 years before he next saw his club play at home.

For the first few months after the Wall went up, he spent Saturday afternoons standing beside it among a mass of East Berlin Hertha fans, listening to the sounds coming from the Hertha ground just a few hundred yards from the frontier. When the crowd at the ground cheered, the group behind the Iron Curtain cheered too. Soon the border guards put a stop to this. Later, Hertha moved to the Olympic Stadium, which lies at the western end of West Berlin, miles from the Wall and out of earshot.

What to do? "We had a "Hertha Society" in East Berlin—illegal of course. We used to meet once a month, in a different place each time. Often we registered as a bingo club, and booked the back room of a café. Every meeting we would get a visit from the manager of Hertha, and sometimes players or directors would come across. I think I've met every Hertha manager of the past few decades. We relied on them to tell us what was going on at the club—not the normal things, because we knew those from Western radio and TV, but the inside stuff, the real gossip. We needed information, because otherwise we were on the moon. The managers must have thought we were a bunch of lunatics, but they always said how sad it was for us. We warned them to keep the meetings secret, but they'd go back and write in the match program that they'd been to see Hertha's loyal fans in East Berlin again. It was plain boasting. So of course the Stasi became suspicious, and they would stop the managers at the border. Once they stripped Jürgen Sündemann naked. Every meeting we'd sit there waiting, wondering whether the manager would get through. It was exciting, an adventure."

"I supported Hertha, Bayern Munich and the West German national team, but really I used to back any Western side against any Eastern side. I was there when Dynamo Berlin played Aston Villa, when they played Liverpool, when Vorwärts Frankfurt played Manchester United. I love Manchester United. I remember a Dennis Law header from 20 yards out that was like another player's shot. When they beat our teams, our papers would write, 'The professional soccer players from England . . . ,' pretending that ours were amateurs!"

It is a minor irony of history that the only match between the two Germanies was won by the GDR: at the World Cup of 1974, they beat the West 1–0. (Jürgen Sparwasser, scorer of the goal, later defected to the West.) Klopfleisch looked away when I mentioned the game. "I just can't understand it," he said. "It was a day of mourning in our house. There were big celebrations in East Berlin, even though it was just a lucky win. The worst of it all was the 300 Party bosses in the stands, waving their little flags with the East German sign, clapping at all the wrong moments because they knew nothing about soccer."

Klopfleisch had had to watch the game on television. He could only travel within the Soviet bloc—and he did. He pulled out a photograph album filled with pictures of himself with various Western greats: Klopfleisch with Franz Beckenbauer, with Karl-Heinz Rummenigge, with Bobby Moore, with Bobby Charlton, with his arm around Roger Milla. The photos are products of his journeys through Eastern Europe to watch visiting Western teams. On a window cleaner's salary? "It was always incredibly expensive, but because I wasn't in a trade union, we couldn't get any other holidays anyway."

In three decades he saw Hertha play once, in Poland, against Lech Poznan. There was a great queue at the Polish border that day, but the East German border guards knew about the match and were turning cars back. Klopfleisch had anticipated this, and had brought his mother along. At the frontier he pointed at her and said, "She grew up in Poland. I'm taking her to see her old home again." It was a lie, but the border guards let him through and Klopfleisch saw the match. He thought he had beaten the system, but the Stasi knew about the trip. The game is listed in their catalogue of his soccer journeys abroad. "The family tries to use all opportunities to experience Bundesliga teams live," warns the file.

The Stasi, sparing no expense, accompanied Klopfleisch everywhere. "K., by his behavior at the People's Republic of Bulgaria vs. the Federal Republic of Germany, has significantly damaged the international reputation of the GDR," an agent reported sadly. It mentions a number of other soccer dissidents who likewise blotted the GDR's noble reputation. Klopfleisch later read in his file that his boss at the private window-cleaning firm had discussed his trip to Sofia with the Stasi. "The comrade was very open and declared himself prepared to support the security organs further," says the Stasi report of the meeting. Klopfleisch had liked his boss.

Bayern Munich visited Czechoslovakia in 1981, and the Stasi took measures "to prevent the arrival of inimical negative forces/criminally dangerous persons, as also negative decadent young people and youths." They failed. Klopfleisch's file reports: "On 18.3.1981 a large number of soccer fans, in large part citizens of the GDR, assembled in front of [Bayern's] hotel. . . . To restore order and safety, the Czech militia was compelled to clear the hotel entrance, through the use of truncheons, among other methods. The action of the militia . . . was filmed from the window of a hotel room by a male person using a cine-film camera."

It was Klopfleisch. The file quotes an extract from a letter he later wrote to a man in Munich, probably a Bayern official: "We hid our souvenirs. They searched us at the border again. It makes you feel like a bank robber. Isn't it a disgrace, just because you go to the soccer to see Bayern you get checked like that."

Then Klopfleisch and the Stasi began to meet head to head. The file contains an account of a "preventive conversation" that Stasi Lieutenant Hoyer held with Klopfleisch on December 12, 1981.

The file reports: "K. arrived punctually, and, so he stated, by public transport, as he does not use his car in this weather [snow/ice]." He was allowed to speak, and did so "in an emotional manner that is founded in his character." He demanded to know why his identity card had been confiscated: it stopped him from traveling abroad. Told to calm down, he raised the topic of soccer, and said "that this was his hobby and was accepted as such by his family. He had gone to Prague for the match." He complained to Hoyer that he had been unable to buy tickets for Dynamo Berlin vs. Vfb Stuttgart. "He claimed that he could not explain this. He asked whether he would be allowed to go to the match even if he did find a ticket. It was pointed out to him that his own behavior would decide this. He replied that he was not a hooligan and condemned their actions, he therefore did not understand why his identity card had been taken away while other troublemakers still had theirs. He mentioned M., who lives at . . . , who is well-known in this respect. He asked whether he was not being confused with M. With regard to a possible match between Bayern Munich and Dynamo Dresden, he stated that for that, too, he would not officially receive tickets. But he claimed he knew the soccer player . . . of Bayern Munich, and if he wrote to him, would be given his tickets. It was then suggested to him that in such a case he should phone and consult Stasi Lieutenant Hoyer, at telephone number 5639289."

Then Klopfleisch began to sulk: "This did not appeal to him at all, he stated that in that case he would lose all pleasure and interest in the match. He already had the impression of being under control."

Other "conversations" followed. Klopfleisch told me: "In the file they call them 'conversations,' as if we were sitting in a nice room and they were saying, 'So, Mr. Klopfleisch, what do you think of that?' Really it was awful. I felt like a hunted animal. Once or twice I was stuck in a cell no bigger than the corner of this sofa," he pointed. "Each time there was a different interrogator. I suppose they wanted to see if I'd tell each one a different story, but that's just my guess. I have no idea. I never knew exactly what they wanted to find out, and whenever I asked, the interrogator shouted, "We ask the questions here!" He hesitated, for in his West Berlin flat, his story seemed barely plausible.

"They always wanted to know who else was in it with me. I made a point of never giving them any names. They probably knew everything anyway, but I wanted them to be sure that they wouldn't get any information out of me. I always said, 'Nothing will ever change in the East, you won't change people's minds, just please let me out of the GDR because I can't bear it anymore.' " "K. possesses a politically labile stance," the Stasi found.

What was it that had made him such an enemy of the system? "I don't know. My grandfather was an anti-Nazi, and he always used to say how terrible the GDR was, so from when I was young I was hearing someone say that. But otherwise, I really don't know. I knew the West was richer but I didn't care about that. I just wanted to be able to read what I liked, to see what I liked, to hear what I liked."

Sometimes he was imprisoned when a Western side came to play in the GDR. "They even locked me up when Schmidt, who was then the West German Chancellor, visited East Berlin in 1981. I suppose they thought I'd go to the airport and wave a German flag or something stupid like that. It was hard enough as it was to get tickets for matches against Western teams. The tickets used to go to Party members— otherwise the whole stadium would have been cheering the Western side. Against Hamburger SV, to make absolutely sure, the tickets were handed out to the comrades just an hour before the match. We always got in anyhow, because most Communists hated soccer, and they'd sell their seats to us." He mimed an idiotic Party member being talked into giving up his ticket.

He was arrested again in 1985. At Czechoslovakia vs. West Germany, he had presented a toy Berlin Bear, the symbol of both halves of the city, to the West German manager, Franz Beckenbauer, and the Stasi had watched him do it. "They stopped my car at the border on the way back and searched it for five hours. They even took the wheel caps off—and they found the photo of me with Beckenbauer." He showed it to me: a few steps behind Klopfleisch, Beckenbauer and the bear, beneath the *"Restaurace"* sign, an unidentified woman stares into the lens, and we briefly pondered whether she might be the spy.

The Stasi took away the soccer souvenirs he had bought in Prague, but noted that "there were no signs of criminal smuggling. K. stated during the control that he was a passionate collector of such things. He said he considered the control to be harassment, and claimed that he had not seen the likes of it previously." Klopfleisch never grasped what it was to live in a totalitarian state: for no particular reason, he always assumed that standards of decency and common sense would apply. Then, he told me, "they questioned me, shouting at me, and I could see they were going to throw me in jail. So I said, 'Leave me alone or I'll call my friend Franz.' Naturally I barely knew Beckenbauer, but this worried them. 'Maybe,' they thought, 'this man really is a friend of the *Teamchef*,' which is what they called him. 'It will be all over the Western papers,' I told them. They were afraid to take the risk, and in the end they let me go."

It was a Stasi principle to tail West Germans who were in touch with East Germans, and I found in Klopfleisch's file a "Request for Information of the Person of" a West German named "Franz," resident in Kitzbühel, Austria. Every German knows that that is where Beckenbauer lives, but because the law says that no third persons mentioned in the Stasi files can be identified, the Western bureaucrats in charge of the files have crossed out the surname. I did not find the information that the Stasi gathered on Beckenbauer.

Klopfleisch was arrested again the next year, just before the World Cup in Mexico, for sending a good-luck telegram to the West German team. "The Stasi asked, 'How dare you wish the Class Enemy good luck?' and I told them, 'Soccer in this country of yours is no better than in Iceland or Luxembourg.' 'Will you stand by that statement?' they screamed, and I said, 'I'll sign it if you like.' Look,

East Germany were rubbish! They only got 5,000 people watching the national team, and even then they had to bus in kids who would have watched anything."

I was getting ready to leave when Klopfleisch's son Ralf came in and sat down beside his father. Now in his early twenties, Ralf forfeited the regime's trust at the age of nine by telling his teacher that his hero was the Bayern striker Karl-Heinz Rummenigge. Rummenigge was a "class enemy," whose uniform Ralf acquired years later. Professor Scherer, President of Bayern Munich, had arrived at the Klopfleisch flat in East Berlin and had begun to undress. "What's this?" Klopfleisch had thought—but Scherer was wearing Rummenigge's Bayern uniform underneath his suit. He had come through customs in it, and he gave it to Ralf.

Ralf grew into a promising soccer player, and at 15 was playing for Dynamo colts and captaining the East Berlin Youth team. Then, at a compulsory Military Defense Training Camp, he fell and tore some ligaments in his knee. Initially he was refused first aid, and later an operation ("because we were 'enemies of the state' ") and he had to retire from soccer. He has never played since. After Klopfleisch told the story Ralf walked out of the room again. "He used to be so happy," Klopfleisch told me. "We used to laugh at the East together. I always thought they tried to play sport like a machine, so we used to shout, "It's the balls, you have to play with them!" He had found in his file a record of a Stasi decision: "The boy will not be taken away from his parents."

The GDR dumped its dissidents in the West. In 1986 the Klopfleisches applied for visas to emigrate, and three years later their request was granted. The Stasi had chosen the moment with care: Klopfleisch's mother was on her deathbed. "I begged the Stasi to let me stay for another couple of days. The doctor had told me that my mother had a few hours to live. I told the Stasi, and they said, "A few hours, we know. Either you leave today, or never." So I went and five days later she died. I wasn't allowed back for her funeral." The Klopfleisch family spent their first year in the West in a refugee camp.

It was just Klopfleisch's luck that having spent his whole life in the GDR, the Wall came down months after he emigrated. But at last he could watch Hertha at home. "When I lived in the East I suppose I had a lot of illusions about Hertha. I thought they were a great club, and I have been disappointed. The Wall fell on November 9, 1989. Hertha's next league match was at home to Wattenscheid, and there were 59,000 people in the stadium! In the second division! The whole of East Berlin had come across. Then, that Monday, we read in the papers that Hertha had invited the directors of Dynamo Berlin and Union Berlin to the match. All those Communists and Stasi chiefs! Because believe me, the big directors, managers and players in the East were all in the Party, whether they admit it now or not. I was a steward for the match against Wattenscheid, and when I saw the Party chiefs march past on the way to their free seats I thought, 'We fought and suffered for Hertha, and then they go and invite the bosses.' Hertha announced at the press conference that these people had been at the game, as if it were something to be proud of. That's why there were only 16,000 at the next match. I immediately resigned my membership, though I still go and watch Hertha. I think they're the only club in Berlin. Even people who never watch them always check their results. Blau Weiss plays better soccer, but they're just not Hertha, are they?"

The balance, he agreed, was sad. "I turn 43 this year. I spent 41 years of my life in the GDR, and now it feels like wasted time, though we lived then, and had fun sometimes. And you know, it was a real consolation that West Germany was so successful. They *always* beat Eastern teams. That meant a lot to us."

CHAPTER 4

THE BALTiCS WANT TO BE iN AMERiCA

BERLIN TO VILNIUS IS a 22-hour train journey. We chugged through Poland, stopped in Belorussia, where two small boys with a plastic bag got on and rifled the carriages, and after about 20 hours, crossed the border into Lithuania. I was standing in the corridor with two Germans, chatting desultorily, when a young Lithuanian outside threw a rock against the window at which we were standing. The glass failed to break in our faces, and eventually we reached Vilnius.

Vilnius, Lithuania. Vilnius has a million inhabitants, a crumbling fifteenth-century center, and crumbling twentieth-century suburbs. Yet by Soviet standards Lithuania was rich, and it was the first of the USSR's republics to gain independence. (When I arrived, in August 1992, most foreign ambassadors were still living in hotel rooms.) The other Baltic states, Latvia and Estonia, had also become free on time to enter the American World Cup, and I had come to see the first two World Cup qualifying matches ever to be played in this part of the world: Latvia vs. Lithuania, and Estonia vs. Switzerland.

In Vilnius, I first made for the office of the Sajudis movement, opposite the cathedral. Sajudis led the drive for independence, and the movement has since become a political party. It was the largest in Lithuania, and a general election was at hand, but as soon as I walked into the office and identified myself as an English soccer journalist I was taken in to see the big boss, the Sajudis executive secretary Andrius Kubilius. Even that was as nothing compared to the young Norwegian tourist who was brought to meet President Landsbergis. Westerners are big shots in the Baltics.

Soccer and basketball games, said Kubilius, had been vital in the struggle for independence. Often, after Zalgiris Vilnius played a Russian team, the home fans would march from the stadium carrying torches and singing folk songs. In the center of town they would meet militiamen with batons—"bananas," the Lithuanians call them. These were virtually the only nationalist protests in the country until the late 1980s. Only when Gorbachev took power and people became freer to speak did sport cease to matter quite so much. "When Sajudis became strong, sport came in second place," Kubilius said. Until then, he explained, large numbers of Soviet citizens could come together and shout what they pleased only at a sports match. The players never joined in, but the Zalgiris soccer players would always first wave to the fans at the southern end of the stadium, where the most vocal Lithuanians sat. "The demonstrations had no consequences, of course," Kubilius admitted sadly. He was sorry when I ran out of questions, and not just because he liked talking sport. Lithuanians love "Europe," which they constantly say they want to "rejoin," and they crave for it to notice them. It matters that a lot of Westerners have never heard of Lithuania: businesses will only start to trade with a nation if they know it exists; tourists will only visit on the same premise, and should the Russian Army march into Lithuania again, Western governments will feel more pressure to act if the Western public knows about Lithuania.

Sport can help. Days before I arrived, Lithuania's basketball team had won the bronze medal at the Barcelona Olympics, thus earning more foreign TV coverage in a month than President Landsbergis had managed all year. Nerijus Maliukevicius of *Lithuanian Weekly* (published in English) told me he had had three foreign visitors in recent months: a journalist each from *Newsweek* and the *San Francisco Chronicle*, both come to ask about Lithuanian basketball, and me. "Everyone comes here for sport," he concluded.

When I asked him about the old demonstrations, he answered hastily, "I participated," and then qualified this to, "I saw. I took my son to see. But then the demonstration would finish, and what could you do? So we would go home."

I left Vilnius the next day. Lithuania was playing Latvia away, in Riga, and I got a lift north in Matvejus Frismanas' Volkswagen van. A Lithuanian with a Volkswagen van is like a Westerner with a private jet: Frismanas is a mega-rich businessman, and also a Baltic calypso character. His passion is soccer, and he told me that he was a director of the Lithuanian side, though his English business card read, more grandly, "Manager of the national team." Frismanas was a bright man.

A Lithuanian hulk drove the van for him, and there were two other passengers: the one Frismanas' brother-in-law, a math teacher by trade, and the other a soccer reporter who had been the sole Lithuanian journalist to accompany the soccer team to Northern Ireland. It had been the country's first ever World Cup match, but the other newspapers had not had the money to send anyone.

Frismanas and his brother-in-law were Jewish, and they quickly established that I was too. "I can never forget," said the brother-in-law in a mixture of Yiddish, German and English, "where my uncles and aunts and grandparents are. In the Lithuanian earth! And it was the Lithuanians who put them there, not the Germans." Frismanas was the sponsor of Maccabi Vilnius, a club which had been Jewish until the war. And now? "Now, only the money is Jewish."

We did a stint on the road, and then Frismanas signaled to the hulk and we stopped for a feast. We had brought our own vodka, it seemed, which we augmented with shashliks bought from a peasant. The journalist handed me a cup of vodka, persuaded me to down it "as a symbol," and then constantly refilled it. I drank lots of symbols. "The Russians taught us to drink," Frismanas lamented. "The Russians."

Guards with machine guns were waiting at the Latvian border. Frismanas jumped out of the van, ran to the guards before they could come to us and handed them a small Lithuanian Olympic flag. He talked to them for a minute or so, the one guard holding the flag, others emerging from the customs shed to stare at Frismanas, and then he trotted back to the car and ordered the hulk to drive on. What had he told them? That they were lucky, he replied. "I said, 'Normally we beat you, but Lithuania does not have all its players fit, so we will draw.' "

Riga, Latvia. I had a slight cold, which worried my companions greatly. We drove straight to the Hotel Riga, where the squad was staying, and went in search of the team doctor, whom we found in a double room surrounded by the entire Lithuanian squad. It was easy to tell which were the stars who played in Austria and which players were still with local clubs: the two men with swish haircuts lying on the beds being massaged were plainly at Austria Vienna, while the boys sitting on the floor with long unkempt hair had to be on a couple of pounds a week.

The doctor was as concerned as my friends, and gave me German pills for my cold. They tasted nice, and I continued to take them after the cold ended. While I was in the Baltics they were often the best food I had all day.

Frismanas and his brother-in-law had asked me whether I felt like interviewing Lithuania's real manager, Algimantas Liubinskas. "This will be no problem," they assured me, and it emerged that Liubinskas was Frismanas' business partner. "But not to put in the newspaper," they added.

The business partner was in his room, wearing a shirt marked "Indiana Refereeing Course" and watching pop videos on MTV with the venerable uniform manager. What kind of a team was Lithuania? "The Lithuanian temperament is not very strong." How had the tiny country, in its first important match since the Hitler–Stalin pact, managed a 2–2 draw in Belfast? "Northern Ireland did not play badly," said Liubinskas, "but they did not know anything about us. We had videocassettes of their matches, but I think they thought, "Lithuania? Where's that on the map?" We know British sides play through the air—we call it, "on the second floor," and we were prepared for that. Though in fact," he smiled, "they scored both their goals along the ground." Liubinskas was better informed than the Lithuanian FA. The table of the World Cup group on their office wall calls Northern Ireland "Airija," and Eire "S. Airija": Ireland and Southern Ireland.

The first World Cup match on Baltic soil was quite an occasion. For me, it was the first time I bought caviar sandwiches outside of a soccer ground. Otherwise, though hawkers around the stadium were selling warm German beer and Agatha Christies in Latvian, I limited myself to the match program with its incongruous picture of Diego Maradona on the cover. It cost eight pence: prices were a great joy to me in my first few days in the old USSR.

The fans were wandering around in shirts with Western logos, any Western logos: one man's shirt said "Royal Mail—Stoke on Trent—MLO." No hooligans seemed to have turned up. A couple of hundred Lithuanian diehards with large beards carried flags and chanted *"Lietuva!,"* and were watched by policemen in Wellington boots.

In the press room I spotted a VIP: the Danish manager Richard Möller-Nielsen. It was two months since his team had won the European Championships, and he was now in Riga to spy on his World Cup opponents. I found him surrounded by Lithuanian journalists and their feeble interpreter. Was it true that he had taken a break from repairing his house to win the championships? Möller-Nielsen grinned, but was keen to get the facts right: "I should have put in a new kitchen, but then we were called away to play in Sweden. But the kitchen is finished now. It took a long time. I had a professional decorator do it." He fended off a question about Michael Laudrup, who was refusing to play for Denmark, and he said that Latvia and Lithuania would be difficult opponents. I thought he was just being polite, and maybe he thought so too, but 50 days later Denmark had drawn 0–0 in each country.

The craze for Western emblems extended to the Latvian FA, who had tacked an enormous World Cup 1994 logo complete with American flag to one of the stands. The World Cup was a kind of mirage— both sides knew they would never actually get to America—but at least the logo clarified that this was not some sort of village match. A Lithuanian folk dance was performed on the pitch, and in this setting it was hardly embarrassing, as Morris dancing at Wembley might have been. The Lithuanian hard core clapped.

The stadium was only a quarter full, which was Stalin's fault. When he invaded the Baltics, he moved hundred of thousands of Russian administrators to Latvia and Estonia, and today Russians make up almost half the population of both republics. Most of the Latvian players that night were Russians, and when I asked people why the stadium was empty they explained that Latvians had no desire to see Russians play, while Russians would not watch a team called Latvia. Latvians had played soccer before the war, but these days most coaches in the republic were Russians, who picked Russian players.

A glance at the two team sheets showed which side was stronger. There were Lithuanians with Austria Vienna and Dynamo Kiev, but Latvians abroad had got no further than Ilves Tampere of Finland, and Lomza and the depressingly named Granit of Poland.

Latvia went 1–0 up, and sustained their lead to halftime, but even by then their earlier defeat to Malta had ceased to be a mystery. After the interval Lithuania equalized, and a few minutes from time Andrius Tereskinas made it 2–1, to end Lithuania's lean spell of over 50 years without a victory. The match was notable chiefly for the number of dives by the Lithuanians who played in Austria, and for the number of players treated for injury. Treatment of injuries, I was to find, takes up a lot of time in former Soviet soccer.

A relieved Liubinskas told the press conference that the match had been "rude and brutal" because it was a Baltic derby, and hence "a match of principle." A journalist then stood up and berated the gathering in Russian. Tickets had cost 30 pence each, he raged. How could they expect people to come to the stadium to pay money like that? He was plainly a Latvian Russian, and was feeling left out of this Baltic festival.

I sidled out and found Möller-Nielsen sitting in the other room, bored and lonely. We shook hands and sat down. *Then* he asked "How are you?," expecting an answer—Möller-Nielsen is a very polite man. We got talking about his passion, England and English soccer. "I like the long-ball game, he claimed. "It gets the balls in front of the goal. Soccer should not be played in midfield. English soccer has a class, a decency to it which does not exist anywhere else in the world. You know, when we won the championships Graham Taylor and Lawrie McMenemy sent me a telegram of congratulation! I am often at Manchester United and Liverpool, and I see how well organized these clubs are, how fair the fans are."

We talked about the Barcelona Olympics, where he felt Ghana had played "wonderful soccer." "Tell me," he asked, "is it negative to say, 'Third World?' Is it an unkind thing to say?" The problem was preying on his mind, and we considered it. "I think a Third World country, an African country, will win the World Cup soon."

Tallinn, Estonia. Two days later, I arrived in Tallinn for Estonia vs. Switzerland. The Swiss press corps and I were handed programs which gave the Estonian squad and the Estonian league table, and the two seemed at odds: though Flora Tallinn had finished fourth in the league, they provided almost all the players in the national squad. Only two players came from other Estonian sides. The Estonians appeared to have selected their squad on illogical principles.

The answer to the riddle was ethnic hatred. Flora were an all-Estonian club. The Russians who live in Estonia are known as *"kolonists,"* and the Estonian players had demanded that no more than three should be allowed to play for the national team, and that these three should be fluent in Estonian. The manager, Uno Piir, suggested picking the best players, but was overruled. The resulting side was hardly the best that even Estonia could muster.

One wonders what FIFA made of this: imagine if England had an official policy of not selecting black players, or Geordies. Scotland, who was in Estonia's World Cup group, might have complained to FIFA, or even refused to play a pure Estonia, but they did no such thing.

The Swiss team, practicing at the stadium, looked happily integrated, with German, Italian, French and English voices mingling. English? No long-lost community of Anglophones has been discovered high in the Alps, but the Swiss manager, Roy Hodgson, is a South Londoner. As we plucked plantain grass from the pitch, he told me that the Estonians played a "Russian" brand of soccer, a view which would not have pleased them. Meanwhile, Hodgson's assistant Mike Kelly was training the two goalkeepers, the Italian Swiss Marco Pascolo and the German Swiss Stefan Lehmann: the one showing off long, dark, Latin hair and unnecessary dives, the other pale, Teutonic and restrained. I was surprised to discover the next day that the quiet man was Pascolo and the flamboyant one Lehmann.

The match went off predictably. Switzerland scored freely, while their fans rang cowbells and exploded stink bombs, which, as one would expect of Swiss stink bombs, did not smell badly at all. At 2–0 up, the Swiss mysteriously started singing "Always Look on the Bright Side of Life." The Estonian fans had only one chant— *"Eesti, Eesti"*—though they had painted a flag in the shape of the Union Jack, but in Estonian colors.

The Estonians were a soft lot. If their style was "Russian," the main thing they had in common with the great Soviet sides of the 1980s was a lack of any will to win. A Dutch journalist once called Dassaev, Belanov, Protassov, and Co. "born losers": he meant that there was no Soviet Stuart Pearce willing to sprint 30 yards to clog an opposing striker and save a goal, no Jürgen Klinsmann who would dive the way to an undeserved victory, no Graeme Souness throttling his teammates for not trying. The Soviets played fair, and always lost when it mattered. Estonia, an infinitely worse side, were in the same mould.

They did attack—all the time, in fact. Once they put together 15 passes without a Swiss player touching the ball, but they seemed to intend this as an exhibition only. They barely tackled, and lost 6–0. The consensus among journalists and managers was that Estonia had been naïve. Hodgson spoke approvingly of Malta, who were "realistic about their ability," and played more defensively. It was sad to think of Estonia curbing their style so as to lose 3–0 instead of 6–0.

One Estonian player stood out. Martin Reim, in central midfield, was only about five feet high, but played like a Baltic Carlos Valderrama. Twice he put teammates in front of the goalkeeper (and calmly watched them miss). He played, of course, for Flora Tallinn. I asked him after the match whether it was right and equitable that the three best teams in the league had no players on the national side. He was disarmingly frank: "There are so few Estonian players. Perhaps it will encourage young Estonians to play soccer? It is true that maybe there are Russian players who could do better now."

Later, in Moscow, I read an article in the Russian *Footbolny Kurier* which called Estonia "not a national team but an ethnic team." The magazine pointed out that Luis Fernandez was of Spanish origins but had played for France; that the Belgian side included Enzo Scifo, son of an Italian, and the Brazilian Luis Oliveira; and that Peter Schmeichel's father had emigrated from Poland to Denmark. Of course the Poles never imposed an inefficient economic system on Denmark; nor did the Brazilians establish large colonies in Belgium, but for the Russians in the Baltics that would be no consolation.

Maybe the defeat by Switzerland would make the Estonians reconsider, *Kurier* sneered. And *Kurier* was right: for recently, scanning an Estonian lineup, I saw a host of Russian names.

CHAPTER 5

THE SECRET POLICE CHIEF

ON MY FIRST NIGHT in Moscow I went to a party and came home in an ambulance. Not that there was anything wrong with me: just that Russian doctors earn about $12 a month, and for a couple of dollars will happily take you wherever you want to go at two in the morning. I sometimes wonder whether my ambulance had been heading for an emergency.

Martin Bormann. Vladimir Shinkaryov and I were sitting in the Academy of Sciences, his place of work, and he was reading me an article from a Russian soccer magazine. The piece was an interview with Valeri Ovchinikov, coach of Lokomotiv Nizhni Novgorod, who without any prompting was telling his interviewer that he habitually bribed referees. "Do you think I am the only coach who does?" Ovchinikov asked. Shinkaryov read this in deadpan tones, and was moving on to the next question in the interview when I interrupted him: "Did this not cause a scandal?" "We have so many scandals in Russia nowadays," Shinkaryov explained, "that it is very hard to get excited about any new one."

I could see his point. After discovering in recent years that Stalin killed millions of his own people, that each Five-Year Plan was not overfulfilled by several hundred percent, and that all Western food aid disappears and later turns up in shops, Russians find it hard to get worked up at the news that their soccer managers pay bribes. Not long before, the 18 coaches of first division clubs had been asked, "Are there arranged matches in our league?" and all

41

18 had replied, "Yes." To the next question, "Does your club play in these matches?" all 18 answered, "It does not."

Corruption is an ancient Russian custom, but only the best informed fans knew that it went on in soccer too. To the rest the news came as a great betrayal. Shinkaryov, an anthropologist who supports Spartak Moscow, told me how happy he had been to hear that Spartak was a rare club that did not pay referees. "A fan wants to believe that when his team wins it is not because they bought the opposition." But he admitted that he might be wrong.

He continued reading the interview. The last question concerned Ovchinikov's nickname. "In soccer circles you are nicknamed 'Martin Bormann,'" said the questioner. "Is this because of your superficial physical resemblance to him?" Ovchinikov thought not: "In our country nobody has any idea of what Bormann looked like. Our resemblance is down to something else. Bormann ran Nazi Party finances, and I will not hide from you that I administer our club's finances. I maintain honesty towards both players and directors."

Kukushkin. Vsevolod Kukushkin, introduced to me as "the little fat guy," is an elderly Russian journalist who speaks perfect, American-accented English. Unlike Shinkaryov, the little fat guy is an insider, and when I asked about Bormann's confession of bribery he shrugged. He replied that there had been a referee in the 1970s who had become famous for *not* taking bribes. The reason for his probity was that he was the director of a big truck company and so rich that no one could ever afford his price. Then there was the club Tavria Simeropol, who had just bribed their way to the Ukrainian championship. "Their coach," said Kukushkin "—well, he is not really a coach, but he is a good dealer."

Even so, I said, surely it was not done to boast to the press about bribery? How could Bormann keep his job having done so? "We are a very special country," answered Kukushkin, almost with pride.

"High-rank officials are exposed as crooks and remain in their posts. Recently, three contracts have appeared for the sale of one player from Torpedo Moscow to Olympiakos Piraeus. One contract is for the Greek tax inspectors, one they show to the player, and the third is the real contract, but no one knows which is which. As I understand it, in a normal country these people would be prosecuted, but here they have kept their jobs." Kukushkin had spent too many decades in Russia to get heated up about things like that: "What's that, when there are wars here, wars there, and the economy has collapsed? Two days ago the deputy health minister was fired and now he is under investigation for bribery." In any case, he said, many referees accept bribes from both sides and then judge the match honestly. Teams pay up simply to get fair treatment. He drew an instructive Russian comparison: "I have to give money to traffic policemen, but I don't get anything for it. I pay a lot of bribes. How many times have you paid bribes?"

At the time I had never paid a bribe in my life, but I did not want to seem a tenderfoot by saying so. In any case, Kukushkin would not have believed me. "In England . . ." I began. "OK, so maybe you don't give money," he allowed. "But you give a guy a necktie or a tiepin and say, 'This is for you, it's a Christmas present.' Sometimes referees here get 'presents.' When the winter is coming you can present him with a fur cap. It will keep him warm, and he can say, 'Money? I never touch money?' " "Referees in England . . ." I started to argue, but Kukushkin interrupted. "When I was a young man," he said, "an older journalist told me, 'Bad referees give penalty kicks or offsides, but good referees know how to stop an attack while it is still in midfield.' That is the only difference. Referees? There are referees everywhere. But there is another Referee up there." He pointed skywards, and I dropped the subject.

* * *

Torpedo Moscow vs. Uralmash. Sixteen days before Torpedo Moscow was due to play Manchester United in the UEFA Cup, I went to watch them against Uralmash. There were only a couple of thousand fans at the ground, and the match was the laziest performance by 22 men I have ever seen. It ended in a 1–1 draw. I told Mikhail Pukshansky of the new *Sport Express* newspaper that Torpedo had no chance against United. He disagreed: "The players are interested in doing well against Manchester because that is important for their futures. They don't care about the league—they want contracts in the West." A month later, Torpedo had knocked out United.

What struck me most about the match was how the fans laughed and laughed at the parade of blunders, as if watching a performance by virtuoso clowns. "People here are very skeptical," Vladimir Geskin, the editor of *Sport Express*, told me. "That is part of the Russian mentality. It has nothing to do with being disillusioned with political systems or living under a dictatorship or whatever. We just like to laugh. Watching soccer here is more like watching the theater. You can't compare us to Italians or Spaniards—we're Northern people."

But there was another, sadder story behind the guffaws. "Why do you laugh at the players?" I asked one young man, who said he was chairman of the Torpedo supporters' club. "The laughter is mutual," he replied. "They are laughing at us too, because they have their dollars and cars and we don't." The Torpedo players were on $500 for a win; the fans earned a few rubles. Worse, at Torpedo the fans really do pay the players' wages, because most of the supporters work at Zil, one of the club's sponsors.

To be fair to Torpedo, when it came to money they were in a bind. On the one hand, in the previous two years alone, they had lost 23 players to Western clubs, and so the treasury was full. On the other, they had no hope of signing anyone because all good Russian players wanted to move abroad. The result was that the club spent its money on higher wages for worse players.

Most English supporters would recognize the Torpedo fan chairman's sense of love betrayed. He told me that he supported all clubs in the world that played in Torpedo's green, white and black, and started to enumerate them before I managed to stop him. Then he told me how, after one match, angry fans had started to overturn the team bus, but had desisted because the damage would have cost their club money. He was a member of the Torpedo Travel Club, and in the days of the all-Soviet league had regularly traveled three or four days to watch Torpedo play Kairat Alma Ata or Pamir Tashkent. They would leave Moscow in midwinter and emerge in Alma Ata in high summer. Now, in the new All-Russian League, one of Torpedo's opponents was a club named Nagodka, from southeastern Siberia, not far from Japan. The chairman had discovered that the train journey would take seven days, so the Travel Club, he told me, would "probably" go by plane.

A fine idea, but ordinary Russians tend to regard flying as a once-in-a-lifetime experience. The Torpedo Travellers were young working-class boys. I asked how on earth they could afford it. "We are also going to fly to Manchester," he replied. So how could they afford that? "We will have to save for some time." On average salaries of £8 a month, indeed. Apparently he meant it, for the Travellers planned to take in an English league match too, and he asked which matches were scheduled in the Manchester area for the weekend before Torpedo's visit. It was bewildering.

The Russian Pelé. In the Torpedo club office (dingy does not begin to describe it), there is a black-and-white photo of a man in a suit, which has been stuck in the trophy cupboard. The man is Eduard Streltsov, who was known to Russians as the "Russian Pelé." Streltsov played for Torpedo in the 1950s, and when the authorities suggested that he join Dynamo Moscow, club of the KGB, or CSKA Moscow, the Army club, he refused. "Streltsov is like a huge mountain, whose whole cannot be known," explained the otherwise rather forbidding Torpedo vice president. For his sins, Streltsov was sent to Siberia and missed the 1958 World Cup. Before that World Cup, the vice president told me proudly, the world's press had written that two teams were greatly weakened: England, who had lost several Manchester United players in the Munich air crash, and Russia, who had lost only one man, the great Streltsov. Streltsov, the vice president added by way of a punchline, was back in Moscow in time to lead Torpedo to the league title in 1960.

Yeltsin's team. There were two matches the next Saturday, and one I missed because it received almost no publicity. In Russia, where it is often impossible to find out the first division fixtures of the weekend, it was only natural that few people knew about the match between the Russian government and Moscow town hall, and though Boris Yeltsin coached the government, only 1,000 spectators turned up. The final score was 1–1, and plans to decide the match on penalties were abandoned when it was found that none of the players could stand. It was a match that would never have been played under Brezhnev or Stalin, and a sure sign that the Russian government was moving closer to its people.

A Soviet disaster. Instead, I went to the Lenin Stadium to watch CSKA Moscow against Spartak Moscow.

The Lenin Stadium is the site of the worst soccer disaster in history. In October 1982, Spartak was playing the Dutch club Haarlem in freezing weather, and all 10,000 spectators were packed into a single section of the stadium. With seconds of the match remaining, and Spartak 1–0 up, the fans were making for the exit, when Shvezov scored Spartak's second goal. Many were already descending the icy, unlit steps behind the stand, but when they heard cheers they rushed back up. Meanwhile, those inside were leaving, as the match had ended straight after the goal. The two groups collided, and could not escape, because police refused to open other exits. What followed was a human avalanche down the steps, and it now seems that as many as 340 people were killed.

It was long rumored that something terrible had happened, but the authorities kept mum for years. The bodies of the victims were carried off straight after the disaster. To keep the sheer number of deaths secret, parents had to take leave of their children 40 minutes before the mass funeral, in the presence of policemen. For a long time afterwards, no matches were played at the Lenin Stadium. The pretext given was that the pitch was in poor condition.

Thanks to *glasnost*, by 1989 *Sovietski Sport* could tell the full story. The magazine also revealed that there had been an identical catastrophe in Moscow's Sokolniki Sport Palace, in 1976: after an ice-hockey match between the USSR and Canada, scores of people were crushed to death because only one exit was opened.

So there we were at the Lenin Stadium (there is a statue of Lenin in front), four of us English and two Russians, ten years on, and this time in midsummer and in broad daylight. The Lenin Stadium is several sizes too big, and yet the Hotel Ukraine towers over it—everything in Moscow is too big. The match, CSKA against Spartak, was the main Moscow championship, their Arsenal vs. Spurs, the main difference being that unlike either Arsenal or Spurs, CSKA is the club of the Russian Army. Spartak, on the other hand, is the only Moscow club without an official backer. That afternoon, there were about 15,000 spectators, and though CSKA and Spartak share the Lenin Stadium, they were virtually all Spartak fans. Shinkaryov had told me: "When I was young I asked my father, 'Father, why do you support Spartak?' and he said, 'Because Spartak is not connected to a definite part of

Soviet society.' " Dynamo is the club of the KGB, his father had explained, CSKA of the army, Torpedo of the Zil plant, Lokomotive of the railways, but Spartak alone were independent. Supporting Spartak was a small way of saying "No." Spartak fans like to call theirs "The Club of the People," though oddly enough, Konstantin Chernenko, the geriatric general secretary who preceded Gorbachev, was also a supporter.

"Horses! Horses!" the Spartakists chanted at the CSKA fans, following the logical link that army equals cavalry equals horses. The four horses in front of us were small boys, which apparently was typical. One young man told us: "We Russians support CSKA until we are 18, because until then we worship army officers. At 18 we join the Army, learn the truth, and never support CSKA again." The text on the boys' hats read "Red Army," written in English. Here a less logical link was at work: Manchester United fans had once named themselves after the Russian army, and now the Russian army team's fans were taking their name from United's fans. We had borrowed the glamor of their Red Army, and they had taken back ours.

The scoreboard gave a phone number for fans to call who wanted to spend a few years' wages on following Spartak away to Luxembourg, for a first round match in the European Cupwinners' Cup. No doubt there would be takers. The crowd at the Lenin Stadium was the only committed one I saw in Russia. Endless Spartak songs were sung, and each time we turned eagerly to our Russian companions for translation. Vassily would explain, "They are singing, 'Spartak is the Best Team in the World.' 'Very interesting. And this one?' 'Spartak Will Win the Championship.' "

It was a gorgeous, sunny day in August (already autumn, in Russia), and I reflected what a perfect tourist event a Russian soccer match was: it was an authentic Russian occasion, for the game was not being staged for our benefit, and nobody even cared that we were there; the setting and the fans' behavior was so familiar that we could recognize differences between it and England; there were real local passions on display; good sport; and all that for three pence.

The match was a placid affair which ended in a 1–1 draw, so that once again it was hard to dispute the referee's fairness, though once or twice the ancient Russian chant, "The Referee's a Pedophile," did sound. Neither team looked very special, and I was taken aback a couple of months later when Spartak thrashed Liverpool in the Cupwinners' Cup, and CSKA knocked Barcelona out of the European Cup. These Russians knew the way to get rich. "I can understand that the current generation thinks mainly about money. If I was still playing I'd do the same," said Anatoly Byshovets, manager of the CIS in 1992. Apparently, even Russian referees do better abroad than at home: abroad no one is bribing them.

The Brothers Starostin. The founder of Spartak Moscow is over 90 years old. Nikolai Starostin was born in 1902, the son of a hunter who died in the typhoid epidemic of 1920. Nikolai, as the oldest son, fed his brothers by playing soccer in the summer and ice hockey in the winter. He went on to captain his country at both sports, to found Spartak, to manage it and the Soviet national team, and to spend ten years in Stalin's gulags. In 1989, he published his memoirs.

The villain of *Soccer Through the Years* is Lavrenty Pavlovich Beria. Beria was Stalin's secret police-chief and one of the least genteel characters in Soviet history. When he was not purging millions of people he was cruising through Moscow in his limousine picking up adolescent girls, or watching soccer. Like all previous secret police chiefs, Beria was honorary president of Dynamo Moscow, the sports club of the secret police, but unlike his predecessors, he cared about soccer.

Like Stalin, Beria came from Georgia, and it was there that he had learned the game. He was a left-half, who, as one would expect, relied on his muscle. He played against Starostin in the early 1920s and was run ragged. Then he began his political rise, and years later, when he next met Starostin, he hissed: "Now here's the little so-and-so who escaped from me in Tblisi. Let's see if you can get away now!"

Starostin founded Spartak in 1935, as a rival to Beria's Dynamo and CSKA. Starostin's three brothers, Alexander, Andrei and Pyotr, also played for the club, and according to Starostin the four became the "symbol of Spartak." Spartak won the Soviet title in 1938 and 1939, and Beria seethed. The story goes that he called the Dynamo coach to his office. Starostin reconstructs the meeting in his book:

> "I have only one question," said Lavrenty Pavlovich. "What is wrong?" These were the words that sounded in the deep frightening silence of the huge room. "Well," and there followed the flash of his famous glasses, "I am waiting."

"Spartak pays higher wages," the coach answered at last. "Really?" Beria was surprised. " 'Feather and Down' gets more than NKVD servants?" And he said to his officer, "This must quickly be rectified!"

"What else?" Beria asked. "There are some problems with the defense, but we hope . . ." Beria interrupted the coach: "Maybe a company of machinegunners would be a good defense? It can be arranged. But remember that they will also be trained at your back. I advise you to think about this conversation."

Starostin spent years waiting to be arrested. At last, one night in 1942, he was woken by a flashlight shining in his eyes and two pistols pointed at his head. He was taken to the Lubyanka, the secret police headquarters, and was interrogated there for the next two years. Rassypinsky, his interrogator, accused him of plotting to murder Stalin. And, in truth, Starostin had had an opportunity.

Red Square looks like a soccer match waiting to happen. On

Sportsman's Day in 1936, a vast green felt carpet was actually unrolled on it, and the Spartak first team and reserves climbed out of a car decorated as a soccer shoe to play a demonstration match before Stalin: Spartak vs. Spartak Reserves. Initially, the game was to have been between Spartak and Dynamo, but the secret police had pulled out their side at the last minute for fear of what would ensue if the ball were to hit the Kremlin walls, or worst of all, Stalin himself.

It was thought to be the first soccer match The Best Friend of Sportsmen had ever seen, and the aim was to put on a great show. The teams had planned a diversity of goals—goals scored with a header, with a back heel, from a corner kick, from a penalty, and so on—and the first team won 4–3. Next to Stalin stood an official with a white handkerchief, which he was to wave to end the match the moment Stalin began to look bored; but the play so amused Stalin that he allowed it to continue for 43 minutes instead of the planned half hour. Possibly, of course, he was simply daydreaming. His perceived delight at the game made Beria all the more jealous of Spartak.

At the Lubyanka, Rassypinsky showed Starostin a photograph that had been found in his flat. The shoe-car, the photo showed, had passed just ten yards from Lenin's Mausoleum, in front of the Kremlin. "It's direct evidence," said Rassypinsky. "Well, what can you say?"

These charges were dropped—the fact that there had been no plot to kill Stalin was a problem—but Starostin and his three brothers were tried all the same, and all four were found guilty. However, they were given just ten years in Siberia each. This was considered such a mild sentence that it was practically a let off. "The future seemed not so gloomy after all," writes Starostin. He knows to what he owed his luck: "The Starostins did not exist by themselves. In people's minds, they personified Spartak. Beria had to deal with the hopes of millions of fans, ordinary Soviet people."

Starostin was the most popular soccer player in the country, and in each of his gulags over the next few years the camp commander tried to appoint him soccer coach. The poet Osip Mandelstam was executed, but no one was permitted to touch Starostin. "Even inveterate recidivists would sit quiet as mice to listen to my soccer stories." He thinks he knows why soccer was so important: "For most people soccer was the only, and sometimes the last, chance and hope of retaining in their souls a tiny island of sincere feelings and human relations." Meanwhile, in the capital, the regime was trying to Sovietize the game. The word *futbol* was changed to *nozhnoi myach*, *gandbol* to *fuchnoi myach*, and *bootsy* to *botinki*. The Starostins were written out of history. The captions to old team photographs would name eight or nine players and list the others as N.N.s—the Starostins.

Starostin missed the war: when it ended, he was coaching local gulag and Dynamo teams thousands of miles from the front. One night in a Siberian camp a few years into the peace, the local Party secretary shook Starostin awake: "Come quickly! Stalin is on the phone!" It was Vassily Stalin, Stalin's son. During the war, at the age of 18, he had become the world's youngest general, and later he was made commander-in-chief of the Soviet air force. He loved sports, and tried to bring together the state's best soccer players in VVS, the Air Force club he had founded. Frequently, he invited sportsmen to his house for chats about sport, and one evening a brave player had suggested that he appoint Starostin as club coach. The idea amused the young Stalin, who loathed Beria.

As soon as Starostin arrived in the capital, Beria visited him at home to give him 24 hours to leave, so Vassily Stalin put him up in his own house. "We even slept together on the huge bed," Starostin reports. "Vassily Stalin always slept with a pistol beneath his pillow." Even when Stalin went to the Kremlin, he left Starostin under guard, and even when Starostin managed to slip past his guards he could see two delegates of Beria sitting on a bench in the park facing the mansion. Once, when Vassily was drunk, Starostin fled through the open window to visit his family. Early next morning Beria's men came for him and put him on a train to the North Caucasus. Vassily intervened, but later the police exiled Starostin to a desert town in Kazakhstan.

The age of terror ended in March 1953, when Stalin *père* became one of the few Soviet citizens of his generation to die of old age. Starostin returned to Moscow. Beria made a bid to succeed Stalin as sole dictator, failed, and was put on trial. He was found guilty of being an "imperialist agent" and of carrying on "criminal anti-party and anti-state activities," both familiar crimes, and was executed. Several million sighs of relief were breathed, one of them by Martyn Merezov. Merezov, as a referee in the 1920s, had once sent off Beria, and he was very upset when the offender became chief of the secret police.

Gathered and free. The crowd of 15,000 at CSKA vs. Spartak was the largest I saw in Russia, but nonetheless distressingly small. A couple of years before, Spartak's average crowd had been 25,000, and a derby like this would have attracted many more. All the big clubs have lost support, and not just in the old USSR, but in all the nations of Eastern Europe. By 1991, the best-supported club in the USSR was a certain Novbakhor, from Uzbekistan in Central Asia, who, though not in the Soviet premier division, was averaging crowds of 35,000. The Uzbeks still care about their soccer, often to the extent of shooting at visiting players.

There are lots of reasons why crowds have declined: the news of bribery disillusioned fans; hundreds of ex-Soviet players are going West; each republic now has its own league, and Muscovites miss opponents like Dynamo Kiev and Zhalgiris Vilnius; and people have less money now. But there is more to it than that.

There are no congenial cafés in Moscow, so one day, trying to answer this question, Levon Abramian and I wandered through Gorky

Park. Levon is an Armenian who leads a full life. He works as an anthropologist, draws celebrated political and erotic cartoons, has turned down an offer to join the Armenian cabinet, and is a soccer fan.

As a sideline to our chat, we were looking for a group of Communist statues. A year before, these statues had stood in the central squares of Moscow, but after the coup against Gorbachev the crowds had torn them down. Now they were thought to be somewhere in the park. Nobody could direct us, but eventually we found them: four or five enormous creations growing old in the grass. The nameplates had gone, but we recognized the statue of Dzerzhinsky that had stood in front of KGB headquarters, and with the help of two women passing with prams, Levon identified the others. Apparently, just as St. Christopher is always depicted with the Christ child on his back, each Socialist hero has certain set attributes, so that a trained Russian can see whether a particular statue is meant to be, say, Yuri Gagarin, Rosa Luxemburg, or Lenin in Switzerland.

The puzzle completed, Levon told me why people no longer watched soccer matches. In a Communist country, he said, the soccer club you supported was a community to which you yourself had chosen to belong. The regime did not send you to support a club, and, perhaps excepting Western teams, you could choose your team. It might be your only chance to choose a community, and also, in that community you could express yourself as you wished. "To be a fan," concluded Levon, "is to be gathered with others and to be free."

Levon had believed, in the 1980s, that if there was going to be a revolution against Communism it would come from the soccer fans. He admitted: "I thought this would happen in Moscow, because only there were there several teams, each representing a different social class." His theory was that only a unified social class could make a revolution, and this idea ruled out fans in the other republics. Zhalgiris Vilnius in Lithuania, for instance, or Yerevan Ararat in Armenia, united the whole nation, and not a social class.

Soccer in Moscow was more fragmented. "Most CSKA fans are army people, so they are a social unit. Most Spartak fans belonged to a low social class, wore a Spartak uniform, were a bit violent, and hated intellectuals—they were a social unit too."

Levon's theory was wrong, but only slightly wrong. The soccer fans did make the revolution, but not the fans in Moscow. "What happened in fact was that the teams of the republics became a focus for national revolutions against Soviet rule." And he told me how this had worked in Armenia.

Armenia is a small pile of rocks which used to belong to the Soviet Union. It is now an independent country that lies between Turkey and Iran, and which is fighting a war with its neighbor, Azerbaijan. Yerevan Ararat is the main soccer club in Armenia. Like many republics, Armenia had only one premier division team—similarly Georgia had Dynamo Tblisi, and Azerbaijan had Nevchi Baku—and this team was seen as the republic's national side. "When we played Georgia . . . ," Levon would say, and I would correct him: "You mean Dynamo Tblisi." "Yes," he would agree, "but we never saw it that way."

Armenia, or Yerevan Ararat, won the Soviet title only once, in 1973, and that year it won the Cup as well. Armenian soccer tends to produce erratic dribblers, but that year everything came right. The winning goal in the Cup final fell in the last minute, so the double was particularly dramatic. "There was a real festival," said Levon, "a national festival, which was permitted because our Communist officials were elated too. Cars were hooting all over the town of Yerevan all night but no one complained. My neighbor, who was a poet, was told by his father to play the accordion on his balcony. He played some songs, and then he played one, which was forbidden, about Kars, a town in Turkey which was once Armenian: 'Oh Kars, when will you return to Armenia?' He was playing the song without the words, but everyone knew them. This was not a nationalist family, just an average Armenian family. But with this feeling of mutual joy, which was not directed against anything, national feelings come up."

In the Soviet era, when Yerevan Ararat won a match, it was customary for fans to walk through the city of Yerevan chanting slogans. Their favorite chant was, "Ararat," which had a double meaning: Ararat is the name of the team, but also the name of a mountain in Turkey that had belonged to Armenia. Yet the demonstrators were not demanding Armenian independence or war against Turkey, said Levon. They were simply saying that Armenia was best.

Then, under Gorbachev, the republics began to taste independence. At matches against Zhalgiris, or against an Estonian team, the Yerevan fans would chant "Lithuania!" or "Estonia!" to show solidarity with their opponents. When a Russian team visited a southern republic, a local policeman would often suggest to the Russians that if they won, there might be a regrettable riot. "To leave these parts in sound health, even with broken glasses, is considered no bad thing," wrote a Belorussian coach.

An Armenian nationalist movement formed at this time, and it borrowed the songs of the Yerevan Ararat fans. One soccer chant was, *"Hayer!"* (meaning "Armenians!") followed by three short claps, a chant copied from the "Ajax!" and three short claps of the Ajax Amsterdam fans; and chants like this were adopted by the crowds at anti-Soviet demonstrations. "I remember," said Levon, "my sister and her friend, who had never been to the stadium, saying, 'There is something romantic, nostalgic in this cry of "Hayer," ' and I thought, 'No there isn't! It's a soccer chant.' "

Armenian women did not go to the stadium, so it was a place for male rituals. "When you go the stadium," said Levon, "you can do some free things." For instance, only in the stadium was it acceptable to curse. There, it was even considered an art to invent terrible curses. Levon told me of the fan who shouted, "Referee, fuck your wife in front of the Lenin Mausoleum!" The point here was that to the provinces of the USSR, Lenin's Mausoleum seemed the center of the world, a place which all could see. The crowd would laugh: they appreciated good curses. "But there was a debate," Levon said, "between those who wanted to invent new curses and those who preferred traditional curses. Once, a man shouted, 'Referee, I piss on you!' Another man turned round and asked, 'Why "piss?"' For this was not a traditional curse. But the other man replied, 'Why not? It's what I feel like doing.'"

The cursing stopped when a bigger ground was built. Now the fans were spread out and their curses could not be heard, and, Levon told me, "people need to be heard, not only to cry. In the old stadium you could make a policeman look up shocked at a particularly awful curse."

In the stadium you were free, to curse, to chant, to be with your own. The normal psychological state of a Soviet citizen was one of frustration. "Now," Levon said, "Spartak fans can go anywhere to express themselves: to a political meeting, to a church, to a rock concert. OK, they don't go to political meetings, but they know that they *can*. Once you know you are free to express yourself as you like, you don't need actually to do it." So attendance dropped.

The Brothers Charnock. Beria's Dynamo Moscow was founded by Englishmen. Hardly surprising, in a way, because Englishmen founded clubs all over the world, but not, one would have thought, Dynamo Moscow.

Of course Clement and Harry Charnock, textile manufacturers, did not call their club "Dynamo." They named it Orekhovo Sport Club. It was Felix Dzerzhinsky, head of Lenin's secret police, who rechristened Orekhovo as "Dynamo." One Charnock tradition survived, and does to this day: Dynamo still plays in the blue and white of the Orekhovo Sport Club. The brothers were Blackburn Rovers fans.

For decades the chiefs of the KGB watched Dynamo Moscow

from the club's equivalent of the Royal Box. Later, when the USSR invaded Eastern Europe, the teams funded and run by the secret police were all named Dynamo: Dynamo Bucharest, Berlin, Dresden, Kiev, and so forth. Dynamos Dresden and Kiev escaped the stigma of the name to become popular clubs, because they were seen to represent their regions—Saxony and Ukraine—and not the secret police. The other Dynamos were hated. There was a startling scene in 1937, when all the spectators at a Dynamo Moscow match spontaneously began to whistle: not at the players, but at the character of the club. At that time, the height of Stalin's purges, the only place where a gathering could express its hatred was in the anonymity of a soccer stadium. Today, Dynamo Moscow has very few spectators, and few of those are fans.

When I first visited Dynamo Moscow, the players were training, and in the parking lot were their Audis, Mercedes, Volvos, and Fords, almost all without license plates as they presumably had not been registered. The stadium was oversized, gray, and uncovered with a running track. On matchdays it sees crowds of two or three thousand. I met the club's chairman, the cheerless Nikolai Tolstich, who told me that he wanted to give the ground an "English atmosphere." He had visited English clubs—he mentioned Arsenal, Liverpool, Manchester United, and Manchester City—and even now, he said, cafés were opening inside the stadium, and the club was planning to get rid of the running track and to build a roof. "We are also currently painting the stadium," he concluded. That would explain the brown patches I had seen on the ground's gray walls: Dynamo was painting their stadium brown! When I told a friend, she pointed out that the undercoat of paint is always brown, but I am still not convinced. Brown is the color that Tolstich would have chosen.

Dynamo Moscow vs. Asmaral. Asmaral was a tiny club named Krasnaya Prenya until a couple of years ago, when they were bought by an Iraqi businessman. Husam Al-Halidi renamed the club "Asmaral," after one of his companies, and pumped in money, which according to rumor he got from Saddam Hussein. I phoned Al-Halidi's office on the afternoon of the match and told his secretary that I was an English journalist who wanted to interview her boss. "An English journalist? How soon can you be here?," was the message. We agreed that I would meet him at the match.

There were, of course, very few people at the stadium, yet we had trouble gaining entry. By dint of seeing thousands of bureaucrats, I had obtained the official Moscow soccer press pass, but I was with a friend from the *Moscow Times* who only had a general pass. The old man guarding the press box stopped us. "Your pass is fine," he said to me, "but yours," he told my companion, "is invalid." Then he threw his arms in the air and yelled in delight: "But it DOESN'T MATTER!" This anarchist then let us in.

The match began as slowly as the Torpedo match had. Every couple of minutes, a player fell to the ground and was treated for an injury. These players were not diving to win free kicks. They were going down out of laziness, and because they were playing so unenthusiastically: their adrenaline had gone skiing, so knocks hurt more. Once, when Dynamo lost the ball up front, just ten minutes into the match, three Dynamo midfield players *walked* back towards their own half, forty yards behind the Asmaral counterattack. They simply could not be bothered.

Gradually, though, the match changed. Dynamo scored a couple, and their players became more interested. They ran into space, chased after opponents, did all the things they previously had not felt like doing, and did them just because they were having fun. Soccer is such a good game, this proved, that even Russian professionals can sometimes enjoy it. Dynamo thrashed Asmaral 6–1. At the start of the second half, I went to the directors' box, where Beria used to sit, to find Al-Halidi, but he had already gone home.

* * *

The President of Soccer. Russian soccer seemed a bit of a mess. The man who presides over it, Vyacheslav Koloskov, is not. Koloskov used to be president of the Soviet Soccer Federation and today he is president of the Russian Soccer Federation. He is renowned for his power within FIFA and UEFA, and travels to the West all the time. A well-groomed character in new clothes that fit him, Koloskov looks considerably less like a Russian than like a German businessman.

It is whispered that Koloskov is responsible for one of the main oddities of the American World Cup: that a European nation the size of France, and with a comparable soccering history, though a disguised one, was not allowed to enter the tournament. That country is Ukraine, for the great Soviet teams of the 1970s and 1980s consisted almost exclusively of Ukrainians. Now Ukraine is raging at FIFA, at Russia, and particularly at Koloskov.

Shortly before disintegrating into 15 republics, the Soviet Union was drawn in a qualifying group for the American World Cup. When the Union collapsed, FIFA decided that there was a place for only one republic to replace the USSR. It chose Russia. I asked Koloskov whether Ukraine was angry. "Georgia is also angry," he shrugged, and took a file from the cupboard that gave FIFA's arguments for its decision. Ukrainians prefer their own theories. As one Dynamo Kiev official told me: "Russia is in the World Cup because Koloskov drinks vodka with the gentlemen of FIFA."

Did Koloskov agree that Soviet soccer had suffered greatly in recent years? "Of course damage was done, very great damage, in all the republics." The problem, as he saw it, was the demise of the all-Soviet league. "Dynamo Kiev of Ukraine, Dynamo Minsk of Belorussia, Tblisi in Georgia, and Yerevan Ararat of Armenia were all very good teams, but more importantly, they were consistent soccer cultures, who enriched themselves by playing against each other." The Armenians and the Georgians were renowned for their skill, the Ukrainians of Dynamo Kiev for their tactical discipline, and so on. Now each republic had its own league, and the level in each league was low.

I asked him about Ovchinikov–Bormann's admission of bribery. "It was a joke," said Koloskov. "Two weeks ago Ovchinikov stood on this very carpet and swore he was joking." Did Koloskov believe him? "There is an old Russian saying: 'He who is not caught is not a thief.'" He added: "We have a match delegate watching every match. If the referee is bad, then this referee is no more. This year, we disqualified five referees for inconsistent refereeing. It is possible that some of them were cheating."

I had one last question. Hundreds of Russian soccer players already played abroad. Did Koloskov have a plan to prevent a further exodus? "Yes, we have a plan." What was it? "Our plan," he grinned, "is to increase living standards in Russia to the level of Germany. At least!"

"Or England," the interpreter suggested politely. "England is not that rich anymore," I confessed. "That is what Dr. Koloskov says," replied the interpreter. Koloskov was a worldly man.

CHAPTER 6

RULERS OF UKRAiNE

A FIRST-CLASS TICKET on the overnight train from Moscow to Kiev cost me £1.50 in September 1992, but would be cheaper now. I shared a compartment with a talkative Chinese man. He spoke no English (and I no Chinese), but with my 100 words of Russian we established that he was the Moscow correspondent of the *Worker's Daily*. "What is the circulation of the *Worker's Daily*?" I managed to convey. "Twenty million," he said.

We arrived in Kiev on a Monday morning. I already had a flat to go to. The woman who had rented me an apartment in Moscow was the daughter of a Red Army officer who had helped conquer Germany. In this officer's regiment there had been a Ukrainian, and this Ukrainian's daughter now lived in Kiev and had a flat to spare—or at least a tenant whom she could easily expel. So the Red Army network got me an apartment.

On the way to and from it I invariably got lost, because all the streets in Kiev look the same. The city was destroyed in the war, and rebuilt in the 1950s, a bad time for Soviet architecture. Kiev has gray flats, wide streets, and the occasional large statue. Everything is on a superhuman scale. One night I decided to eat in a restaurant that I knew to be further along my street, and I got on a bus. It trekked ten miles down the road until it reached a forest. By then it was dark, and raining. The restaurant had to be a little further along, but was the forest safe at night? Would the food be worth it?

And so I took the bus home again. I stayed alive because, inexplicably, Kiev street vendors sell New Zealand kiwis, and Dynamo Kiev runs a snack bar. Once, struggling through its Soviet cuisine, I watched the club president's secretary pass carrying an electric kettle. Not much good in the West, I know, but in Kiev the kettle was the difference between Them and Us.

Ukraine has 50 million inhabitants and is poorer than Russia. Kiev has four million inhabitants but no McDonald's, and is a one-club town. Valeri Lobanovski, the great postwar Soviet manager, turned Dynamo Kiev into one of the best clubs in Europe, and led them to the European Cupwinners' Cup in 1975 and 1986. "Loba," as his players never dared call him, liked discipline. Once, seeing a player drunk, he set him to work as a groundsman for five months, and then sold him to a lesser club. When *perestroika* came, the Dynamo players moved west and flopped: Alexander Zavarov at Juventus, Igor Belanov at Borussia Mönchengladbach, Alexei Mikhailichenko at Sampdoria, and he and Oleg Kutznetsov at Rangers. They could not cope without Loba.

Everyone who saw the Dynamo of the mid-1980s came away talking of robots. The players were constantly moving off the ball, yet found one another without looking, and appeared fitter and quicker than other soccer players. It was said that Dynamo had been using science, and it was true. On my first morning in Kiev, I changed money with my landlady's 14-year-old son, a hard bargainer, and made for the city center. About five minutes from the Dynamo Stadium, in the basement of a rare ancient house, I found Professor Anatoly Zelentsov.

Lobanovski was a trained plumber, but at heart he was a scientist. In 1967, when he was manager of Dnepr Dnepropetrowsk and Zelentsov was dean of the Dnepropetrowsk Institute of Physical Science, the two became collaborators. "Our aim was to invent the science of soccer," the professor, a robust, cheery man in a large sweater, told me. In his basement, he and his assistants think up ways of improving Dynamo's game.

That morning we talked only briefly. He outlined the science of soccer, and stressed that it is highly practical. When Lobanovski said things like, "A team that commits errors in no more than 15 to 18 percent of its acts is unbeatable," he was not guessing: Zelentsov's team had collated statistics. Zelentsov worked from the premise that since a fraction of a second's thought can be too long in modern soccer, a player had to know where to pass *before* he got the ball. To this end, Dynamo's players had to memorize set plays, as if they were American soccer players, and had to run off the ball in set patterns. As to the superman look of the players: Zelentsov pointed out that when players train for stamina, their speed drops, and vice versa. To assure both qualities, a coach had to alternate training exercises in a certain sequence, and Zelentsov devised a training model. He told me that Italy had used the model to win the 1982 World Cup.

Then he took me to a room where an assistant was watching the latest Dynamo match, on a screen divided into nine squares. Here, Zelentsov said, a computer program automatically analyzed each game Dynamo played. The squares on the screen were there to measure how often each player went into each part of the pitch, who should replace him when he left a zone, and how much work he did with and without the ball. It also showed which players were compatible with one another. In the West German team of the 1980s, for instance, Manni Kaltz and Hans-Peter Briegel disliked each other but combined well on the field. It was a fertile program: Zelentsov handed me a computer printout that measured, for each Dynamo player in the match, "intensitivity," "activity," "error rate," "effectivity" ("absolute" and "relative") and "realization," and awarded each player a final mark computed to the third decimal point. It almost put to shame the stars *Match Weekly* hands out.

Science, boasted Zelentsov, had made Dynamo the most successful club in the USSR. So good were they that they often masqueraded as the national side, and at the 1976 Olympics "Dynamo" (he meant the USSR) had won bronze. But that was a catastrophe—it should have been gold—and Zelentsov began to mutter about the referee.

He had something special to show me, but I had to go to the club. I arranged to come back to see him on Thursday morning, the day after Dynamo was to play Rapid Vienna in the UEFA Cup.

A dolphinarium stands in front of the Dynamo Stadium, and shaven-headed men in tracksuits directed me to the club offices. Dynamo offer various sports, and these characters did not play Ping-Pong.

Inside, in an office with a view of the pitch, I met a neat, gangling young man named Roman Obchenko, head of international relations at Dynamo. Like many other people, I had thought that Dynamo were a sports club. Roman was to tell me how wrong I had been.

The club, he told me, was the richest in the old USSR: "That is like an axiom which does not need stating." Each player earned about $1,125 per month, almost all of it paid in dollars, and 14 members of the squad drove a Mercedes. Victor Bezverkhy, the Dynamo president, drove two. By way of comparison: the Ukrainian President Kravchuk earns around $40 per month, paid in Ukrainian coupons.

Roman spoke perfect English, so I said, "You speak very good English." He nodded: "I have an Oxford degree." I had an Oxford degree too, and we became friendly. We discussed England—he had disliked it—and then I ventured: "Journalists in Moscow tell me that Dynamo are in with the mafia." I had spoken the password: Roman suggested we continue our chat over a drink. It was a pleasure to find the old boy network at work here.

We were taken to the Hotel Intourist in a Mercedes driven by a

Dynamo chauffeur, whom Roman asked me to tip. I gave the man $2 (which I was sure was a fortune to him), and paid for the beers in Deutschmarks. Roman and I settled down on brown armchairs, German businessmen all around us.

Roman proved the best single source I met all year, a lazy journalist's dream. I have often wondered what made him talk to me, but I suspect this: that he was simply bursting to tell someone what he had seen at the club. For Roman had become quite Western, and the ways of Ukraine could still surprise him. As well as in Oxford he had lived in Canada, where his father had been a Soviet diplomat. Also, he wanted my book to do well. He was writing a novel himself, about life after Communism, though he really wanted to become a politician. "The route to the top must be short for someone like you," I suggested, and he replied: "That's correct!" The children of the old *nomenklatura*, with their contacts and foreign languages, will be the next rulers of the old Soviet countries. Roman's father was one of President Kravchuk's seven advisors.

Then Roman began to talk. "The mafia in this part of the world is very old," he said. There was not one big mafia in the old USSR, but several thousand small ones. "When the Party was responsible for everything, the mafia made money by producing legal things illegally. For instance, the Odessa mafia bought cotton in Turkey and produced with it jeans in state factories, by paying the factory workers to do overtime." The early mafiosi were often sportsmen, he told me. "This is because the first stage of mafia activity is always racketeering—demanding money from private businesses with threats—and for that you need strong men, who are sportsmen." I thought of the shaven-headed people at the stadium.

He then began to tell me about Dynamo. The Ministry of the Interior controlled the club in Soviet days, but Lobanovski, who was considered to be club president as well as manager, had striven to free Dynamo from the ministry's control. He wanted Dynamo to turn "professional," to make its money from sponsors, like the clubs he saw in the West.

Dynamo had fans in high places. The late Vladimir Scherbitsky, leader of the Ukrainian Communist Party, used to sit in the government box at the Republican Stadium. If he said, "Take that player off," off the player would go. To thank him for his tactical tips, Dynamo built Scherbitsky a secret *five-story underground palace* in a town near Kiev. He was touched, and persuaded Ygor Ligachev to lobby the other members of the Politburo for permission for Dynamo to go professional. "But Ligachev was a conservative," I objected. "He hated capitalism." "Ligachev was a conservative," agreed Roman, "but he was also a friend of Scherbitsky's."

Ligachev did the trick, and in 1989, Dynamo became the first fully professional club in the USSR. Soon after, Lobanovski went off to coach in Saudi Arabia, and Dynamo got a new president. Victor Bezverkhy came with friends, who joined the board. "They decided to make the club rich, which was a good idea," Roman said. "In Communist society that could be done legally, by observing formalities, which takes a long time and is expensive. They decided to do it another way."

(Roman really did talk like this. He knew exactly what he wanted to say, and said it simply. This was a lecture he had been a long time in preparing.)

The first step Dynamo took was legal: they set up joint ventures, companies in which they put up part of the capital and a Western firm put up the rest. The profit from these is tax free, because in theory Dynamo is a sports club. A lot of money came in. The main joint venture, Dynamo Atlantic, made a profit of $1.5 to $2.5 million a month, in a country with one of the most disastrous economies in Europe. "It became plain," said Roman, "that the club could be successful without even playing soccer." To safeguard the joint ventures, Dynamo invited leaders of the mafia to join: Party officials and their families. "This was easy," said Roman, "as most sportsmen had mafia ties."

Then Communism fell. "Dynamo Kiev is a famous soccer club, but now Western businessmen know Dynamo too. The word passes around among them that when you do business in Ukraine, the club can help, as it has ties. Take Zgursky, the ex-mayor of Kiev: he is now head of a commission responsible for renting premises for industry. These premises are in high demand. Zgursky gets a *very* large amount of money in dollars to give premises to people who have references from the club. Dynamo gives him money too."

"Bribery," I said. "But what is a bribe?" Roman countered. "In this country you can bribe someone by taking him abroad. Zgursky comes on all Dynamo's foreign trips. If someone asks, you can say that he is a fan who will shout, 'Dynamo, score a goal!' "

Rapid Vienna was visiting Kiev that Wednesday, and the return in Austria was two weeks later. Roman produced an expensive American laptop—I instantly regretted paying for the beer—and called up on the screen the list of guests accompanying Dynamo to Vienna. It looked as though the plane would be full, and the 90 or so names on Roman's list read like the Ukrainian *Who's Who*. There was Alexandre Denissov, head of the board of trustees of a major bank; "my name-sake, Roman Romaniouk," son of the presidential envoy in a Kiev district where Dynamo is renting premises cheaply, or buying them, "which is very profitable now." "Wait a minute," said Roman, "I will find the name of the guy who is the boss of the mafia in Kiev." He searched, but said he could not find it, which was perhaps the one sign I got that Roman was at all afraid.

"Were they all in the Party?" I asked. "You can judge from their age," he replied, for with customary efficiency, he had listed dates of birth. "Can it be that all soccer fans are born before 1940? No, but all the important people in Kiev were." It was the ageism that he resented, not the corruption. There were only a few young guests on the list, all of whom were women. "Girls serving the interests of the bosses," Roman explained.

In the winter of 1990, when it was thought that the USSR was starving, I had read an article by a German aid worker who had driven a truckful of food to Kiev. On reaching the city, he and his friends were given a banquet by the local great and good. At the end of it, the great and good leaned back in their chairs and said to the Germans, "Well done. Now give us your truck, and we will distribute the food to the poor." The Germans thanked them for the offer and rejected it. "Were the people at that banquet the Dynamo directors and their guests?" I asked Roman. He burst out laughing, delighted by the childish greed of it all: "very likely!"

The Dynamo mafia was doing nicely, he said, and it paid as few taxes as it could. "Did you notice the driver who brought us here? His main job is driving money from Odessa to Kiev, and then from Kiev to Berlin. Usually he takes $600,000 to Kiev, and $2 million to Berlin, all in cash. He is guarded by the mafia. If you have money in a Ukrainian bank, and you transfer it to a foreign bank, you have to pay taxes on it. But if you carry it in cash to a foreign bank you avoid taxes. Our prime minister said on TV recently, 'The government only has $20 million to spend on all its programs. We know that some organizations have ten times as much money to spend as we do, but they keep their money abroad.' Now, if he is right that the government has $20 million to spend, then we could buy the government. But there is no need to." Why not? Because there were still lots of legal ways to launder money. Ukraine, a young nation, was busy framing its laws, and for the moment there were plenty of loopholes.

In the Mercedes, on our way back to Dynamo, I asked, "Don't you ever need to rely on corruption in the cabinet itself?" "No," said Roman. "Not at all?" He laughed again: "Isn't that enough?" A country in which even the president earns $40 a month, while a local business has tens of millions to spare, is sure to be corrupt.

"In fact, you could afford to pay the players far more than they earn now," I said. "You could pay salaries to compete with the best in the Bundesliga, or in Britain. You could bring the best British players to Kiev." "It's true," said Roman, "but if we paid salaries of £30,000 a month, the government and the Ukrainian public would get angry. It would be seen as tactless. Also, the people who run this club have a policy that to invest in the team is risky: to invest in production is safe."

The team was a source of income: Dynamo bought players cheaply in the old USSR and sold them at a profit to the West. To help me with an article I was writing for *World Soccer*, Roman gave me a list with each Dynamo player's name, weight, height, age and the period his contract still had to run, all of it in English: a catalogue for foreign buyers. Recently I read that Dynamo Kiev might be about to go bankrupt. Perhaps the directors had decided that it was time to ditch the team.

We tend to think of Dynamo as a soccer club, and yet their role in Ukraine makes sense. The country is backward, but thanks to Lobanovski, Scherbitsky, and various soccer players, its soccer club is modern and rich. European soccer has an economic system of its own. Juventus paid £3 million for Zavarov. How many other Ukrainian products do the Italians want to buy? From soccer, Dynamo had the initial capital they needed to bribe officials, buy protection, and put up money for joint ventures. Thanks to their regular European matches, the club's officials already knew directors and sponsors of Western clubs, and Western TV executives and advertisers: in short, Western businessmen. They also knew the local political leaders, who hung around the club because they liked soccer. Probably no other Ukrainian company was as well placed.

That Wednesday, a few hours before the Rapid match, I spoke to Roman for the last time on the pitch of the Republican Stadium. Dynamo athletes were running around the track, and Roman, guided by Austrian yuppies, was stapling advertisements onto boards. Many were for Dynamo's joint ventures. "Will you beat Rapid?" I asked, and he admitted that soccer bored him. Instead he said: "Our joint ventures are not real." What? "Foreign companies provide all their capital. Dynamo only lends its name, because if a company is a joint venture it pays less taxes, and Dynamo Kiev's name helps in the Ukrainian market." The foreign company then pays Dynamo around 50 percent of the sum it saves in taxes.

It was then, in my last few minutes with Roman, that he told me the most interesting club secrets. He was going to Berlin on business the next day, and would not see me again. "Dynamo," he told me, "has licenses to export nuclear missile parts, two tons of gold per annum and metals including platinum." He asked me not to mention the gold, and I promised, and in the rest of the book I have honored such promises, but not in this case. "How did you get these licenses?" I asked. Through bribery. Also, he explained, if you publicly give the government $1 million, as a present to the nation, the government might be encouraged to give you a license to export goods worth far more.

This was unfortunate: not only does a soccer club that exports nuclear missile parts endanger the world, but Ukraine needed its gold. The country was giving up the Russian rouble to establish its own currency, and only gold reserves could prevent the new currency from inflating. Two tons a year is a lot of gold, and inevitably, Ukrainian inflation is even higher than Russian.

Outside the stadium, just before the match, Roman and I ran into Victor Bannikov, president of the Ukrainian Soccer Federation, who agreed to see me at ten the next morning. I arrived at quarter to ten to watch him drive off in a Lada, waving at me as he left.

"Have a good time in Berlin," I said to Roman, and he shook his head. He would be living modestly, he said: "The other guys, when they go abroad, spend $5,000 a day on their hotel, their limousine and their private helicopter." We shook hands and I went to the press-box. It was the last I saw of him. I trust his career is thriving.

It poured with rain that night. The Republican Stadium has no roof, which would be fine were it in Africa, and the few thousand spectators huddled at the back of the stand, where the rim of the tier above gave a modicum of shelter.

In the pressbox, an Austrian journalist looked up in disgust. The woman in charge of the telephones had just put him through to the Viennese police. "Nothing has changed," he announced, meaning that the fall of Communism had not made his life easier. "Nothing," a colleague agreed, and the poorly connected one said, "The phones are as bad as ever, it still smells like it used to, and the place is still a ruin." The exchange would have bemused the men who run Dynamo. A lot *had* changed. For one thing, they now earned several times more than Austrian journalists.

Yet it was true that the parts of Dynamo that did not relate to business were still mired in Communism. The soccer team, for instance: no new Blokhins and Belanovs here. But the famous running off the ball was still largely intact, and Rapid was often made to look like old men. Dynamo won 1–0, with a goal from Pavel Yakovenko, one of two survivors from the Lobanovski years. At the final whistle the fans sprinted out of the stadium, sopping wet.

The next morning, Professor Zelentsov sent his chauffeur-driven Lada round to collect me from the Dynamo Stadium. He was keen to see me, for now that Communism was gone he hoped to sell his ideas to Western clubs. As he put it: "I would like to pass on my methods, though only to reputable buyers." I hope I can repay him for his help. Any soccer manager who happens to be reading this can write to Zelentsov c/o Dynamo Kiev, Kiev, Ukraine. No need for a more complete address: Dynamo is well-known over there.

The problem with theory, Zelentsov began by saying, is that soccer depends on the players you have: "There is an idea, and there are executors of the idea." So he had devised a scientific way of identifying the best players.

He showed me his assistant, who now seemed to be playing a

computer game. "There are many methods of measuring the capacity of a player," Zelentsov said. "You can test his blood control, how he runs, how he jumps. I prefer to work with non-contact methods: to avoid getting AIDS, and so as not to give the player so much work that it tires him. There are lots of ways of testing, but I prefer the computer. For the player, also, it is interesting to work on the computer." He had invented computer games to test soccer players.

I asked: "Is it correct that you used these tests to pick the Soviet squad for the 1988 European Championship?" Zelentsov's son-in-law had told me so. "There were 40 candidates, and with these tests we selected the first 20," Zelentsov agreed. The squad he picked had baffled the press, but the USSR had reached the final. Zelentsov chastised me for citing just one instance. The tests were used often. If Dynamo was thinking of signing a player, the man took the tests, and the Dynamo squad was tested regularly.

The assistant at the computer ran the first test. A line ran down the screen, a dot moved across the screen from left to right and the assistant tried to press a key just as the dot crossed the line. It was a test, Zelentsov explained, of reactions, nerve and balance. The assistant tried to place around ten dots, each of which moved at a different speed, and was given a score.

Then it was my turn—my chance to see whether I could play for Dynamo. I did badly. The first time I scored 0.34, and the second time 0.42. Dynamo players, said Zelentsov, would normally score between 0.5 and 0.6, with higher scores ranging from 0.6 to 0.8. When a player was in form, or felt good (Zelentsov spoke of his "psyche"), he would do better than otherwise.

In defense of my scores, I want to say that I think I distorted the exercise. When I placed a dot badly, I would become nervous and press the keys a few times, thus placing my next dot well off target. Admittedly, one of the qualities the test measured was nerve. Even so. Zelentsov looked downcast.

I was resolved to do better on the next test, a typing test that measured endurance. I had to press one key as quickly as possible for a few seconds, to establish my maximum speed, and then I had 40 seconds to get in as many more presses as possible. The aim was to stay as close as possible to my maximum speed during the 40 seconds, which (try it) is a long time to press up and down on a key. This time I am sure I distorted the test. While I established my maximum speed Zelentsov told me not to lift my finger off the key, as this wasted time. From then on I kept my finger on the key and did better. Because of this, my speed barely fell off the maximum during the 40 seconds. I hope Zelentsov knew about problems like this, because otherwise strange choices might have crept into that 1988 team. Perhaps he was also measuring intelligence: if you took the tests in the wrong way, you failed. I got marks for endurance, the way my muscles work, my ability to achieve speed and my resistance to tiredness.

Then came a memory test. The screen was divided into nine squares, and a different number under 100 appeared in each square and vanished after a few seconds. I had then to type the right number in each square. According to Zelentsov, this tested the ability to remember where teammates and opponents are on the pitch. (Perhaps he was a charlatan—I cannot say.) I played three screens and got all numbers right, scoring 97 percent. Of course I did: the kind of memory required was very like the kind used in academic work, to remember names and dates and so on, and I had just finished a university degree. The test suggested why good passers—Osvaldo Ardiles, Glenn Hoddle, Ray Wilkins, Graeme Souness, and most quarterbacks in American soccer—tend to be more intellectual than other players.

The next test was very simple. The screen would suddenly flash white, and as quickly as possible after that I had to press the keyboard: a test of reactions. The average time I needed was 220 milliseconds, and a jubilant Zelentsov announced that this score would have been acceptable from a Dynamo player at the start of a season. I can honestly say that I have never felt prouder in my life.

The last test I found impossible. A dot would trace a complicated trajectory through a maze, and then I had to retrace the path, using a joystick. But I could never remember the route, and the maze was so narrow and mazy, and moreover constantly in motion, that I was always bumping into walls. It was, of course, a test of coordination and memory, and it made me realize how extraordinary professional soccer players are. Not after years of practice could I have negotiated that maze.

Using the scores, Zelentsov could tell the coach which aspects of a player's game needed work. I said, "I see that these tests measure abilities required in soccer. But surely there are some abilities they cannot test?" He agreed: "Speed, for example, also depends on running technique. We can measure that elsewhere." "And," I said, "what if Zavarov and Belanov did these tests badly? They were still your best players. You had to pick them." "Zavarov and Belanov," replied Zelentsov, "even when they were out of form, had far higher results than the others." Which players in the current side did best on these tests? "Did you see the match last night?," he responded. "Then you have seen it for yourself." "Yakovenko?" I guessed. "Yakovenko! Leonenko! Luzhny! Annenkov! Shmatovalenko!"

Dynamo was good to me: along with Barcelona, Cape Town Hellenic, and the USA team, they were the nicest club I dealt with that year. (Orlando Pirates of South Africa and Sparta Prague were the rudest.) That Friday, on my last day in Kiev, President Bezverkhy made time to see me.

His office was simple: brown walls, brown chairs, Communist furniture, and house plants. I mentioned this to Max, my interpreter, who replied scathingly: "But you don't think his house looks like that!" Max had no time for Dynamo. He wore a ponytail, of which the shaven-headed disapproved, and he had learned to walk the other way when he saw tracksuits at night. The CinCin Cafe, opposite the Dynamo Stadium, is where these characters hang out, and when you next visit Kiev it is a place you might avoid.

Bezverkhy was friendly, but then he was a contented man. "Thank God our club was created two years before the market came to our country," he told me. The ministry of sport had wanted all clubs to go pro simultaneously, which would have been the Soviet way. Dynamo made a lot of money before their rivals became independent.

I asked why it was rumored that Dynamo was connected to the mafia. "It's news to me that we have links with the mafia," Bezverkhy replied, but the topic seemed to appeal to him, and he grew talkative. Did the mafia do much work in soccer itself? "Two mafia men came to a Russian club, said that two players had to transfer to another club and it was done." Why did the mafia care? "The mafia understands that transfers can be profitable to it." And in Ukraine? "There is a process of arranged matches in Ukraine. I can't be sure. I can only suspect." Did Dynamo have experience of this? "Two years ago, there was an attempt to dictate the result of a match here in Kiev. We were able to evade it, not thanks to links with the mafia, but thanks to our links with the KGB." What had happened? "One member of our team was approached in the street, and was told that the next match had to end in a draw. It was pointed out to him that players had wives and children in Kiev. The situation was clear. To avoid these situations, we have created two organizations of bodyguards, who guard not only the players, thanks to our joint venture with the British firm Securitas."

Even with bodyguards you could never be sure. Not long before I arrived, "Vata," a Kiev mafia boss, speaking to a man in his car at the Dynamo Stadium, suddenly found himself riddled with bullets. Vata had 16 bodyguards, and only let people near him whom he trusted, so the murderer must have been a friend. Vata was a big Dynamo fan, and the whole squad attended his funeral. Bezverkhy stayed away: given Vata's reputation, to attend would have been unseemly. Instead, reported one newspaper, on the day of the funeral the president cried in a five-star restaurant.

On Friday afternoon—within hours I would be on a train to the West—the Dynamo press officer dug out his umbrella and walked me to the statue in front of the Dynamo Stadium. It depicts four men, all ten feet tall with conservative hairstyles, who stand arm in arm gazing into the distance. There is not a soccer ball in sight, and no accompanying text either, but the clue to their identity is that they wear shorts. This is a monument to a soccer match.

On invading Kiev, the Germans arranged a match against Dynamo. The spectators were all German soldiers with machine-guns, and when the Ukrainians took the lead the soldiers began to fire at their legs. Though several players went down, Dynamo hung on to win. After the final whistle the whole team was executed. It was, in short, *Escape to Victory* with an unhappy end. In fact a famous film was made of the match, and the actor who played the goalkeeper looked so much the part that a club offered him a contract.

The press officer told me the story of the game, and then asked me not to write it: because it was not true. The match was a myth concocted after the war by the local Communist Party. No doubt some kind of game had taken place, for one survivor, age 86, lives in Kiev, but sensibly he keeps mum.

It was time to go. I had spent six weeks in the remains of the Soviet Union, and to celebrate my departure I blew $3.00 on the *Guardian* international edition. It told me that the day of Dynamo vs. Rapid had also been Black Wednesday, the day the pound dropped out of the ERM. I waited at the station from midnight to 5 A.M., and let a group of Pakistanis studying in Moscow read the *Guardian* cricket reports. Meanwhile I watched two old women with the worst job in the world: cleaning the waiting room at Kiev Station on the 3 to 5 A.M. shift.

Perhaps because of the state of the currency markets, perhaps not, the woman at the ticket desk refused to take my British pounds. Minutes before the train left, at five in the morning, the Pakistanis changed my pounds into dollars, taking a sizeable cut for themselves.

Fifty-six dollars to go from Kiev to Prague is a bargain, if you consider that the journey passes through a large swathe of Europe and takes 48 hours. I slept for the first day, waking up every few hours to see exactly the same countryside as before. It was soothing. At 2 A.M. we reached the border with Czechoslovakia. A Ukrainian border guard who looked about 15 told me that my visa was invalid (it was valid). He swiftly added: "No problem, no problem. How many dollars do you have?" I had three. "Two," I said. "You give me two dollars, no problem." It was my first ever bribe, and I thought of Kukushkin in Moscow. Back at the train, another border guard asked me, in deliberate tones, for he had memorized the sentence: "Do you have a present for me?" I said not. I asked for the Prague train, and he directed me to it. I waited in it for five hours, in cold weather, and when it finally left it made for Bratislava. Two trains and 12 hours later I was in Prague, and it looked like the West to me.

CHAPTER 7

LONE SKINHEAD
SAVES NATION

I TOOK A TRAIN from Prague, passed through Bratislava again at three in the morning, and arrived in Budapest a couple of hours later to find soccer on the front pages of all the newspapers. A shame they were in Hungarian.

Twelve days before, Ferencváros of Hungary had visited Slovan Bratislava of Slovakia to play a European Cup match, and 15 Hungarian fans had landed up in the hospital. Soccer hooliganism had nothing to do with it. I was in Budapest for the return match, and revenge was in the air. Ferencváros vs. Slovan looked like it was turning into something more than a soccer game.

In Bratislava, Slovak anti-terrorist troops in black masks had repeatedly stormed Ferencváros fans who may or may not have been chanting, "Greater Hungary" and "Give us Southern Slovakia back." The troops had used tear gas and wooden clubs, and had been thorough. The Slovak crowd had applauded. Tibor Nyilasi, Hungarian legend of the past and now manager of Ferencváros, had thought of the Heysel. And, he told *Kurir*: "I'm not afraid to say that it reminded me of the cruelties of the fascists." At the final whistle, Slovan had thanked the troops over the loudspeakers ("a peculiar and repulsive act," said the Hungarian consul), and then police had chased Hungarians in the streets around the stadium while Slovak fans stoned Hungarian cars and buses. Slovan won the match 4–1.

"This is not a soccer roar, it is a political question," said Gyula

Horn, the Hungarian elder statesman. Within three months, Czechoslovakia was to split into the Czech Republic and Slovakia, and Bratislava, scene of the beatings, was to become the Slovak capital. Independent Slovakia, under President Meciar, showed signs of becoming a nasty little nationalist state. Meciar, often seen at Slovan matches, liked to say that Slovakia had been "truly free" only as a puppet state of Nazi Germany during World War II. He blamed all problems on "enemies" at home and abroad. "I wonder who is playing this dirty game at our expense?" he asked when bugs were found in the American Embassy in Bratislava.

The 600,000 Hungarians who live in Slovakia were frightened. Meciar was already complaining about bilingual road signs in Hungarian areas, and they feared that worse was to follow: no more Hungarian schools, a ban on their language, and one day perhaps even "ethnic cleansing." Yugoslavia, after all, was just down the road.

The Hungarian diaspora is the largest in Europe. It spreads across Rumania, Slovakia and the Ukraine, and politicians in Budapest fret over it. The year before, Hungarians in Rumania had been killed in a pogrom. When Slovak troops beat Hungarian soccer fans, Budapest protested immediately, but Meciar retorted that the fans were hooligans who had got what they deserved.

Meciar knew exactly what he was doing. A Slovak nationalist (who used to be a Communist), Meciar wanted to show both Slovaks and Hungarians that he would stand for no nonsense. He deliberately chose a soccer match to deliver his warning: people who pay little attention to politics watch soccer on TV, and the only place in which Slovaks and Hungarians appear in opposing mobs is a soccer stadium. The problem with using soccer was that the West watched too. CNN sent pictures of the match around the world, and Western governments and businesses reminded themselves not to deal with the brutish Meciar.

Meanwhile Ferencváros was still hoping to reach the second round. On the afternoon before the return leg, I spoke to the club's general manager, Mihály Havasi—though only for three minutes, as he was about to meet the Hungarian home affairs minister. Havasi claimed that three of his players had had their wives and one his father in the crowd in Bratislava, and he mimed to me how they had played: looking briefly down at the ball, and then lengthily up at the stands. He had asked UEFA to overturn the 4–1 defeat and have the match replayed, but instead UEFA had fined both clubs 15,000 Swiss francs. "It's a typical Western decision," commented a Prague radio station (the Czechs remained neutral). "Faced with an annoying Eastern European phenomenon, instead of investigating and deciding according to the facts, the West gives both mischievous children a slap and tells them not to do it again." Later Ferencváros appealed the fine, and it was lifted.

UEFA had ranked the return leg as an "A" on the danger scale. "A" seemed an understatement. Most Slovak journalists had decided to give the match a miss, and Slovan was begging their fans to stay at home too. Even the team was planning to arrive in Hungary only just before kickoff. "Where are they arriving?" I asked one Czech journalist, and he smiled and said, "I'm sorry, I can't tell you." I tried to ask the Ferencváros president, a red-bearded giant, whether he expected trouble, but all he would say was, "Soccer is here, and politics is there." Then I went to look around the club museum. The curator spoke only Hungarian, but when he gathered I was British he produced the largest bottle of Johnnie Walker I have ever seen. It was noon.

Outside the metro station by the Ferencváros ground that night, I passed five or six boys in black balaclavas, all leaping up and down and shouting, in English, "Fuck you Slovan, fuck you!" at a pack of press photographers. I was led into the ground with a group of

Czech and Slovak journalists. We were searched and then escorted by police past Hungarians shouting abuse. The Ferencváros support cares.

The little stadium is one of those corners of Eastern Europe that the Communists never got round to spoiling. The stands do not dwarf the crowd, as stadiums in Russia do; they are not in gray concrete, but painted green and white, the club colors; and there is no running track. All quite British, in fact, and the fans were trying to be Britons too. They wore English club scarves, waved Ferencváros flags in the shape of Union Jacks, and the chant to which they always returned was, "Fuck you Slovan, fuck you!" Yet they never quite mastered our style. They sang in Hungarian accents, and I saw two boys in Chelsea scarves kiss each other on both cheeks. Even the Union Jack has another meaning in the East: there, it evokes the West, pop music, and above all, soccer hooliganism. Our thugs may have hurt Britain's image abroad, but to one section of every society they are heroes.

The stadium was packed. In the press stand, which is behind one of the goals, were 200 journalists, for most newspapers had sent both soccer and political reporters. I could see no Slovan fans, though Czech radio had said that more than 200 had crossed the border.

The Slovan players took the pitch first, to warm up, and were whistled at nonstop for half an hour. They were separated by a fence and a few fat stewards from 30,000 people who hated them, and as 4–1 leads went theirs did not look safe. "I've never seen an atmosphere like it," I told a Hungarian journalist. He asked, "Have you never seen Liverpool against Manchester?" which is what Continentals call Manchester United. That was different. English fans enjoy their rivalries; this crowd *loathed* Slovaks.

And then, though Slovan had returned inside, the crowd suddenly began to bay again. Below me, at the bottom of the press stand, a small skinhead in dungarees was carefully tying a blue-and-white Slovan flag to the fence.

We journalists pounced on him. The skinhead declared that he was 16 years old, spoke no Hungarian, and had travelled alone from Bratislava. The manager of Slovan was alerted and walked over to tell the boy, "We are grateful."

It later transpired that five other Slovak fans had made the journey, but the "Lone Slovak Hero" story lost little of its shine, and the boy gave interviews and posed for photographs throughout the match. He was a pleasant enough skinhead, and now he was a national hero. Though our grandstand was an all-seater he watched the match standing, presumably from force of habit.

Ferencváros proved a slow team even by Eastern European standards, and stirred themselves only when it came to kicking Slovaks: no Nyilasis in this team. The crowd stopped chanting, and the political reporters grew bored and began to talk politics. The match ended scoreless, so Slovan went on to the next round, where AC Milan was to thrash them. But first they had to get out of Budapest.

Outside the changing rooms, Nyilasi gave interviews and the Slovan players sat on their bags and waited for their bus. The skinhead, still on his feet, was among them, for he had been invited to fly back with the team and had graciously accepted. The reporters surrounded him, ignoring the players.

The Ferencváros fans were outside awaiting their prey. I went to join them. After an hour, a bus came out, its telltale Czechoslovak number plate ineffectually covered by a plank. The fans rushed it, only to find themselves face to face with worried middle-aged Czechoslovak journalists. Then policemen on horses came galloping out of the gateway, the fans ran away, and the Slovan bus tore out of the gate. The Hungarians went home, but now and then I read in the newspapers that Meciar is still bullying his Hungarians. Slovakia and Hungary are rearming.

CHAPTER 8

GAZZA, EUROPE AND THE FALL OF MARGARET THATCHER

WE IN BRITAIN TEND to divide soccer players into two classes: one class is "British," and the other "Continental." Tony Adams, David Batty and Tony Cascarino are British players, and Chris Waddle, John Barnes and Eric Cantona are Continentals. It was the same in the past: there were Englishmen like Jack Charlton, Norman Hunter and Nobby Stiles, and Continentals like Liam Brady, Glenn Hoddle and Ossie Ardiles. The terms have so little to do with geography that Ron Greenwood could even call the Brazilians "those marvelous Continentals." (In fact, the Brazilians are more Continental than the Continentals and want to change).

The Briton and the Continental tend to differ not only as players. Often, the Continental is a more cultivated character. He discusses soccer, reads books, and may move abroad and learn a foreign language. Hoddle and Liam Brady are examples.

Not Paul Gascoigne, the most Continental player England has today. Gascoigne is, perhaps, more commonly known as Gazza ("Guzzle" to one fanzine) and is the subject of Gazzamania.

When the soccer fan dies, he goes to Italy, where he finds the best players in the world, matches shown in full on public TV and numerous daily sports newspapers. Nice weather, too. In October 1992 I reached Rome and went to the Olympic Stadium to watch Lazio Roma (complete with Gazza) play Parma. It was Gazza's first home game in Italy.

Aron Winter, Lazio's Dutchman, had filled in the Dutch magazine *Voetbal International* on Gazza's start in Rome:

> Gascoigne is here with his brother, his best friend, and his bodyguard. And as long as Paul plays here, they stay in Rome. Each one has his own flat. But take last night . . . It was a little over half past twelve, and Yvonne and I had just decided to go to sleep, when there's a knock on the door. I open it, Paul's there. Completely naked, wearing only a very small pair of glasses. "If you need something, call me," he says. This morning he had the police in his room. A policeman had tied up his friend with handcuffs which they just couldn't get off. Tied to a chair. The four of them always drive around Rome together, escorted by a police car with howling sirens. He's just absolutely mad.

Apparently Gazza's friend had already been fool enough to make a telephone call without covering his back, and had been urinated on, but Winter refused to confirm the story. Winter's business manager added: "It's a bit of a pose of Gascoigne's, he acts a bit. Because if you talk to him alone, he's quite normal, but as soon as his friends come in, he starts again."

Mussolini built Gazza's home ground, and on the forecourt is an imitation Roman mosaic, bearing the text, over and over again, *"A Noi Duce."* Sitting in the Curva Nord among the more intense *Lazioli*, I felt as though I had trespassed into a Fascist rally. By the fence at the front of the stand stood four men, their backs to the game, who took turns with a microphone to dictate chants to the masses. Sometimes the chant would be "L-A-Z-I-O, Lazio," each letter accompanied by the thrusting forward of right arms in a familiar salute. Sometimes, instead of a chant, one of the leaders would utter a string of shrieks and groans into the microphone, to which the *tifosi* would respond with fast handclap.

The match was fantastic, as was Gazza. There was a moment when he had the ball in midfield, while Thomas Doll ran into space on the right wing, marked by the Parma left-back. The back saw that Gazza was planning to thread the ball past him, and blocked off the space expertly. Yet Gazza put the ball, over 30 yards, inches over the defender's left shoe and into Doll's stride. The thugs around me rose in adoration. The English boy was their hero, and they sometimes seemed to shout the opera title La Gazza Ladra—"The Thieving Magpie"—at him. Opposition fans prefer to call him "Ubriacone con l'orecchino"—"Drunkard with an earring." Lazio won 5–2.

The next day, the Lazio man at the daily *Il Messagero* explained to me that the fans liked Gazza because he was an extrovert. I agreed that Gazza was an extrovert, but pointed out one thing he had in common with British failures in Italy like Luther Blissett and Ian Rush: he speaks no Italian. Rush left Juventus after two sorry years saying, "It was like playing in another country," while Blissett, at AC Milan, complained, "No matter how much money you've got, you can't seem to get any Rice Crispies." *Il Messagero*'s Lazio man nodded. It was true that Gazza spoke no Italian, and of Lazio's Italians only Fiori spoke English. Fiori and Gazza were pally. "But," said the Lazio man, "Blissett and Rush were like this": and with his hands he made a tunnel before his eyes. "Gazza is like this": and he threw his arms out wide and waved them about.

I said to the paper's sports editor, "Italian clubs insist that their players behave in public. Gazza does not behave." The Italian papers were not like the British tabloids, he replied. He himself had been offered a photo of Gazza, standing in the showers, holding a teammate's private parts and waving at the camera, but had turned it down, and so had all his colleagues. Why had he? "The picture was not elegant." I asked whether the Lazio fans were known for a somewhat Fascist style. He said: "The *Nazi-skins* are Lazioli, but not all Lazioli are *Nazi-skins*. Not all Germans are Nazis."

In January 1991, six months after the World Cup, I had written the following article in the *Berliner Tageszeitung*, a German daily. There are as many interpretations of Gazza as of Hamlet, and this is mine.

Gazzaland

Every year Britain's feared satirical magazine *Private Eye* elects the Bore of the Year. The winner is the person who in the previous twelve months gained the most publicity with the fewest achievements. This year the election will be a formality: the soccer player Paul Gascoigne is going to win his umpteenth title of 1990.

Nobody calls the fat little soccer player Gascoigne anymore. Since the World Cup probably even his mother calls him "Gazza"—I didn't ask her, because nowadays she charges £300 per interview. England's adoration of Gazza has taken on unheard-of, ridiculous forms. There are a number of Gazza books and newspapers on the market; his single, the worst of all terrible soccer players' songs, reached second place in the charts; and the British tabloids live off him. The *Sun* has even published the Gazza family albums, which chart his development from small, fat, ugly, red-haired kid with freckles into small, fat, ugly, red-headed international with freckles.

Each country has the heroes it deserves. Why do the English worship Gazza? I must admit that even to many of us it is a mystery. Gazzamania, that much is clear, took off after the World Cup semi-final between England and Germany in Turin. There were only a few minutes left to play when Gascoigne committed an unnecessary foul, got a yellow card and was thus suspended for the hoped-for final. Gazza began to cry.

The TV cameras captured the sight perfectly, and on millions of English sofas tears began to fall too. Gazza's tears even inspired the intellectual TV station Channel Four to make a successful documentary series about men who cried in public.

Admittedly, Gazza's crying is uncommonly moving. He admits in confidence that he sometimes cries tactically. There is the famous story of his first meeting with hard man Jack Charlton, now manager of Ireland. When Big Jack became manager of Newcastle, he called in the teenaged Gazza and threatened him with the sack unless he lost weight. The meeting ended in mutual tears. "The lad has had a hard life," Charlton defended himself afterwards.

Gazza comes from the poor city of Gateshead in the Northeast of England, where his father has been unemployed for almost 20 years. It is often said that Gazza grew up on fish and chips, but in fact, in his neighbourhood fish was an almost unattainable luxury. Nowadays he plays for London's glamor team Tottenham Hotspur, but every week he drives home to drink at his father's working man's club.

He is a man of the people and the people know it. To the English, he is the true Englishman, who matches the Continentals without behaving like a Continental. He does not speak a word of a foreign language, has no desire to learn either, and yet he has an un-English skill and tactical intelligence. That is why he is beloved: he is precisely the symbol that Britain needs today. Before Gazza, the English were always being told that "the Europeans" were rich, spoke languages, kept their streets clean and played clever soccer. Our country had an inferiority complex. Only a few still believed in Margaret Thatcher's constant claims of British superiority. That is why she was replaced by John Major: like Gazza, he plays European and yet remains unmistakably English.

Shortly before her fall, in a desperate attempt to identify herself with the new Britain, Mrs. Thatcher invited Gazza to Downing Street. Apparently they hugged each other, and Gazza later revealed that the prime minister was "nice and cuddly, like me." But then he does tell tales about women. Until this tête-à-tête, Mrs. Thatcher was probably the only person in Britain who was not familiar with Gazza. All she knew about soccer was hooliganism.

Many believe that Gazza will soon be lying beside Mrs. Thatcher on the scrap heap. His predecessor, the brilliant Northern Irish winger George Best, was also ruined by hysterical publicity. The chairman of Newcastle United, Gazza's first club, has called Gazza "George Best without brains." Gazza in turn has said that Best is "scum," to which Best has replied that at least he was by far the better player of the two. But then Gazza's fame does not have much to do with soccer.

Beneath the article the *Tageszeitung* printed a picture of Thatcher and Gazza with the caption: "Margaret Thatcher with Paul Gascoigne. Shortly afterwards she was forced to resign."

Years have passed and some passages from the article read strangely now. Gazza has learned a little Italian, but the main problem is that John Major today hardly seems a prototype of European élan. I accept that he and Gazza are by no means identical characters, and they may never become close friends, but when Major replaced Thatcher and promised to deal with the Continentals, he stood for a Britain that would be less out of things and yet would remain thoroughly British. The nation loved him. Major and Gazza came in on the same ticket, and within five months of each other.

We can now see that at the time of my article Gazzamania was at its peak. When Gazza appeared on the television talk show *Wogan* soon after the World Cup he was introduced as "literally the most famous and probably the most popular person in Britain today." The person still periodically delights us by advising Norway to fuck off, or by belching at Italian journalists, or even by scoring for England, but nothing he has done since crying in Turin and driving through Luton in false breasts has excited as much joy in millions of English people with no interest in soccer.

The World Cup was Gazza's stage, and not just because he played well and England won matches. The tournament was the best opportunity we have had to contrast him with the Continentals. The first thing one noticed was that, fat and red-faced, he did not look like them. Nor did he even want to: he told Ruud Gullit, the suavest Rastafarian in the business, that he was "a long-haired yeti." The Continentals spoke to the press in several languages, while he refused even to speak in one, and somehow he contrived not to seem as rich as they did. "What did they pay for you then?" he asked Ronald Koeman, Holland's Continental *libero*. (Frank Rijkaard laughed and replied, "A hell of a lot!")

As a player, Gazza did to the Continentals what they normally do to Tony Adams. When he back heeled his way past two Dutch defenders, English friends explained to me that it was the "Cruyff turn": the supposed speciality of Johan Cruyff, the Continent's most cosmopolitan soccer thinker. Gazza had proved that we did not need to *be* like him to play like him.

Gazza's crowning moment at the World Cup was his foul on Berthold. He did slide into Berthold, but then, as Continentals do, Berthold played dead. The German bench rose in pretend horror, and the referee, whose name was Wright but who was a Brazilian and therefore a Continental, produced the famous card.

Then Gazza cried. Continentals cry too—Maradona does—but they do it on purpose, like characters from their operas. Gazza cried because a nasty thing had happened to him. He probably also hoped that Wright, upset at the tears, would take back the yellow card, but that hardly qualifies as scheming. These were the tears of a child, and they were seen by more Britons than had ever watched a single TV program.

I say Gazza was our two fingers up to the dreaded Europeans. I may be quite wrong. What is undeniable is that anyone writing a mental history of postwar Britain will have to explain Gazza's tears.

CHAPTER 9

A DAY WiTH HELENiO HERRERA

THE MAN WHO TAUGHT the world how to play defensive soccer is Helenio Herrera, and I was delighted when he agreed to speak to me.

As I see it, there are four approaches to soccer that dominate today. There is the long-ball game, played particularly in Britain. There is total soccer, spread by the Dutch to teams like Barcelona and AC Milan, Dynamo Kiev and São Paolo. There is the happy-go-lucky style that we associate with Brazil, but that I was to see at its purest in South Africa, where it is known as "piano and shoeshine" soccer. And there is *catenaccio*, the defensive system with the Italian name. Few teams play pure total soccer, or pure long-ball soccer: most borrow elements from all the styles. In the dourest defensive team, an unpredictable winger can provide the Brazilian touch. However, every team in the world tends to one or other of these four basic systems. In other chapters, I try to explain why the Dutch, the British and the Brazilians play the way they do. In this chapter, I ask how *catenaccio* arose.

I took a night train from Rome to Venice, wandered around the city all morning trying not to spend money, and then met Herrera's wife, who took me to their medieval *palazzo* on a canal. She is a fashion journalist, and it was plainly she who had chosen the house: it was the most beautiful private home I have ever seen, though Herrera and his son had broken many of its windows playing soccer indoors. The *palazzo's* interior was an unusual mix of *objets d'art* and caricatures of Herrera, many of them depicting him as a magician. As he was to remind me several times, his nickname had been *Il Mago*.

I found Herrera daydreaming in his study, with its view over the canals. A stocky figure with neat, grizzled hair, he is in his seventies but looks 20 years younger, and behaves 60 years younger. These days he is a soccer pundit on Canale 5, Silvio Berlusconi's TV channel, and he had come a long way to Venice: "My parents were poor Andalusians, so they went to Argentina, where I was born. But they were poor in Argentina too, so when I had four years we moved to Morocco, which was French then. My school was almost totally French, and now there are only Arabs there." He seemed astonished that such a great change had managed to occur without his participation. "From 14 or 15 years old, I played with the Arabs, Jews, with the French, with Spaniards. That is a school of life. Then, at 17 or 18, I went to Paris, because I was a good soccer player."

He became a manager, and in the 1950s and 1960s he was the most famous manager in the world. In his three years at Barcelona, he won two Fairs Cups and two Spanish titles, but he had to leave when *Barça* lost to Real Madrid and fans assaulted him outside the team's hotel. At Inter Milan, he won two European Cups and three league titles. He also managed Spain, France and Italy (not at the same time). Asked once where he would finish in an Italian popularity poll, he replied: "Behind Sophia Loren, but only because she has a better figure." It was in Italy, with Inter, that he earned his place in history.

Catenaccio has become a synonym for the defensive style. In Italian, the word means "padlock." In soccer, it describes a system in which the sweeper stays behind his defense, and his team marks man to man, forming a padlock in front of the goal, and letting the opposition attack. It is boring soccer, but as we see at every World Cup, it works. Most nations draw from it, but it is an Italian speciality: the *Azzurri* won the World Cup of 1982 with Giacinto Scirea, their sweeper, spending whole matches in his own half. My aim was to find out what it was about Italy—its culture? its history? its soccering culture?—that made *catenaccio* thrive there.

"I was the first player ever to play sweeper!" he told me. "It was when I was in France, it was, oh, about 1945"—Occupation or no Occupation, for Herrera dates have a strictly soccering significance— "and we were playing like this." He drew the old W–M formation on a file. "With 15 minutes to go, we were winning, 1–0. I was him," he pointed at his paper, "the left-back, so I tapped him, the left-half on the shoulder, and said, 'You take my place, and I'll go here behind the defense.' (Already when I was a player I thought like that.) And we won, and when I became manager, I remembered that."

That's what he says. According to Brian Glanville, it was the Swiss coach Karl Rappan who invented *catenaccio* in the 1950s. When Herrera came to Inter, the club was playing a moderate form of it. Herrera refined and exaggerated the evil system, won European trophies with it, and thus spread it around the world.

The logic behind *catenaccio*, he said, was that in the old W–M system the lone central defender was helpless if two forwards came through the center: "So for hard matches I used a sweeper. Away is hard." But he had also said, I quoted, that *catenaccio* was necessary to combat lesser teams. "Yes, against the bad teams also," he conceded. "But my critics, they all used a sweeper! The English criticized most, but Wright played sweeper." Whether he meant Mark Wright at the Italian World Cup—Bobby Robson's bow to Herrera—or Billy Wright in the 1950s, I do not know.

I suggested that he had made soccer a duller game. "*Catenaccio* is much criticized because it has been wrongly used." He drew another formation. "In my system these two"—the center backs in front of the sweeper—"were markers, but the fullbacks had to attack," and he energetically drew long lines forward from the back positions. "Facchetti, Giacinto Facchetti, could attack at Inter because of me. When I put Facchetti in the team he was a teenager, and everyone said,

'Ohohoh!' " He threw up his hands in mock horror. "I said, 'This man will play for Italy!,' and he was captain of Italy 70 times! But the managers who imitated me did not let their backs attack, and they used *catenaccio* as a defensive system." He shook his head in grief.

Who had given him his ideas? "Gabriel Hanot (the Frenchman who invented the European Cup) is the only one who is better in intelligence"—better than Herrera himself. And which managers had he influenced? "All, in some way," and he nodded sagely. "I have a TV here, and I see managers say, 'It was M. Herrera who gave us the ideas to win matches.' " Had his cosmopolitan background shaped his ideas? "Ideas come from the intelligence. From nowhere else."

As well as giving us *catenaccio*, Herrera had introduced to soccer unique methods of motivation. "I invented training camps. When I started at Inter, I used to get phone calls at two on Saturday night from *tifosi*, fans, saying, 'Balbo is still in the disco!' But also, at most clubs it was like this: you come in for practice in the morning," and he mimed, at top speed, a player shaking hands, nodding to teammates right and left, exchanging a word here, a word there, running like a cartoon character onto the field, running back, showering and running home. Herrera dismissed the image with a shake of his head, and intoned his mantra: "One team, one family." "When I came to Inter," he told me, "there was a terrible ambience. There were boards everywhere about past championships, very impressive you understand, but so distant."

So, "on Friday evening we would go into seclusion. We would go for a walk, to take in oxygen, and I would talk to players individually: 'How's it going? How's your wife?' and so on. I hung up boards in the changing rooms saying 'SPEED' and 'TECHNIQUE,' and later we had great speed with Jair and Mazzola. I told the masseur, 'The players will talk with each other while they are lying on your couch. Tell me what they say, but only what concerns the club. The rest,' he added grandly, 'does not interest me.' "

And: "I don't like the restaurants in this country, where there is a table here, a table there, a table over there. I wanted," he spread out his hands, "one big table for the whole team. I would sit at the head, and we would talk: 'How's it going? How's your wife?' and so on. Then, on the day of the match, I would sit down with the whole team and . . ." Nostalgia overcame him, and he produced a magnetic board, a referee's whistle and a small case of magnetic soccer players. Using me as his imaginary team, he mimed a tactical talk.

It was at this point in the presentation that Herrera would introduce his more eccentric methods. Glanville writes that he would throw a ball at each player in turn, while yelling, "What do you think of the match? Why are we going to win?" The players had to shout answers like, "We'll win because we want to win." Finally, Herrera would hold out a soccer ball, and the players would extend their arms towards it and shout, "It is the European Cup! We must have it! We shall have it! Ah ah ah!"

"It is important to touch the ball before the match," Herrera explained to me. "The players are nervous, it is a big match, there is a big crowd, but the ball: that is their life. Then I made the players hug each other. Not kiss, just hug! And I told them, 'We are all in the same boat!' They would hug, not *so*," he mimicked a tentative embrace, "but—" and he threw himself into imaginary action, and repeated several times, "I have confidence in you, and you have confidence in me. Then they would start throwing themselves at each other spontaneously! Then they would get changed, and I would say, 'Speak to each other! Defense, speak among yourselves! *Une équipe, une famille.*' "

At Inter, Omar Sivori grew so riled that once, during a game, he blasted the ball straight at Herrera on the bench. I told Herrera that Gerry Hitchens, an Englishman at Inter, had said, "Mr. Herrera is a genius, but leaving Inter for Torino was like coming out of the army"; in fact Hitchens never said the part about genius. "Hitchens, is he still alive?" Herrera asked curiously. "Yes it is true," he agreed about the army, "but we often sang too. When we lost a match I would say, 'Now we'll sing!,' and we'd sing for hours on the bus home. When we lost in Sevilla once, we danced on the bus." He took a few steps. "The flamenco."

Yet his methods worked: he was not *Il Mago* for nothing. Even when Inter replaced him, they chose a man named Heriberto Herrera, always known in the press as HH 2.

As well as winning two European Cups, Inter reached the final in 1967, when they lost to Jock Stein's Celtic in Lisbon. At the banquet after that match, on order from Liverpool's Bill Shankly, two Celtic coaches sat abusing Herrera. Shankly had a grudge against Herrera. In 1965, Inter had knocked out Liverpool in the semifinal of the European Cup thanks to two dubious goals in Milan: Corso scored directly from an indirect free kick, and Peiro kicked the ball out of the keeper's hands for another. It seemed as if Dezso Solti had been at work again.

Solti's job, Glanville has shown, was to buy referees for Inter. The Hungarian is a blot on Herrera's Italian triumphs, but I did not bother to raise the topic with Herrera himself. I merely asked him if soccer was an honest world, and he said yes. Certainly he has no Olympic spirit in him: so competitive was he that Shankly, the man who thought soccer was much more important than life or death, called him "a cutthroat man who wanted to win."

Cutthroat was not the half of it. Told by doctors at AS Roma that his young forward Taccola had a heart murmur, Herrera heard the news with faint interest. Then, when Roma visited Cagliari, he took Taccola along for the ride, but made him train with the squad on a cold beach the morning before the match. Taccola caught a fever, watched the match, and died.

Herrera and I stopped for lunch, and at the table he pressed food on me. "Don't torture him. He's not one of your players," chided his wife. Herrera looked ashamed. They were kind. We had a mutual friend in Leeds, and I asked them about their holiday there. "Leeds!

What is there to say about this city?" exclaimed Mrs Herrera. "Nothing. It's pleasant enough." "I liked the stadium," ventured Herrera.

After lunch, we walked through the streets to his dentist. He seemed activated by the familiar situation, and clasped my arm and began asking me about myself, as if we were preparing to play Real Madrid. A dictator, yes, but a solicitous dictator. He told me that his favorite player had been Real's Alfredo di Stefano. "Cruyff is not in Pelé's style, he is in Di Stefano's, but at a lower level. Di Stefano was the greatest player of all time and I'll tell you why. People used to say to me, 'Pelé is the first violinist in the orchestra,' and I would answer, 'Yes, but Di Stefano is the whole orchestra!' " He was in defense, in midfield, in attack, he never stopped running, and he would shout at the other players to run too. He'd say, 'You're playing with my money!' Because Di Stefano was like this," and Herrera rubbed forefinger and thumb together in the international sign for money.

I mentioned the rumor that as manager of Spain at the World Cup in 1962, Herrera had had a personality clash with Di Stefano, who played not a minute at his only World Cup. "No, he was injured," Herrera insisted. "It is true that the first time the team came together, at the Soccer Federation office in Spain, Di Stefano refused to shake my hand. The press in Madrid was attacking me because I was Barcelona manager, and because I had picked almost the entire Barcelona team. Of course I had kept my eyes open over the years," he made the gesture, "and collected my people. Also, Di Stefano was not happy at first because in those days it was the players who ran the teams. You had the team of Di Stefano, the team of Mazzola, the team of Sivori, and the trainer was the man who carries the bags," and he mimicked an overburdened porter. Herrera was a gifted mimic, and I wondered what he did as a TV commentator. "I changed all that. I said, 'I am the manager, so I am the boss.' And after that managers started to earn good money," and gleefully he rubbed finger and thumb together again. "Later Di

Stefano said, 'I understand now that *Señor* Herrera is a great manager.' But at the World Cup, he was injured."

Herrera was managing Spain in 1962 because he had had to resign as assistant manager of Italy. There had been rumors that Inter players were taking drugs, and Herrera had celebrated too openly when Inter's rivals Juventus were knocked out of the European Cup. He could make Brian Clough look shy at times. On taking over at AS Roma, he had told the press that the club had won its one league title, in 1941, only "because Mussolini was the manager." The fans were upset. I asked whether a manager could afford to be controversial. "It hurts if you are a little manager. A manager like me, forgive me for saying it, can tell the directors, 'If you have confidence in me, *bon*. If not . . .' "

Club presidents, he added, "are all mafiosi! Well, not all. They sit there to earn money. If it is two million, they write down one million and stick the other million in their pockets." Barcelona, I said, had a particular tradition of directors interfering with managers. "They were jealous of me," replied Herrera, "they were jealous of Maradona too. I always said, 'It is my team,' " and he cupped his hands protectively. "I am the only one who talks to the players."

It was time to ask again about the place of national character in soccer, about Italy and *catenaccio*. Herrera is a Cosmopolitan. He is trilingual in Spanish, French and Italian (and speaks passable Arabic), and he has worked with the best teams and best players of various countries.

I began by reminding him that he had been a scourge of the British game. "You in England," he had told journalists at Birmingham Airport in 1960, after his Barcelona had beaten Wolves 5–2 at Molineux, "are playing now in the style we Continentals used so many years ago, with much physical strength, but no method, no technique." I quoted this back to him and he smiled fondly. "Yes," he agreed. "Now, there is still dispute about where the modern game was invented. 'It was in China!,' 'No, in Italy!,' 'No, in England!' There is no doubt that modern soccer was invented in England, and English railway workers brought it to places like Huelva and Bilbao. They would play, and Spaniards would think, 'Oh, that is a good pastime,' and run off to do it also. That is why when I came to Spain, my players called me '*Señor* Mister': they thought 'Mister' was the word for coach, because until then their coaches had always been Britons!" (In fact managers in Spain are still known as "Mister.")

"But," he added sternly, "when it came to modern soccer, the Britons missed the evolution. That was the case when we played Wolves. Though they have caught up now, and now sometimes Italy is best, sometimes Germany, sometimes the English. It changes, as it should." Why had the English missed the evolution before? "The English are creatures of habit: tea at five." Later, quite by chance, his wife brought us tea at 5 P.M., and he shouted with delight as if his point had been proven.

We were where I wanted to be. I asked, "So players from different countries have different characteristics?" He agreed. At Barcelona he had played his tricky foreigners in attack, and in defense, "my big Catalans. To the Catalans I talked, 'Colors of Catalonia, play for your nation,' and to the foreigners I talked money." He smiled whenever he mentioned the word. "I talked about their wives and kids. You have 25 players, you don't say the same thing to everyone."

What were the differences between the nationalities? "Hungarians are more reserved." He hunched his shoulders and screwed up his face in imitation, "so I mixed them, not Czibor and Kocsis together in one room. I wanted all to be the same, I wanted friendship. That is why we retired to training camp, why we ate together. And it created a new category of players: before, you had players who took a whisky, a whore, even though they were married! Mazzola and Facchetti, at Inter, were a new generation, serious and well-mannered. (When you return to England, I advise you to marry.) Once, I took the wives on holiday with us!" He took as an affront my suggestion that he had failed to make his players identical.

Going from *Barça* to Inter, had he found a difference in mentality between the two teams? "No, the Latins are alike. When I was sitting at the head of the table at Inter, I would look at the players and think, 'Is this Inter, or *Barça*?' "

He then dismissed the question: "You know, in soccer the drive is *gagner*"—a word that means both to win and to earn. But had his Cosmopolitan background shaped him? "Yes." Then suddenly he said, "Perfectionist." I was baffled. "Perfectionist," he repeated, "that is the word I have been searching for all the time!"

I tried once more: Did different tactics suit different nations? "No, I always put the same imprint on a team, wherever I was. The secret is putting players in the right place, because if you put Pelé in the wrong place he is only 30 percent."

But by his own admission, I said, Herrera had used *catenaccio* at Italy and not at Barcelona. "It is true," he said unhappily. "In France I was the first *libero* who ever played. I abandoned that in Spain, but when I came to Italy they had copied *catenaccio* from France where it had become general." Some theorists, I said, argued that *catenaccio* suited Italians because they were supposedly physically weak. Herrera was scornful. So each nation does not have its own style? "No. If things are right, the system is the same everywhere."

The previous Sunday, the day I had seen Lazio and Parma score seven goals, 48 were notched in all of *Serie A* to break an Italian matchday record. At that stage of the season, the goals-per-game average was 3.45; the best for a whole season stood at 3.32 for 1949–50. "It is the Death of *Catenaccio*," was the headline in *Il Messagero*, and certainly Milan, with Baresi at *libero* playing in front of his defense, must have irked Herrera. He shook his head. You *had* to have man-to-man marking, he told me. Milan took too many risks. "When you play away, you have to watch out!" he said again. Then he suddenly made a pragmatic point: "You have a tactic, you concede a goal, tactic—*pfff.*"

CHAPTER 10

FC BARCELONA AND THE SCOTTISH QUESTION

FC BARCELONA'S MOTTO IS "More than a club," and next to *Barça*, Juventus looks like a village team. Juve does not have a weekly satirical BBC TV program devoted to them, and nor do they run an art competition so prestigious that Salvador Dali once submitted an entry, nor boast the Pope as season-ticket holder no. 108,000. Even the *Barça* museum is the best attended in the city: more visitors than the Picasso Museum.

I arrived in Barcelona in October 1992, which was a good time for the city. The loudspeakers in the metro played genuine music, and every day shop signs in Spanish went down and were replaced by Catalan signs. The city had just staged an Olympic Games free of terrorists, drugs and boycotts, and was growing richer by the day, while that May, against Sampdoria at Wembley, *Barça* had won its first ever European Cup. A week after leaving Barcelona I returned to post-Black Wednesday in Britain, and noticed a different mood.

Fittingly, Barça's Nou Camp stadium is in the center of town. One weekday morning I looked down from the fourth tier of the empty stadium, and felt that a team that dared face *Barça* here must regret it the moment they peered out of the tunnel. The stadium is a city in itself: it seats 120,000 people, or the entire population of Norwich, and is currently being enlarged. "There comes a point when the people in the top tier need telescopes, and then you have to stop building," laments the club.

In the catacombs of the Nou Camp that morning, 25 journalists were waiting by the changing rooms for the squad to emerge after practice. These men and women have a hard life. Every day, they must wring quotes from *Barça* players who are trying to say nothing, and then improve the spoils. When half an hour had passed a senior quote collector shrieked, *"Cruf!,"* indicating that Johan Cruyff, the manager, had appeared, and that if caught quickly would surely reveal great secrets. A couple of hopefuls charged forward and returned to derisive laughter. Eventually Michael Laudrup appeared, tastefully dressed for a man of his income. Denmark was playing Ireland that night, but Laudrup was still refusing to play for his country, so the journalists asked him about Möller-Nielsen. Naturally he answered in platitudes, which were eagerly noted. Then a club official announced that Cruyff would not be seeing the press that day. So who was going to fill the papers?

FC Barcelona may be the biggest club in any country, in any sport, in the world. Why is this? There is a reason for everything.

I was granted an interview with Nicolau Casaus, first vice president of *Barça*. I was told he had no English, but while waiting outside his room I heard him repeat several times, in an American accent, the word "Siddown!" He seemed to be practising. When I came in he spoke Spanish and had a big cigar in his mouth. I remarked on the club's motto and asked whether it referred to FC Barcelona's status as a political item in Spain. Casaus denied *Barça* any political significance. He said that people of different parties and religions supported the club. Why, then, that motto? "Barcelonism is a great passion," he answered vaguely.

Club directors—at Rangers, at Celtic, at Barcelona—always prefer to say that their club is just a club. Nor do players tend to worry about their employers' political status. But what players and directors think is beside the point, because a club is what it means to its fans. *Barça* has fans everywhere—they have a fan club in

Tianjin, China—but they belong to Barcelona, and to Catalonia, the region of which Barcelona is the capital.

The Catalans feel Catalan first and Spanish second, and to prove it they have long fought wars and made revolts against Madrid. Until recently they always lost. This century, for instance, in the civil war of the 1930s, Catalonia held out longest against General Franco, but then suffered under his yoke until he died in 1975. Now Catalonia has its own regional government, the *Generalitat*. But the five million Catalans want more: a state of their own, perhaps. "Catalonia is the most powerful nation without a state in Europe," Jordi Torrebadella, a young Barcelona economist and *Barça* fan told me. "You can't compare us to Scotland, because we're far more powerful within our state than Scotland is in the UK. We subsidize the rest of Spain, whereas Scotland is subsidized by England." Or as Cruyff learned when he came to play for *Barça* in 1973: "We earn it, and in Madrid they eat it up."

I asked Professor Lluís Flaquer, a Catalan sociologist, if he could recommend any books on *Barça*, but he could only come up with one, and it was 20 years old. I asked why academics had neglected the club. "There are some subjects," said Flaquer, "which are considered too sacred to write about, and there are also subjects that are thought too profane." I took it he was going to call soccer profane, but he concluded: "*Barça* is still too sacred."

Barça is a hundred times more famous than Catalonia itself, and is the main source of Catalan pride. When Franco ruled Spain, they were the only source. Why, I asked a Catalan woman bored by soccer, do you care about *Barça* beating Real Madrid? She replied: "Franco destroyed our autonomy and forbade our language, and he supported Real Madrid." It was said that *El Caudillo* could recite Real lineups going back decades, and when Real visited Barcelona during his reign there were always banned Catalan flags in the Nou

Camp. *Barça's* fans went home from these matches as exhausted as the players. "You couldn't shout 'Franco, you murderer!' on the streets," explained Flaquer, "so people shouted at Real Madrid players instead. It's a psychological phenomenon: if you can't shout at your father, you shout at someone else." Only at the Nou Camp did Catalonia still exist, and the only Catalan symbol Franco never dared touch was *Barça*.

It is natural that when a region is silenced it turns to soccer. Yet Franco is long dead and *Barça* remain the symbol of Catalonia. "When I go to the Nou Camp, I feel as though I am suddenly back in the days of Franco," one woman told me. In 1992, when Barcelona introduced a new strip design that included a thin white stripe on the famous red and blue, there was an uproar: white was the color of Real. "I brought in the stripe," Josep Lluís Núñez, the club president, argued paradoxically, "because I don't want to be known as the president who introduced shirt advertising here." (To preserve the sanctity of their colors, Barcelona refuses to wear advertising.) Even today, Catalans confuse Real with rule from Madrid, and find it confusing that a few cabinet ministers now support *Barça*. They take bias from Madrid for granted, and the Nou Camp often subjects referees to a hail of cushions. Cruyff and Núñez like to speak of political refereeing. After all, José Plaza, ancient boss of Spanish referees, is a self-confessed Real fan.

The passion persists, which becomes even harder to explain when you know that a great many citizens of Barcelona—fans of the club—are not even Catalans. So many, that some say there is no such thing as a Catalan working class: the lower classes in Barcelona are migrants from the rest of Spain. The typical migrant arrived in the 1960s, when the Catalan boom began. He jumped off the train, took a room where he could, found a job, and then made a choice: either to support *Barça* or Español.

* * *

Español is the second club in the city, and they play around the corner from the Nou Camp, in the Sarria Stadium. Their founders, in 1900, chose the name Español—"Spanish"—as a gibe at foreign *Barça*, whose founder, Joan Gamper, was Swiss. From Messrs Harris, Parssons, Wild, and Witty in 1899, to Gary Lineker, Mark Hughes, and Steve Archibald in the 1980s, to the present day, *Barça* has always depended on foreigners. I asked Torrebadella whether Catalans would prefer to win without help from outside. "Ah, of course!" he replied. "But that is what we call Catalan *'pactisme'* "— our capacity to make pacts with other peoples. Because we are a nation without a state, we have always had to make such pacts if we want to win championships, or achieve anything at all."

Barça is undeniably foreign, but the name "Español" proved a blunder. As *Barça* became the symbol of Catalonia, so the smaller club came to stand for Spain. Español attracted many Catalan families, but also the migrants who continued to feel Spanish, and particularly the civil servants, soldiers and policemen whom Franco sent to run Barcelona. Inevitably, the club has close ties with Real. They often invite Real to their summer tournament, and when *Barça* plays Real at the Nou Camp, there are fireworks when *Barça* scores, but also when Real scores. Español came to be known as the Fascist club, and their hooligans, *Las Brigadas Blanco y Azules*, are still that way inclined.

When I went to the Español offices to get a press ticket, I found men chatting, children hanging around, and after the behemoth that is *Barça*, a quiet, subdued mood. Español struck me as a small family club, a Spanish Ipswich, and, in Catalonia, a club of outcasts. A couple of days before, the Español president had complained to the press again that people undervalued his club. I saw Español draw with Seville, who had an off-form Maradona in their ranks.

Yet many migrants chose *Barça* rather than Español, and understandably so. It is hard for a Scot to move to London, but it is even harder for an

Andalusian to come to Catalonia, because the Catalans speak a different language. *Barça* President Núñez, himself a migrant, speaks abominable Catalan.

If the migrant to Catalonia wants to belong, his best chance is to get behind the symbol of his new home. It gives him something to talk about at work, and becoming a *socio* makes him a little more like the middle-class Catalans who dominate the Nou Camp. "Barcelona has 110,000 *socios* . . ." I was saying to Torrebadella, when he interrupted me: "I am not a *socio*, but I have watched *Barça* a hundred times and I have never yet paid for my ticket. A father will buy cards for his wife, and for all his kids when they are born, even though a *socio* card costs at least £300 a year, because that is a kind of tradition. Maybe his family never goes to watch, but they all have cards, and I borrow them."

FC Barcelona is the symbol of Catalonia, and historically they have underperformed. Just as Madrid ruled Barcelona, so in the Franco era Real Madrid won all the soccering prizes. Barcelona has now won one European Cup; Real have six. In the league, Helenio Herrera took *Barça* to two championships in a row, but in the 30 years after the fans chased him away the club won only two more, one of them under Terry Venables. "What did you think of Herrera?" one *Barça* fan asked me, and I said, "He has a high opinion of himself." "I know," replied the man. "All our coaches have a high opinion of themselves. They need it, to take this job." Cesar Luis Menotti (who failed in Barcelona) called *Barça* "the most difficult club in the world."

The men to blame for the Catalan failures are the directors. They are ambitious, any defeat is a disaster, and so they interfere. Chief culprit is President Núñez. He has held his post since 1978 and has seen off coaches like Venables, Menotti and Udo Lattek. I asked one *Barça* fan why a millionaire businessman like Núñez was so keen to be president of a soccer club. "You know the Small

Man Theory of History?" the fan asked me. "Well, Núñez is very small."

Often, he has only narrowly survived. In 1979, when *Barça* brought home the European Cupwinners' Cup, he waved the trophy around at the airport and carried it into the team bus as if he had clinched it personally with a hat trick. The watching fans were livid. Núñez had just refused to renew the contract of Johan Neeskens, their Dutch idol, and they chanted, "Núñez no, Neeskens yes!" Núñez burst into tears and resigned on the spot, and Neeskens, moved by the chants, burst into tears beside him. But the *Barça* directors talked their president into staying, and Neeskens left for the New York Cosmos.

Sixte Cambra, a Barcelona businessman, challenged Núñez in the *Barça* presidential elections of 1989. FC Barcelona's elections always matter, for the winner becomes a big player in the city, but this one was particularly momentous. The Catalan Nationalist Party backed Cambra, which meant that a victory for him would link the club to a political party—rather as if, because Liverpool is a left-wing city, a Liverpool league title were to bring glory to the Labour Party. The Socialist Party backed Núñez, though he is personally more right-wing than Cambra, and the city filled up with rival banners and adverts. Núñez pointed out that Cambra was married to a woman from Madrid, and boycotted the television debate, claiming that Catalan TV was partisan. He won the election.

Now *Barça* is one of the best teams in the world, and from 1991 to 1993 they won the Spanish championship three times in a row. The man who has tamed Núñez is the Dutchman Johan Cruyff. Cruyff played for Barcelona in the 1970s, and returned to manage the club in 1988. By now Barcelona is his adopted home, and he can often be seen whizzing through the city on his motorbike. His wife, Danny, likes Barcelona because although the stress is as bad as in Amsterdam, the weather is better. Their son, Jordi, named for the patron saint of Catalonia, is in the *Barça* squad, and Chantal, their eldest daughter, has married one of the club's goalkeepers and is already a force in one of the *Barça* factions. The Cruyffs are as good as Catalan, except that Cruyff himself has failed to master the local language. Even his Spanish is suspect, and the weekly satirical TV program on *Barça* portrays him constantly repeating his favorite phase, *"en un momento dado."* Cruyff uses it to mean "at a certain moment," but the phrase doesn't exist in Spanish.

On his first day at *Barça*, Cruyff told Núñez (in Spanish): "The changing room is for me and the players alone." The president resisted in vain. For perhaps the first time, a *Barça* manager had defeated the board. "Cruyff," I was told by Pilar Calvo, of the daily *Sport*, which devotes most of its pages to the club, and which is owned by Joan Gaspart, another *Barça* vice president, "has won because of his playing career. Venables was a nobody when he came to Barcelona. Menotti had a name, but he also had a personality more open to manipulation than Cruyff's." Cruyff never compromises. He says, "I am better off than the club, financially and in my private life," and he knows he can resign if he wants. Herrera, the last *Barça* manager to succeed, was another strong man who kept the directors out. (It upsets him that Cruyff alone has won the European Cup.)

Naturally, Cruyff's European Cup immediately became a political tool. Because Cambra lost to Núñez, all parties can still use *Barça* for their own ends, and they do whenever *Barça* wins a trophy. When this happens, the players display it to the crowd at the Plaça Sant Jaume, a square with two political buildings: the *Generalitat*, and the Town Hall. At the celebrations, Jordi Pujol, president of the Generalitat, a sharp-featured character in a suit, always shouts from his balcony: *"Visca Barça, visca el Cataluña!"* Which, the nuances no doubt lost in translation, means, "*Barça* wins, Catalonia wins!" The crowd always cheers. But the city's Mayor in 1992, Pasqual Madragall, *socio* no. 107,024, was a Socialist, and thus opposed to separatism. So when the European Cup arrived, and Pujol had had his shout, Madragall told the crowd: "*Barça* is no longer 'more than a club,' and it has become the best club in Europe."

And he was right. Cruyff has changed *Barça*. No longer are the fans happy as long as their team beats Real. Now they demand proper success. And by changing the club, the Dutchman has changed Catalonia. When *Barça* was ailing, this hurt Catalonia in the way that the royal divorces hurt Britain. The symbol of the nation was tarnished. Now that the club is doing well, the political impact is immediate. The city is suddenly confident. In 1992, after the Wembley victory and the Olympics, Madragall officially proposed that Spain become a federal state with two capitals, Madrid and Barcelona. "So winning the European Cup helps Madragall make this proposal?" I asked Torrebadella, and he replied, "Absolutely."

It is rare for Barcelona to make a concrete proposal to Madrid. For a decade now, the Catalans have argued among themselves over whether they should seek independence from Spain. Pujol himself is unsure. He may call himself a Nationalist, but he has never called for secession, though he hints at it a lot. The debate goes on endlessly, but what is at issue became most clear during the Olympics of 1992. (How did Barcelona get the Olympics? Juan Samaranch, head of the International Olympic Committee, is *socio* no. 7,965.)

From the first, Pujol tried to make it clear that the Games were being held in Catalonia and not in Spain. The Catalan crowds at the opening ceremony gave an extra cheer to teams from newly independent nations like Lithuania or Croatia, and politicians in Madrid panicked. The Spanish Olympic soccer team dreaded Barcelona. The full Spanish team never play there—for Catalans, *Barça* is the national team—and the fixtures for the Olympic team were arranged so that they could play in Valencia as long as they kept winning. But came the final, against Poland, and the Olympic eleven had to move to the Nou Camp. A Catalan demonstration was feared, or an empty stadium. Instead, *Sport*'s daily rival, *El Mundo Deportivo*, could describe the crowd as "95,000 spectators . . . with Spanish flags." Spain won 2–1, and later that night fans were heard chanting, *"Pujol nos engaña/Cataluña es España"*—"Pujol is deceiving us/Catalonia is Spain." It appeared that Catalans do not despise Spaniards after all, or at least not if they win gold.

(On the other hand, Catalan TV made time during the Games to show in full *Barça*'s pre-season friendlies against northern Dutch provincial teams.)

When it comes to it, few Scots want to leave the Union, and few Catalans do either. They have done well enough as part of Spain. "Most people here would say, 'We don't need a state, but on the other hand we're more than just a region,' " Torrebadella told me. "It's more a matter of symbols." The Catalans do not want a state of their own, but they do want something vaguer than that, symbols to prove that they are a separate people. During the Games, many foreign observers read the Catalan flags that draped Barcelona as a demand for independence, but in fact the flags themselves satisfied people: all Catalans want is the symbols of a nation. When Pujol stands on the balcony and shouts, *"Visca Barça, visca el Cataluña,"* he is doing nothing more than restating Catalan symbols. People like to hear him say it. It makes them feel good.

And that is why *Barça* is possibly the biggest club in the world, why they have 110,000 *socios*. They are the symbol that this nation needs in lieu of a state. "And," one Catalan told me, "some people watch *Barça* because they like soccer."

CHAPTER 11

DUTCH AND ENGLISH: WHY BOBBY ROBSON FAILED IN HOLLAND

BOBBY ROBSON MANAGED THE Dutch club PSV Eindhoven from 1990 to 1992. He failed at PSV because he failed to understand the Dutch.

Before I start, I must establish that Robson did fail in Holland. He himself would disagree: after all, he won two league titles in his two years at PSV. Here is his first failure to understand. In England, the league championship is the prize every club wants most. In Holland, it is not. Robson never understood that PSV took the Dutch championship almost for granted—they had won it three times in the four years before his arrival—and wanted European success.

"PSV OFF BUNGLER BOBBY," opined one British tabloid when news of the England manager's impending move leaked a few days before the 1990 World Cup. The Dutch press was quite as dismayed. *Voetbal International*, an intelligent soccer magazine read by professional soccer players, managers, and directors (I know of no British equivalent) ran an editorial headlined, "Why Bobby Robson?" It claimed that Robson "is a typical coach of the British school with too little tactical baggage to fathom continental soccer."

To the Dutch, Bobby Robson stood for the Insular Englishman. He ran one of the less sophisticated international teams, occasionally wore a cloth cap, and spoke only one language. (He studied Dutch for a while, but never got far.) He arrived in Holland with a buffoonish image and never shed it.

At PSV, he took over a group of players that even more than most in Holland was used to having its say. The season before, the squad had split into rival factions whose members hardly even spoke to one another, and this cost Robson's predecessor his job. Kees Ploegsma, PSV's general manager, was looking for a coach who would keep the players quiet. A Briton was the obvious choice.

The British game has a code of honor. If a player comments on tactics, he is "bringing the game into disrepute." If he quarrels with his manager, he is transferred. He never speaks out of turn, except when he retires and runs out of money and sells his "story" to the *Sun*. Alex Ferguson will not let Ryan Giggs speak to journalists, and Manchester United players generally give few interviews (most of them to John Motson). Brian Clough terrified adults like Des Walker and Stuart Pearce out of talking to the press altogether. A British player obeys his superior. He is a soldier. Before the Dutchman Ray Atteveld came to England for a trial with Everton, he phoned John Metgod, formerly of Nottingham Forest and Spurs, to ask his advice. "Get a haircut, wear a suit, and yell a lot at practice," Metgod told him. Everton took Atteveld.

By contrast, foreigners who come to Holland all make the same discovery: "The coach doesn't say that much. It's always the players who are talking," marvelled Ajah Wilson Ogechukwu, a Nigerian at Roda Kerkrade. Dutch players love to talk, and interviews in soccer magazines run to four pages. When the Dutch go abroad they carry on talking, and in the vernacular too. They advise their managers on tactics and team selection. The AC Milan manager Arrigo Sacchi reported that Ruud Gullit, Frank Rijkaard, and Marco van Basten had given him "new ideas and views," and he said it was largely down to them that "a new style was introduced that diverged from the traditional, Italian mode of thought and style of play." (Later, when Van Basten decided that Milan needed an even newer style, Sacchi had to leave.) But usually the Dutch advice is unwanted.

John van't Schip joined Genoa and was dropped from the team for five weeks for debating tactics with his manager.

"I've got a reputation of having my own opinion and they don't like that in Great Britain," reported Hans Gillhaus, who spent four years with Aberdeen. "As a soccer player there you're just a number and you do what the boss says. That's what you call the manager: 'Boss.' At halftime or after the match, it was customary for the manager to swear for a while at a couple of players. Most players accepted it. The Dutch boys would go against it, and then there'd be a row."

"We Dutchmen are pigheaded," summed up Johan Cruyff, the greatest of them all (and the most pigheaded). "Even when we're on the other side of the world, we're always telling people how to do things. In that respect, we're an unpleasant nation."

Unpleasant perhaps, but successful. Dutch soccer works. It seems that if you let players think for themselves they win soccer matches. Over the last 20 years, no other small nation (and of the large nations, only Germany and Argentina) has won as much as Holland. No one else has played as gloriously. It is precisely because the Dutch talk so much that they can play the way they do. A player must understand his role. He has to know when to overlap or to cover for the man in front of him, when to leave his man and chase the ball. British players play the British brand of 4–4–2 from childhood on, and so they have little to learn about it. By the age of 20, a British fullback knows, for instance, that he must cover his center backs when there is an attack over the other wing. The system is simple. When he has the ball, he can always hit it into space over the top of the opposition's defense, and when he is in trouble he can hit it into touch. But if the player is called upon to play in a new way, or to do more difficult things—to keep the ball in the team, for instance—he has to learn again. He can learn a lot from just playing the new system, but not enough. One Genoa manager tried to make his team play total soccer like Ajax, and failed. Vant

Schip commented: "To play the Ajax system you have to under-stand it, and especially talk about it a lot."

The drawback to talking a lot is that personality clashes happen. Holland in 1990 could have won the World Cup, but the players preferred to squabble. The PSV squad that Robson inherited was torn by rows: Wim Kieft versus Gerald Vanenburg, Romario versus the rest of the squad.

It was all new to Robson. The English method barely gives players a chance to argue: there is simply no debate, and so team spirit is the best in the world. It does seem that the England squad at the 1990 World Cup helped persuade Robson to use a sweeper, but that was nothing compared to the power of the Dutch squad. It refused even to go to the World Cup with its manager, Thijs Libregts, and Libregts was fired. The difference is down to Dutch working-class culture. The Dutch working classes value debate. They are Calvinists (even Dutch Catholics have strong Calvinist traits) and Calvin told the faithful to ignore priests and to read the Bible them-selves. The result is that a 20-year-old Dutch soccer player assumes that he is as likely to have the Truth as his manager. The British view is that the manager is the manager. He is older than his players and so he must be right. That is why, when Robson is heckled, he cites his record and the number of years he has been in the game.

"The players are all much more interested over here in tactics—how we play and how we change things," he told *World Soccer* after 18 months at PSV. He spent most of his time in Eindhoven trying to decide whether the club should play a British-style 4–4–2 system or not, and his players entered the debate energetically. Only PSV's sweeper, Gica Popescu, shared Robson's attitude: "I think soccer players should play soccer, and apart from that shut up. The coach must talk, we must listen." Popescu grew up in Ceaucescu's Rumania.

Robson told *Voetbal International*: "An English pro accepts the manager's decision. After every match here, the substitutes come and visit me." He pulled off John Bosman against Montpellier and Bosman asked for an explanation, but Robson would only say, "Players only understand substitutions when they become managers." Dutch players demand proper reasons. English players always do their best, but when the Dutch disagree with the manager they sulk, as Holland did at the 1990 World Cup.

Robson got on best with PSV's most "British" players: the eager teenager Twan Scheepers and the muscular stopper Stan Valckx. He took Valckx with him to Sporting Lisbon where he even made him team captain, despite Valckx's utter inability to speak Portuguese. Robson said of Scheepers: "He's got strength, he runs very well, he's strong in the tackle, and he's got desire. You can see it in his eyes." Those are the qualities with which Robson feels comfortable.

People talking about soccer tend to draw their metaphors from one of two fields: from art or from war. Brazilian soccer has "the rhythm of samba," and the British have "fighting spirit." Robson always compares soccer to war. Speaking of Bryan Robson, he told Pete Davies, author of *All Played Out*: "You could put him in any trench and know he'd be the first over the top . . . he wouldn't think, well, Christ, if I put my head up there it might get shot off. He'd say, c'mon, over the top." When Terry Butcher broke his head in a match against Sweden and played on, Robson was delighted. "Have a look at your skipper. Let none of you let him down," he told the other players while the doctor stitched Butcher up at halftime. The tabloids liked it too: "YOU'RE A BLOODY HERO SKIPPER." The idea was that only a British soccer player would carry on with a cracked head. This may be true. Frits Kessel, the Dutch team doctor, explains: " 'Work soccer players' can deal with pain much better than super-skillful players, who depend more on their coordination. Marco van Basten, for instance, can take absolutely no pain. If anything at all is troubling him, he's no use to anyone. He says so himself." Since most British players are "work soccer players," they can play on with broken skulls. Managers like Robson admire their grit, and continue to pick them. Robson's British colleagues talk about war only slightly less than he does. After the USA beat England in 1993, his successor, Graham Taylor, told the press: "We are in a battle, aren't we? It's a battle we'll stick out together." Naturally, Taylor was more inclined to pick David Batty than Chris Waddle. As Robson said, in the days when he was reluctant to play Gazza: "You have to be utterly reliable." Soldiers are reliable, artists are not.

At PSV, the players complained nonstop about Robson's training methods. Robson believed in "functional training," a form of practice that relies on dry runs of moves. A midfield player puts the ball out wide, a fullback comes up the wing and crosses it, and a striker runs in to head the ball, all without opposition. Functional training may make sense, but since the players were sceptical of Robson from the start they laughed at it. Johan Cruyff, as manager of Ajax, had also made players do new things—he brought in an opera singer to teach them how to breathe—but Cruyff commanded respect. "The sarcasm about Robson went on all season. About Bobby Robson!" exclaimed Frank Arnesen, his Danish assistant for a year at PSV. "A manager with a career behind him that is practically unequalled in the world. I think that's very Dutch. Holland is an extremely tolerant country, but on the other hand the Dutch have no respect for anyone."

The players also thought that Robson trained too lightly. English clubs often play three matches a week, and so they tend to make do with a few gentle exercises. Asked by Pete Davies whether British players thus had less chance to learn the skills of a Rijkaard, Robson agreed. Yet in Holland, where training matters, he would not change his ways. This almost led to disaster in his first season at PSV. With two games left, PSV and Ajax were neck and neck for the title, and PSV's penultimate match was a tough one, away to FC

Groningen. Robson decided that his players needed rest, and took them to Israel for a few days on the beach. The team returned tanned and rested, and proceeded to lose 4–1 to Groningen. Robson's defense was characteristic: "We often did it when I was at Ipswich and the players there loved it." He was saved by Ajax, who lost to lowly SVV that day, and the next week PSV won the title. His players were unimpressed. Celebrating after the final match, they dunked Ploegsma, the general manager, in the players' bath, while Robson stood by untouched.

Had he understood the Dutch press better it might have taken his side more. When he first arrived in Holland he seemed determined not to impress the journalists. Eight years as England manager had got to him, and in his first months at PSV he often answered questions on soccer with, "None of your business." During an interview with *Voetbal International*, he jumped up from his chair at one point to hiss: "Listen fellow, British coaches are the best in the world." At post-match press conferences he did little more than repeat the claim that the game had been "superb," even when this was manifestly false. But in time, he understood the need to change. Dutch journalists, he explained to *World Soccer*, "are more like soccer reporters, rather than journalists looking for a headline. Here, they all think they are little coaches. It took me a while to adjust!"

He never quite adjusted to Dutch tactics. "In England mostly everybody plays 4–4–2. Tactically, the English game is completely predictable. But here you never know quite what you will come up against," he confided to *World Soccer*. "Sometimes they'll come at you with one central striker; sometimes they won't play a striker at all but play with two men wide. Then, midway through a match you have to ask yourself what do you do with your two center backs who have no one to mark?" Robson never seemed sure. He had PSV playing first 4–2–4, then 4–3–3, 3–3–4, 5–2–3 and 4–4–2. "Our play worries us," said general manager Ploegsma, at a time in

Robson's second season when PSV were still unbeaten in the league. Then Robson fell ill, Arnesen took over, and suddenly PSV were playing 4–2–4 every week.

PSV officials came to sound defensive when talking about Robson. "It was a period when there wasn't much on the market," Ploegsma admitted to *Voetbal International*. "We asked ourselves, 'What are we looking for?' " Values like discipline, experience and respect were important to us. Then we looked at who was available." PSV approached Franz Beckenbauer and Dick Advocaat before offering Robson the job. "Whether Robson is tactically, and all that sort of thing, suited to PSV, I don't know," said Ploegsma. "We didn't ask ourselves that. We had a different priority."

Months before Robson's contract expired, Ploegsma was promising Dutch journalists off the record that it would not be renewed. It was, in fact, *Voetbal International* who broke it to Robson that he would be leaving PSV. When he left, the magazine called him "the amiable Briton," and quoted PSV's chairman Jacques Ruts as saying that Robson had had problems "as a *foreigner*." Ruts explained: "If an Englishman says, 'I'm afraid I would have difficulties with that,' a lot of Dutchmen think he means, 'I'll do it, but I have problems with it.' " Not bloody likely! The Englishman is saying, politely, that he is *absolutely* against it. Well, I've spotted that sort of problem in the relationship between Robson and the squad." But PSV's fullback Berry van Aerle had the last word. He told *Nieuwe Revu*: "Robson's a nice man, really a very nice man. But the only thing he taught me in two years was English."

CHAPTER 12

AFRICA (iN BRiEF)

"I say that magic, in soccer, cannot exist. The proof is Cameroon. It is not the strongest nation in magic, and it is better at soccer than the countries where magic is strong, like Benin, Togo, or Nigeria." Roger Milla in France Football, *1981.*

HERE ARE THE FACTS, being the African history of the World Cup.

The first African nation to play in the World Cup was Egypt, in 1934, when any team that turned up was welcome. Egypt played one match, losing 4–2 to Hungary.

Later, World Cups became events for which teams had to qualify, but for decades FIFA arranged no qualifying rounds for Africa. Eventually FIFA gave way, and the modern African history of the World Cup starts in 1970, when one place was reserved for the continent. Morocco won it, and at the finals in Mexico, they lost 2–1 to West Germany, 3–0 to Peru and drew 0–0 with Bulgaria. Poor results, but no walkovers.

In 1974, Zaire became the first Black African team to qualify for the World Cup. The Zairean performance in West Germany is the worst by any African team at the World Cup so far, and the European press loved it. Zaire seemed to live up to the crude European stereotypes. Journalists spread stories that the players had taken monkeys with them to eat during the tournament, and that they had the tactical grasp of savages. Zaire lost 2–0 to Scotland, 9–0 to Yugoslavia and 3–0 to Brazil, and the Zairean kleptocrat President Mobutu (still in office today) may have considered recalling the team.

The players had other problems too, many of which came to light when Mulamba Ndaie was sent off against Yugoslavia for kicking the referee.

When the Dutch magazine *Vrij Nederland* asked Zaire's Yugoslav coach Blagoyev Vidinic for his view of Ndaie's expulsion, Vidinic said the offence warranted a red card. He added: "I have only one small reservation. It wasn't Number 13 who kicked the referee, but Number 2, Ilunga Mwepu."

Ndaie said: "You can tell from the referee's behavior that they can't tell us apart. And they don't try to either. I cried terribly when I was sent off. I told the referee that it wasn't me, and Mwepu said, 'I did it, not he.' But the referee wasn't interested. All the referees here are against the black race, and not only the referees. Scotland's Number 4, the captain, shouted at me a couple of times during the match, 'Nigger, hey nigger!' He spat at me too, and he spat in Mana's face. Scotland's Number 4 is a wild animal." Scotland's Number 4 was Billy Bremner.

The press also asked Vidinic to explain why he had substituted his goalkeeper, Kazadi, when Zaire were only 3–0 down to Yugoslavia. The substitution had helped start rumors that Vidinic was a Yugoslav agent, and the rumors persisted when Vidinic refused to discuss his decision at the post-match press conference, saying only that he would explain all the next day. He kept his promise: "Mr Lockwa, the representative of the Ministry of Sport, said after the third Yugoslav goal, 'Take that keeper off.' I did."

"These are my specific problems," Vidinic sighed. "But I assure you: I'll never again give the government permission to make changes in my team. When I trained Morocco (he had taken them to the 1970 World Cup) I also rejected interference by the Moroccan king. Shortly before one match he gave me a note with his preferred lineup. I said, 'In that case, I leave straight away.' 'All right,' he said, 'but if Morocco loses in your formation then things will happen.' " Vidinic paused. "Well?" demanded the assembled press, "what did happen?" "Oh, we won of course. Better yet, against our arch-rivals Algeria."

These interviews all took place outside the Zairean hotel. Vidinic and the players would not talk to the press inside the hotel, which was full of officials from the Ministry of Sport.

Zaire was the only African team ever to justify the tag of "minnow." They were an odd lot in any case, but undoubtedly, also, African soccer improved after 1974. Professor Paul Nkwi explained to me in Cameroon: "We can now see how people play. On the radio you had to *hear* how a player swerved past four players. Everyone sits around the TV in the *quartier*. When my little boys watch France they know the differences between the high balls of the British, and the small passes of the French and Germans, and they have brought that into Cameroonian soccer. The Zaireans were not aware of the difference."

Zaire withdrew from their qualifying matches for the 1978 World Cup, the nation's Sports Minister citing "certain deficiencies" in the team and the "unpatriotic behavior" of some players. Tunisia qualified in 1978, beat Mexico 3–1, and were unlucky to lose 1–0 to Poland and to draw 0–0 with West Germany. In 1982, Cameroon drew with Italy, Poland and Peru, while Algeria beat West Germany and Chile and lost to Austria. Both African teams failed to reach the second round because of marginally inferior goal differences. In 1986, Algeria did badly, earning just one point from three matches, but Morocco won England's group to reach the second round.

In 1990, Egypt drew against Holland and Eire before losing to England, and you may remember Cameroon. After winning their group they beat Colombia, and then lost to England. It was a needless defeat, but Roger Milla told *France Football* that it pleased him: "I'll tell you something: if we had beaten England, Africa would have exploded. Ex-plo-ded. There would even have been deaths.

The Good Lord knows what he does. Me, I thank Him for stopping us in the quarter finals. That permitted a little pliancy."

The African results at World Cups make an interesting tally. From 1978 to 1990, African nations played 24 World Cup final matches in which they gained 23 points. (I am awarding two points for a win and one for a draw.) During that period, their performance did not improve. If anything, it very slightly dipped: in 1978, Africans gained three points from three matches, in 1982 seven from six, in 1986 five from seven, and in 1990, eight from eight. Remember also, that because African teams are seeded as minnows, they never meet true minnows like El Salvador or New Zealand. Every point the Africans earn is fiercely contested. In short, it says little for the world's bookmakers that Cameroon could startle them as late as 1990 by reaching the quarterfinals.

"There's still an idea here in Europe that Africans can't do anything better than the whites," complained Alloy Agu, the goalkeeper of Nigeria who plays for Club Liège in Belgium. "Don't look at color, look at what we can do! Black, white, yellow: we're all the same. Still, if you're black, you're well-dressed, and you drive a nice car, they want to see your papers."

For a long time we said that Africans could not play soccer. After 1990, we invented an explanation. Africans can play, we said, because they were born that way. They are naturals. They have no idea of what they are doing. "If they can get their organization right off the pitch, their natural ability, athleticism, flexibility and the way they play the game will be far too much for us," the then-England manager Graham Taylor told the *Independent on Sunday* in 1992. Even some Africans believe this: Alloy Agu claims that African players "have a natural suppleness." He fails to understand that though Roger Milla, Lakhdar Belloumi, and Peter Ndlovu are natural athletes, Trevor Steven, Les Ferdinand, and Nigel Winterburn are too. The Africans played soccer a lot as children, and so did our players.

We also believe that Africans have no notion of tactics. "They go out there to enjoy themselves," say our commentators. Remember how defensively Cameroon played in the "Group of Death" in 1982, and against Argentina and Rumania in 1990? When three Cameroonians hurled themselves at the Argentine striker Claudio Caniggia, and Benjamin Massing was sent off, newspapers described the fouls as "stupid," or cited excess enthusiasm. When three Uruguayans bring down an opposing striker making for goal, we call them "cynical."

Africans never train and have no tactics. They have magic instead. European journalists always ask African players about witchcraft. ("I'm the witchdoctor around here," answered Vidinic. "I touch them on one leg and say, 'You score with him.' ")

Certainly, faith in witchcraft is strong enough for the Botswanan FA's mouthpiece, the *Botswana Sports Magazine*, solemnly to warn its readers that, "There is no evidence that matches can be won using *muti* alone." Almost every team in Africa practises *muti*, or *Juju* (though the Zairean FA once banned it).

Muti takes various forms, often spectacular. A team's witch doctor cuts players with his knife, players urinate on the ball, animals are killed, and potions are sprinkled on jerseys or boots or changing-room doors. If a winger needs speed, the witch doctor might sacrifice a fly. In Zambia, when Profund Warriors had a long home winning streak, visiting teams stopped using the changing-rooms and changed in their minibuses instead. To avoid using the main entrance, they would then take the pitch by jumping over the perimeter fence, and *voilà*, Profund suddenly began to lose at home. In wealthy South Africa teams fly witch doctors to matches, and in many countries they earn more than players.

But though many players believe in the rituals, many others do not. Also, needless to say, the value players set on *muti* depends on their mood. Mark Williams, a feared goal scorer in South Africa, told me that he had had no time for his manager's *muti* while he was at Mamelodi Sundowns. "Maybe it's psychological," Williams said, "that if you don't like someone you won't eat his food, because at Cosmos we had a *muti*-man and everyone accepted it and got on with things, but with Tshabalala I hated it. The boots would always be prepared with the potions and sometimes I would take my own boots with me, because I felt happy in them—I always used to score in those boots, always—and you'd be quietly trying to put them on and he'd be looking at you and you'd think, 'Oh no.' "

For most African players, witchcraft is little more than their form of superstition. No one I met in Africa began telling me about witchcraft, though when I asked, I got answers. If you ask Italian players if they are carrying rosaries, a few will say yes, but that does not mean it is their only hope of winning matches. Witchcraft matters less than we think. The manager of South Africa, the Peruvian Augusto Palacios, told me that as a devout Catholic he refused to stage *muti* ceremonies. "Any player can practise *muti* in his home if he wants to," he said, "but not here in camp. I try to explain to my players that I respect their culture but that *muti* is superstition and is only psychological." Would he stop a player from using *muti*? "It is part of their tradition. If a player cannot afford the materials for his *muti* we would pay for them, but there will be no team ceremonies." Witchcraft on the expense account. Had any player asked for a *muti* ceremony? "Never." By cross-examining every Black African World Cup team about witchcraft the moment they step off the plane, we imply that they are believers first and world-class soccer players second. "We hate it when people ask us if we burn chickens before a match," the Cameroonian François Omam-Biyik said during the 1990 World Cup. Omam would probably not mind if this were the tenth question he was asked, but it is always the first. (The second is, "Did you play barefoot as a child?")

Of course, you don't have to be African to believe in magic. The

Dutchmen Ruud Gullit and Marco van Basten have a personal medic-cum-psychologist, Ted Troost, who punches them, orders them to feel as light as a feather, and grabs them by the testicles. They feel better for it. Gullit and Van Basten are two of the most written about players in the world, but foreign journalists rarely mention Troost. Bryan Robson, injured again at the World Cup of 1990, flew in the faith healer Olga Stringfellow to cure him. (She failed.) Terry Paine, the former England player, now manages Wits University in South Africa, and when I asked him about *muti* he began telling me about British *muti*: some players take a hot bath before a match, some put on their right shoe before their left, and some insist on going out of the tunnel eighth. Playing 825 league games in England had given him great respect for African witchcraft. He told me a story of his team arriving at a ground in Durban: Paine was unlocking the dressing-room door when his players begged him not to. "Look!" they pointed. "There's *muti* on the door!" Paine opened it regardless. "That day we lost 1–0, after 17 matches undefeated," he recounted mournfully.

Gary Bailey, the former England goalkeeper, learned about *muti* at home in South Africa. To support his weak right knee, he said, "They would tie strength-giving things to it," and a "third ball" would be slipped down his shorts. Then he moved to England, and in his first three Wembley finals with United he let in seven goals. For the replay of the 1983 FA Cup final, against Brighton, he took the advice of a South African witch doctor, tied a red-and-white ribbon to his goal and fixed a lock and key to the netting. At half-time, he moved the padlock to the other goal. United won 4–0. Naturally, he used *muti* again in his next two Wembley finals. United beat Liverpool 2–0 in the Charity Shield of 1983, and they beat Everton 1–0 in the 1985 FA Cup final.

If the manager is popular, witchcraft rituals can help unite a team. If the whole team prepares for a match by taking a bath in oxen blood, it concentrates their minds—as long as the skeptics wash in the blood too. As manager of Kaizer Chiefs, Palacios had forced another strict Christian to join in the rituals. As manager of Lecce in Italy, Zbigniew Boniek ordered his team to attend mass before a match, and when Pietro Paolo Virdis refused, Boniek exploded. Julia Beffon of South Africa's *Weekly Mail* even suggests that African *muti* rituals, if cleverly hyped, could unsettle European opponents, as the New Zealand All Blacks' *haka* dance does in rugby.

Gaborone (or "Gabs"), Botswana.. As World Cup qualifiers go, Botswana vs. Niger lacked glamor. Nonetheless, with my Dutch photographer, Willem, I crammed into a minibus, a type of vehicle that is constantly involved in fatal accidents in South Africa, and drove the five hours north from Johannesburg to Gaborone, capital of Botswana.

A former British colony with just 1.3 million inhabitants and 26 percent of the world's diamond wealth, it is usually counted as the one stable democracy in Africa. However, the Botswanan national team, the Zebras, are possibly the worst in Africa, and had just lost their first ever World Cup match 6–0 to the Ivory Coast. F.S. Chalwe wrote in the *Botswana Sports Magazine* that if his experience was anything to go by, "I would say we have eight to ten years before we can be considered to be among the best in Africa." The Nigeriéns are better at soccer than the Botswanans, but are poorer and live in an even larger desert.

The little Gaborone National Stadium lies between a tennis club and a mosque. The stands are pretty, in their light blue and white, but they lack a roof. Not to stop the rain—sadly, it never rains in Botswana—but because watching a soccer match in 95-degree heat is irksome. Some supporters carried umbrellas against the sun. I sat in the only covered stand, which was considered so desirable that even the footrests between the seats were packed.

Life on the field was more relaxed. We watched various officials traipse across the field, most spectacularly the obese Ashford Mamelodi, secretary-general of the Botswanan FA, while the Niger players had a kickaround with Willem. We stood for the two national anthems. Then we sat down, but Ismail Bhamjee, president of the BFA, gestured to us to stand again. It seemed that the first anthem had not been Niger's. The fans remained seated, and no new anthem was played, so the Niger team sang their anthem without accompaniment, their hands on their hearts.

The kickoff was scheduled for half past three, not by chance. The *Botswana Sports Magazine* was frank: "It is not hard training alone that wins international games. . . . There should also be something prepared for the visiting team so as to make it difficult for them to win." The magazine suggested that Botswana make use of its hot weather by scheduling games in the afternoon. As it was, the match only kicked off at five to four, and since Niger lies in the Sahara the ploy could have only limited effect. But the heat certainly did for Willem.

The match was poor. The ground was bone hard and, despite Mamelodi's walkabout, desperately uneven, so the ball bounced like an unpredictable jumping bean. Both teams seemed to have decided to play without tactics, but the players were astoundingly athletic: flying volleys abounded. Without any further evidence, I could have deduced from the match that the British had colonized Botswana and the French Niger, for the Botswanans played like an English third division team while the Nigeriéns showed distaste for all physical contact. African soccer has its Dover–Calais divide too. Against the run of play, Niger scored just before the final whistle to win 1–0. "Niger don't deserve winning," protested the Botswanan manager, the Zambian Freddie Mwila. What about the next match against the Ivory Coast? "They're the African champions; we are part of Africa."

In Niger's dressing room I met a man in robes and a high West African hat who was rolling a soccer around beneath his shoes. "Are you the Niger manager?" I asked. "No," he replied, "I'm the minister for sport." I was impressed. In Africa, a sports minister is at least as senior as the minister for home affairs. I suggested that the match had been a clash between the British and the French styles of soccer. "The Francophone style," corrected the minister, by which he meant the French-speaking African nations. I asked whether he picked the team. "It comes with the job," he said.

It is hard to buy a pair of soccer shoes in Gaborone that is not sold by Ismail Bhamjee. The day after Botswana vs. Niger, I interviewed him across the counter of one of his sports shops.

An Indian who left South Africa for Botswana to escape apartheid, Bhamjee is one of the men who run African sport. He is, among many other things, an executive member of the Confederation of African Soccer, CAF. "I have so many hats, I'm always away, I'm never here," he sighed, giving me his Botswanan Olympic Committee card. "That's why I don't even know the prices in my own shop."

He told me CAF was lobbying FIFA ("we always are") for more World Cup places for African teams. Currently, the continent has only three of the 24 places at the World Cup. (An American Peace Corps volunteer in Niger complained to me that while in Africa he was challenged on this issue all the time.) Africans reckon that Nigeria or Ghana could have given Costa Rica as much of a game in 1990 as Scotland or Sweden did. As they see it, the West excludes them from the World Cup just as it does from the UN Security Council—but the World Cup matters more.

I asked Bhamjee to outline his case for me. "FIFA's argument has always been standards, and now we're as good as the Europeans. FIFA says, "But African sides have never got past the quarterfinals"—but obviously they're not going to excel that much with only two teams out of 24. The Europeans had 14 teams and so they had far more chances to win it. Those boots are 75 pula, sir." Look at FIFA's youth tournaments, said Bhamjee. The Africans have a fairer chance of qualifying for those, and both Ghana and Nigeria have won youth World Cups. Yet he remained pessimistic about the real thing. When it came to a vote, he said, "the white countries gang up to stop the black countries." On the FIFA executive, "the vote just goes black against white." So he was 'very, very upset, but not surprised," when FIFA awarded the 1998 World Cup to France rather than Morocco. Why did he think the Europeans were so recalcitrant? He said that though he understood that more places for Africa would be at Europe's expense, he also felt that racism played a part.

"Racism" is a vague word, but it takes specific forms, and in this affair I can suggest two. Firstly, Europeans are used to treating Africans as beggars with nothing to offer. The World Cup is ours, and we let in outsiders only if we so desire. We are the world. The second form of racism was best expressed by Brian Clough: "If the African nations get their way, and only one British team plays in tournaments in future, I think I'll vote Conservative. Think about it, a bunch of spear throwers who want to dictate our role in soccer. They still eat each other up . . ." Old Big 'Ead was merely echoing the soccer journalist who once explained to Papua New Guinea that the British were entitled to four national teams because they were playing soccer when the Papua New Guineans were still running around in woad. Many less cultivated people than these sit on FIFA committees.

The first lesson of the African history of the World Cup is that the Africans have done better than we realize. The second is that only rich, stable African countries do well. The seven African nations that have reached the World Cup since 1970 are Morocco, Zaire, Tunisia, Algeria, Egypt, Cameroon and Nigeria. Of these, measured by African standards, only Zaire—the one World Cup flop—is a poor country. The spread of wealth in Africa closely matches the spread of soccering success.

The four nations that founded CAF in 1957 were Ethiopia, Sudan, Egypt and South Africa. Of these four, the only one to succeed at soccer in the decades since is Egypt. South Africa was excluded from the international game by sanctions, and Ethiopia and Sudan quite as effectively by famine and war.

Ethiopia was one of just 27 African countries to enter for the World Cup of 1994 and to complete its qualifying fixtures. The team's first game was away to Morocco. The Ethiopians flew via Rome, where their five best players sought political asylum. That left a squad of eight players to play the match. The reserve goalkeeper, the assistant manager and a friend filled in, and Ethiopia began the game with a full side. By halftime, however, two of the ringers had dropped out exhausted, and Morocco led 5–0. Early in the second half three more Ethiopians gave up, and with just six away players left standing, the referee stopped the match. Ethiopia did not qualify for the World Cup.

But the nation that suffered most for its lack of funds was Zambia. The Zambian national team died when their plane crashed into the Atlantic off the coast of Gabon, on April 28, 1993. They had been on their way to play a World Cup qualifying match against Senegal. It turned out that the plane designated to carry them 3,000 miles from Lusaka to Dakar was a short-haul military carrier: the Zambian FA had been unable to afford a regular airliner. The news incensed Zambians at home, particularly as cabinet ministers and investigators had flown to pick up the bodies in a presidential DC-8. "I will never forgive the Soccer Association of Zambia for what has happened," said Albert Bwalya, who had been left out of the squad thanks to a quarrel over money.

Money was not the sole cause of death. Burkhard Ziese, a German who had managed Ghana, explained: "For the officials and players it's more lucrative to travel in a military plane. Then they don't have to go through customs and everyone can buy unlimited and cheap luxury soap, perfumes, gin and whisky, and sell them at a profit in Ghana."

Next to African FAs, European FAs look organized. Senegal is a rich nation and good at soccer, but its FA clean forgot to enter for the 1990 World Cup. (People shrug and say, *"C'est l'Afrique."*) Or take Nigeria, another rich country, with more than 100 million inhabitants, where from time to time the government fires all the officials of the FA. This last happened a couple of years ago, when the Nigerian kit manager forgot to take the team's shorts along to a home match against Burkina Faso. People ran about looking for spares, but none were found. Instead, tracksuit bottoms were cut off at the knee, and in that outfit Nigeria won 7–1. But the wire services sent the story around the world, and another batch of officials fell.

Nigeria qualified for the 1994 World Cup by beating Algeria away. A few days later, the sports minister, one Chief Akinyele, appeared on national TV to sack the team's manager, the Dutchman Clemens Westerhof. Then there was a military coup. Akinyele lost his job, and Westerhof was given back his.

In all, over 20 African nations either did not enter for the World Cup of 1994 or failed to complete their qualifying matches. For most, the obstacle was poverty or civil war (or both), while Libya could not travel due to a United Nations air embargo.

An African nation that is not at war, and that can afford to enter the World Cup, and that remembers to do so, and that completes its schedule, turning up at every match with at least eleven able-bodied men, has already outdone most of its competitors and has a fair chance of reaching the finals.

It is hard to fathom what it means for an African nation to have to withdraw from the World Cup. For come the tournament, the entire population of every *quartier* in Africa spends a month in front of the local TV set. Soccer is the one chance Africa has to beat the world. Before the crash, the only time in recent history that Zambia had made international headlines was when its soccer team beat Italy 4–0 at the Seoul Olympics. After the game, one Italian newspaper published a map of Africa to show its readers where Zambia is. "Before the match, the Italian players were walking straight past us. Afterwards, they came to our hotel to ask for autographs," said Kalusha Bwalya, who hit a hat trick in the match and who is still alive. The World Cup matters to Africa, and not only to Africans but also to black Europeans like Frank Rijkaard. Politicians understand. Chief Moshood Abiola, a candidate in the Nigerian elections of 1993, vowed that if elected he would ensure that Nigeria reached the World Cup. He won, but the election was annulled by the Nigerian dictator, General Ibrahim Babangida. Babangida was nicknamed "Maradona," in tribute to his skill at evading challenges.

Walter Winterbottom, in 1962, became the first man to say that an African country would win the World Cup. Richard Möller-Nielsen made the same prediction to me in Latvia, Graham Taylor made it to the *Independent on Sunday*, and almost every article on African soccer cites Winterbottom. It is a prophecy that pundits like to make: it sounds grandiose, is kind to the Third World, and cannot immediately be disproved. Also, at every World Cup Africa surprises us.

But Joachim Fickert thinks African soccer is going to get worse, and he should know. Fickert, a German, is the technical director of the Congo national team, and he has been coaching in Africa for over a decade. "The scissors of European and African soccer will separate even further," he told me.

I met him in Gaborone, just before Botswana vs. South Africa. He was spying on the South Africans, the "Bafana Bafana," who were sharing the Gaborone Sun hotel. We spoke just two hours before the match, as South African players, journalists, fans and officials ate and chatted and mingled around the pool. Fickert, who was sitting inside, a neat figure, told me he disapproved: the sorrows of a German in Africa.

He thought African soccer would decline because Africa was getting poorer. "Soccer is not on an island. In terms of medicine, of feeding, these countries will have ever greater disadvantages. If you talk about winning the World Cup, well, it's just possible that one of the North African states could do it one day, because of their better economies." For the same reason, he tipped South Africa, currently a weak team. Elsewhere, times were hard. He told me the Congo's neighbour, Zaire, could no longer even afford to call its players together for training in the capital, Kinshasa. The coach of Ghana has to beg gasoline from the minister of sport before he can drive into the bush to look at players.

I asked Fickert whether ministers interfered with his work. He replied: "Not in Congo. I have had six ministers of sport in two years, and the top civil servants change all the time too. Ministers just give speeches and don't bother about daily affairs. There is no positive intervention either. This is the sixth month in which wages have not been paid." For the recent away match against South Africa, his FA had only been able to afford to fly over two of Congo's European-based players, and the pair got no match fee. The young Congo team lost 1–0 and were knocked out of the World Cup. Their forthcoming home match against South Africa was meaningless.

So how could Fickert afford to fly to Gaborone and stay in this fine hotel, just to watch the Bafana Bafana play? "African nations take these matches very seriously," he replied. Here was another official on a junket.

CHAPTER 13

ROGER MiLLA AND PRESiDENT BiYA

CAMEROON HAD SLIPPED OUT of the news rather since the 1990 World Cup, so until I visited their embassy in London to ask for a visa I had no idea how bad things had got there.

When I rang at the embassy, a man opened the door two inches and peered around it. "What do you want?" "A visa." "Wait here." He shut the door again, returned with forms to fill in and explained the procedure to me on the doorstep. Each time I visited the embassy I was blocked at the door. At the time I took this for rudeness, but as I found out later, the embassy was barring strangers for fear that they might be creditors demanding money.

Not the colonists, but a Sierra Leonean photographer named Georges Goethe brought soccer to Cameroon, when in the 1920s he started juggling a soccer in the streets of Douala after work. We were all grateful to the great German poet in 1990. Recall the images the Italian World Cup has left in your mind: there is Gazza in tears, and Lineker pointing at his own eyes to alert the England bench; the mad glint in Toto Schillaci's eyes; and Frank Rijkaard spitting at Rudi Völler; but most images you have will be of Cameroon. There is Roger Milla tackling the Colombian goalkeeper Higuita, and grinning massively even as he dribbles towards goal; Benjamin Massing clogging Lineker; the three consecutive Cameroonian assaults on Claudio Caniggia, timed like gags in a comedy routine; and Milla's post-goal corner-flag belly dances.

The Indomitable Lions fell in the quarterfinals, when they lost 3–2 to England despite outplaying the English for great swathes of the game. England's fans rendered an inapposite "Rule Britannia," and the Italians gave the Lions an ovation. "They're unlucky to be out," Bobby Robson conceded.

Roger Milla later said that the image of the World Cup he treasured most was that of Paul Biya, the Cameroonian president, shaking hands with other heads of state after Cameroon had beaten Argentina. "Do you appreciate that?" Milla asked *France Football*. "An African head of state who leaves as the victor, and who greets with a smile the defeated heads of state!" The magazine objected that this was not an image of soccer. "It's thanks to soccer that a small country could become great," retorted Milla.

Cameroon lies at the corner of West and Central Africa, almost due south from Britain, but the cheapest flight there goes via Moscow and Malta. I spent twelve hours in Sheremetyevo airport, another hour in Malta, and on arriving in Cameroon I was pleased to be greeted by a porter. He threw my backpack on his back, and rushed me straight past the customs officer.

Out at the other end I tipped him, and he said I owed him another ten pounds. He had, he explained, bribed the officer to let me pass unsearched. "But I didn't ask you to do that," I protested. "I have nothing to hide and am happy for him to search my bag." The fact that I was carrying nothing illegal was irrelevant, replied the porter. If a customs officer wants to make trouble, he makes trouble. In any case, the official would be wanting his money. If I did not pay up, he, the porter would have to. I handed over the money.

Then I opened my backpack and found that my travelers' checks were gone. Ah, said the porter, one of the baggage handlers must have taken them, but not to worry: his own brother was head of the handlers and would find the checks for me. It seemed a happy coincidence—I only found out later that a Cameroonian's "brother" is simply any man from his village.

The theft shocked the porter's brother. "There is nothing you can do with travelers' checks! All the boys know that!" he told us. He asked around, but failed to identify the culprit, and the porter and I proceeded to other business. The task at hand was to get me from Douala to Yaoundé, Cameroon's political and soccering capital. The porter, by now motivated purely by kindness, advised against going by train or road, since as a white man I would probably be robbed. I flew to Yaoundé.

Yaoundé is a cool, hilly city, quite how large no one knows. The last map of the capital dates from 1972, and that one is unfinished, because the Swiss technician who was drawing it left when the money ran out. It is thought that Yaoundé has 650,000 inhabitants, but no one has gone into the slums to count. Of the inhabitants at work, most are civil servants, soldiers, or drivers of the yellow Toyota taxis that form the Yaoundé public transportation system.

No one in Yaoundé seems to produce anything. There are few shops, among them a clothes emporium named "Bobby Robson"— the memory of *Italia '90* lives on—and there are hundreds of unemployed people selling junk at the central market. As one of the only whites who ever went about on foot, I was their main hope, and every time I ventured into the central square the joyous cry went up, *"Le petit français!"* Back in London later, it was odd to pass shops without causing comment. Many men on the streets wear soccer shirts, and some Cameroonians wear political clothes: dresses, for example, with President Biya's face printed on front and back. *"L'impossible, ce n'est pas camerounais,"* as the saying goes.

Yaoundé is poor, but could be much poorer: no one starves in Cameroon, a fact due less to enlightened rule than to the rainy season. There are always enough bananas to go around. Yaoundé even has its rich suburbs, including one known as "Santa Barbara," because it looks like a Hollywood film set. One Santa Barbara family owns twelve Mercedes.

On my first morning in Yaoundé, I discovered why Cameroonians are good at soccer: they play it a lot. Forget all the nonsense about African suppleness. To explain the Lions of the 1990 World Cup, all you need to know is that at lunchtime, in the evening, and all weekend, Yaoundé turns into a soccer pitch. Some kickarounds draw dozens of spectators, and the quality of play is rare.

On the small, bumpy playground next to my hostel I watched matches at least as fast, as violent, and as sophisticated as lower division professional soccer in Britain, except that the style of play reminded me much more of the Lions in Italy. Had Massing and Milla donned old uniform and turned up they would have slotted in nicely. All players attacked and defended and clattered opponents into the perimeter fence, from which bits of wire protruded frighteningly inwards. Close control was perfect, as it had to be in that space, and as well as the total soccer on show, the sudden switching from one wing to another would have enchanted a qualified coach. A scout would have run out of notebooks.

President Biya plays golf. In Yaoundé, there are many posters of Biya. To judge by the posters, he is a man with a moustache. The accompanying text describes him as "Courage man, Lion man." Each day, to remind citizens what he looks like, the *Cameroon Tribune* prints a Biya snapshot and a wise Biya saying on its front page. The *Tribune* is the government newspaper. "Beyond your affiliations," it quoted on my first day, "beyond your alliances inherent in a democracy, beyond all differences, I am, and will remain, the President of all Cameroonians without exceptions."

Biya was worried. Africa's foreign aid donors had suddenly discovered the virtues of democracy, and tyrants wanting more money had had to hold elections. Biya had won 98.75 percent of the vote in the 1988 elections, but some felt that was because he had been the only candidate. Just before the 1990 World Cup an opposition party, the SDF, had been launched, and the month before I arrived, in October 1992, Biya had felt obliged to organize the country's first ever multiparty elections. His CPDM lost to the SDF, though the government had prevented two million people from voting. A quick thinker, Biya then told local chiefs to throw away the votes they had counted. The nation found out and turned nasty. The Anglophones turned against the government, and a civil war looked possible.

There are over 200 distinct ethnic groups in Cameroon—"a treasure house of cultures," the tourist brochure calls it—but the main divide is between those who speak French as a second language and those whose second language is English. The Anglophones live in the west, and the Francophones, who make up three-quarters of the population, in the east, in the area that includes Yaoundé and Douala. The Anglophones call Biya's CPDM "Chop People Dem Money," and in the election they voted *en masse* for the Anglophone leader of the SDF, Ni John Fru Ndi. When Biya rigged the vote they rioted, and so he declared a state of emergency in Northwestern Province. Biya's soldiers began to torture (Fru Ndi's mother was one victim) and to kill in the rebel region. The British Embassy easily dissuaded me from paying a visit.

Western nations began to demand new elections; there was talk that Biya would give up chopping people dem money, and would go and live in some of his houses in France, or in the USA, or in the hospital he owned in Germany; it was said that the treasury was finally bare; there was lots more talk.

But Yaoundé was still quiet, and the only signs of the times were the smoking heaps of rubbish everywhere: the government could no longer afford to pay the garbage collectors, so the locals had tried to burn the refuse themselves, with little success. Chickens and tiny dogs grazed in the piles.

I listened to the radio news in English at ten every evening, out on the *Mission Presbyterienne*'s porch with the proprietor, chiefly because I could do nothing else at night. Going out after dark, as a white man in those bad days, was thought an insupportable risk, like jumping off a cliff, or driving on the Yaoundé-Douala highway. The news was dull. The state of emergency was never mentioned, and almost all items (delivered in West African English) were announcements of official events, so that one night we would hear that, "A seminar on government work goes underway in Yaoundé tomorrow," the next, that the seminar was up and running, and the night after, that it was into its second day.

On my second day in Yaoundé I went to the Omnisports Stadium. It has an official capacity of 70,000, but (as custom once was in Britain) far more cram in for big matches, which in this city of 650,000 often draw 100,000 people. The ground is one of just three or four grass pitches in all of Cameroon. That day, the Indomitable Lions were training on it.

Each player was dressed in a uniform of his own choice; one even wore a Dutch national team shirt. It was a terrible training session. The squad practiced crosses, most of which went behind the goal, while the manager, a Cameroonian named Jules Nyongha, commentated from the center circle. The exercise was set up in such a way that only four of the 25 or so players could do anything at any one time, and they all grew bored. Two goalkeepers took turns in goal, one a competent performer, the other a fat, short, aging man who at one point ran ten yards out of goal to punch the ball backwards toward his own net. He may have been the team's bus driver, but on the other hand he may have been the first-choice goalkeeper. Had I come to the right practice? My neighbor on the stone slabs (which in the Omnisports count as seats) reassured me. These were the Indomitable Ones.

To get closer, I went to sit with some fans on the grass next to the athletics track. Then a small moustachioed man in formal white robes appeared, shooed the fans into the stands, and berated two passing workmen with spades, who trudged on. He threw me a nasty glance, but left me where I was. White skin may make you a thief's target in Cameroon, but it saves you from the worst bureaucratic bullies. Even so, I retreated to the stand, pointed at the bully and asked one of the evicted fans, "That's not Milla, is it?" "Yes it is," he replied sullenly.

Roger Milla is the son of a railway worker. His father probably took his name from a German named Muller. The boy turned out to be blessed with the balance of an American soccer running back and was voted African Soccer player of the Year in 1976. A year later he went to play in France, and for the next 12 years he moved from one mediocre French club to another. He was 38 in 1990, playing Indian Ocean soccer in Réunion and bound for oblivion, when Biya picked him for the World Cup squad.

It was an arbitrary presidential act that paid off. The born extrovert (he shaved his head before the England match, just in case anyone was forgetting him) won the title of Most Entertaining Player of the World Cup (a choice that must have given FIFA three seconds' thought) and became the idol of middle-aged men everywhere. He scored four goals. When he strolled into press conferences after games, Cameroonian journalists would wave their yellow and green caps and cheer, *"Bravo, Roger, bravo!"* "No one," says Milla, "has forgotten the moments when I was on the pitch."

For a year after the World Cup he travelled the world, playing exhibition matches and negotiating with clubs. Every now and then it would be reported that he had signed for a team in Mexico, or in Germany, or in South Africa, or somewhere on the far side of the globe from all these places, but each time the deal would collapse on his demands. At Cape Town Hellenic, he demanded 65 times the pay of any other player. In this phase of his life he charged for interviews, and refused to play for Cameroon against England at Wembley, in February 1991, when the English FA would not pay him a special appearance fee. A Nigerian chief awarded him a trophy, which was meant to be an annual prize, but when the time came for Milla to return it he held tight. The chief had to have a new trophy made. Finally, accepting that no club in the world could afford him, Milla retired to Yaoundé. He claims he scored over 1,000 goals in his career, but no one really knows.

The day after he chased away the fans, I met him again. This time he was wearing soccer uniform (a team shirt with Arabic letters) and was descending the steps of the Omnisports on his way to train with the Lions. "You see," he said, pointing to his outfit, "I'm keeping fit for 1994!" I was not about to bet against it, but he laughed uproariously. He had become general director of the Lions, a post Biya had invented for him.

The general director agreed to an interview (for free) and the next day I found him in his office. It is basic and battered and located in the basement of the Omnisports Stadium, just a few doors down from the room where he kept 120 pygmies from the Cameroonian rainforests locked up last summer. Milla had invited the pygmies to play a few games at the Omnisports, to raise money for their health and education, but he imprisoned them there, issued them with guards (one of whom wore a Saddam Hussein T-shirt) and seldom fed them. A tournament spokesman explained to Reuters: "They play better if they don't eat too much." As for the imprisonment: "You don't know the pygmies. They are extremely difficult to keep in control." The Omnisports cook concurred: "These pygmies can eat at any time of the day and night and never have enough." The little hunters themselves were too frightened to comment.

Their tournament was a disaster. Team names included Beesting of Lomie and the aptly named Ants of Salapoumbe, but only

50 fans bought tickets, and most of these came strictly to shout abuse at the pygmies. On the last night of the tournament, Milla staged a charity concert for the pygmies, at which he sang himself. (When *France Football* asked him, "Can you sing?," he replied, "Let's say, if they rectify my voice in the studio, then yes, I can sing.") Thousands attended the concert. A month later, with the pygmies safely back in their rainforests, Milla proposed a charity game between them and the Bushmen of South Africa. The pygmy reply is not recorded.

I did not dare discuss pygmies with Milla. With his enormous, cropped head, his military moustache, the photograph of Biya above his desk and the sense he emitted of pent-up force, he resembled the leader of a Fascist party. In fact, the Biya photograph is customary in Cameroonian offices, and though Milla growls rather than speaks, he is friendly. Dressed in shirt and tie, he was also the smartest thing in his office. Hammering went on constantly above us.

I began with the World Cup. Was Cameroon's success Africa's success too? "Not just the success of Africa, but of the whole Third World, because the Third World supported Cameroon." This was no idle boast. When England knocked out the Lions, a Bangladeshi man died of a heart attack and a Bangladeshi woman hung herself. "The elimination of Cameroon also means the end of my life," said her suicide note. What Milla did for Cameroonian migrants in southern French provincial towns surpasses imagining.

Had Milla's own success in Italy surprised him? "Maybe, because it was after all a World Cup. But I was a star in the French league, I was a star in Africa." Already he was rewriting history: Milla was a respected player in French soccer, but no star. Until the World Cup he could have ridden the Paris metro in peace, and even Cameroonians were amazed by his play in Italy. Why, I asked carefully, are some African greats nonentities at their European clubs? "Because when Africans arrive in Europe they are taken for monkeys. The clubs must give the players confidence." He claimed that his spell at Monaco "brought me not to play in big clubs in France because I told them the truth: that they must accept players as they are." He was saying, in other words, that he played for minor clubs by choice. How much racism had he found in French soccer? "Let's say that maybe now this racism has disappeared, but when we arrived in the 1970s we suffered racism. I have been told to go and look for bananas in the forest."

He said sorry about the Wembley match, and blamed his absence on "machinations" by the president of the Cameroonian FA of the time. But this was the new Milla speaking, Milla the diplomat. Milla at the end of the World Cup found himself a great player who had made no money out of his career, and he was bitter. He says he never made more than £3,000 a month. This, he claims, is because he is African. "I have been deceived by France," he told *France Football*. He admitted to me that he had still not received all the money he was owed for the 1990 World Cup: Cameroon took 80 people to Italy, the largest delegation from any nation, and £400,000 went missing. Joseph Bell, the team's first-choice goalkeeper, was dropped on the eve of the opening match for complaining about the missing money, which is why Thomas Nkono enjoyed his second World Cup. (For his rebellion, Bell earned himself the nickname "Nelson Mandela.") Yet some say that Cameroonian soccer is the best organized in Africa.

Why had Milla quit his global quest for money? "Friends advised me to stop at my peak," he said, and the president had given him this job. I pointed to the photograph of Biya. In 1990, when Milla was voted African Player of the Year, he had dedicated the prize to him. You are an admirer of the president, I said. "Yes: he's our president," said Milla. "When he goes there will be another president whom I will admire."

Now that he was a general director of the national team, what did he do? "I administer the team, I call the national team together for training camps, I prepare water, balls, uniforms, and so on for their practices, I prepare the fees for the training camps." And was that fun? "Everyone must be happy where he is and we must not refuse without judging first in the field," he replied piously. "I like the job because it keeps me in contact with my old comrades in the national team."

Ah yes, his old comrades. Before the World Cup, they objected to the retiree being added to the squad. After the World Cup, many of them complained that Milla had taken the credit for Cameroon's success. "We played, but Milla won," sulked François Omam-Biyik. Milla was reticent to me, but two years before he had told *France Football*: "Omam-Biyik has understood nothing. It was not the manager or the minister who chose me to play in the World Cup, it was the people. I accepted the verdict of public opinion, relayed to me by the head of state, President Biya, who ordered the minister to send me to Italy. I did it all for them, for the young lads. If I had done it for me, I would have descended upon the Champs-Elysées in an open-top car and I'd have said, 'I am the greatest!' " And indeed, he never did descend upon the Champs-Elysées in an open-topped car and say, "I am the greatest!"

Could the new Lions do as well without him? "No one is indispensable. Without Pelé Brazil won matches, but the presence of Pelé in a team motivates the other players. My presence had the same effect."

Pelé wanted to become president of Brazil. How ambitious was Milla? Would he like to become, say, manager of Cameroon? "To become a manager you have to be appointed, and since I must wait I am content with my current post for the moment." What about minister of sport? "Beeeh," he growled. "Since to become minister one must be appointed, one must wait. I would not refuse if they asked me to contribute something." It was an exciting time for him: after his post-career panic, he had found a post that seemed to offer a bright future, and at 40, he was starting a new life. It was why he spoke to me for free, apologized for Wembley and even refused to insult Omam-Biyik. The young man who had fought with critics on the streets of the Yaoundé had become a careerist. But I was told he was kidding himself: he has no education, and thus no chance of becoming a minister.

Finally, could he describe Roger Milla? "You journalists must do that. I cannot say Milla is this or that, but I am a man who likes to have contact with everyone, my nature is to discuss with everyone, no matter what they are. And further: I am a simple boy, as you see."

A number of Cameroonians I met told me, "You have a very good player in your country. Paul Parker!" Cameroonians follow black players, and I was often told that Africans were the best players in Europe: Abedi Pele at Olympique Marseille, George Weah at Paris St Germain, Peter Ndlovu at Coventry. Certainly Africans have done well in Europe, but the striking fact is that no Cameroonians have. Milla did little of note, Thomas Nkono spent ten years with the second club in Barcelona, Español, and most other players from the 1990 side are still with minor European clubs. Makanaky, a star at the World Cup, was not even a Toulon regular in 1990. "We were watching the match against Argentina, with some friends," says Peter Bosz, a Dutchman who played with Makanaky at Toulon, "and I told them, 'Watch that number 20, he plays for us but he's useless.' " And then I see him beating men and helping his defense, unbelievable."

African players in France face constant humiliations. Toulon had trouble finding a flat for Makanaky because landlords would not accept a black tenant. It is therefore natural that, as Bosz says, Makanaky was an isolated figure at the club. "I can't judge whether all the Cameroon team are like that," Bosz added, "but it's obviously not for nothing that none of them play for big clubs. They're very private. Joseph Bell, the goalkeeper, who played for us for a season, was like that too. Always alone in a room. A bit antisocial really. But apparently they don't behave like that when they're together." Soccer is about confidence, and it is easy to see how Africans in Europe might lack some. A manager picking a team has no trouble leaving out his African, who has no allies among the players and no name in Europe.

But if that is why Cameroonians have failed, then why have so many other African players succeeded? Professor Paul Nkwi, a Cameroonian anthropologist, suggested the answer to me. The players who have done best in Europe, he pointed out, are from the Anglophone nations of Africa: Abedi Pele is Ghanaian, Stephen Keshi (Anderlecht's sweeper for many years) is Nigerian, Charlie Musonda of Anderlecht is Zambian, George Weah is Liberian, and Peter Ndlovu is Zimbabwean. The only Francophone African who has done as well is Youssouf Fofana, the Ivorian of Bordeaux. The former English colonies have provided the successes, the French colonies, the flops, and the difference, said Nkwi, is down to their styles of government.

The British colonials in Africa lived in "reserved areas" and spent their time in "special clubs," away from the natives; the French preached that all men are equal. Each French colony was nominally part of France, and the professed French purpose was to turn Africans into Frenchmen by means of education. British colonization being openly racist, Africans from these colonies learned to expect racism. "Look at me," said Nkwi, who is a Cameroonian Anglophone. "I studied in Switzerland for six years, I knew there would be racism, there was, and I could deal with it." Or as Nii Lamptey, a Ghanaian, puts it: "You can piss on me, you can shit on me, I don't care." Lamptey made his debut for Anderlecht at 16 and scored in each of his first five matches.

The funny thing is that Cameroonians believe that players who go to Europe get worse. The Anglophone TV presenter Ignatius Fon

Echekiye, Cameroon's Desmond Lynam, cited Nkono. "Before he went to Europe," said Fon Echekiye, "until the ball has hit the net, don't be sure you have scored—his reflexes were that good. But now Nkono says to his defenders, 'You stand there, I stand here.'" In Europe, players learn to minimize energy expenditure. So players who come back from Europe no longer have the same kind of endurance, and though their raw talent is shaped, we feel they come back worse."

With only 12 million inhabitants, Cameroon is the most successful soccering nation in Africa, but Cameroonians think they should have done better. They see the 1982 World Cup as the one that got away.

When Cameroon set off for the Spanish World Cup, they were determined not to be a second Zaire. Zaire's debacle in 1974 had inspired the theory that the Black African game was embryonic, and Cameroon's sole instructions in 1982 were not to lose too heavily. Black Africans must not be made fools of again.

At the World Cup Cameroon was hailed as a marvel. The country nobody could find on the map gained three draws and failed to reach the second round only because their goal analysis of one for, one against was worse than Italy's two for, two against. Cameroon just defended. Their 0–0 draws with Poland and Peru passed with hardly a chance for either team, except that Milla scored a goal against Peru that was disallowed (even though the Peruvian medicine men themselves had predicted that Peru would lose. Also, it was never a foul). Against Italy, the Lions were heading for another 0–0 when suddenly the Italians scored. The Africans equalized immediately, and then shut down the game, against the team that went on to win the World Cup. They went home the only country never to have lost in the World Cup, but home they went, and they saw that they should have done better. They blamed the coach. Initially, Cameroon had appointed the Dutch manager Kees

Rijvers to take them to Spain. Rijvers was an eccentric, but he had a coaching pedigree. On the way to Holland to sign the contract, the Cameroonian delegation stopped in Paris. The French showed them a man named Jean Vincent and persuaded the Cameroonians to sign him. "The French care about Africa because it's the only place where they can flog their stuff," says the South African journalist Mark Gleeson, overstating the case.

Vincent was a bad choice. The French in Cameroon have tended to learn the intricacies of tribal politics rather quickly. Every player, minister of sport, and assistant masseur tries to get players of his own tribe into the Lions, and a manager who plays their games will not be picking the team on merit. The goalkeepers' debate of the past decade—should Bell play, or Nkono?—was in part tribal. To have appointed a Cameroonian would have been like making Graham Taylor England manager in the knowledge that he would fill the team with players from Lincolnshire. A Frenchman was almost as bad. The other argument against Vincent is that he came from the French second division. The French pushed him solely because he was a Frenchman. He was the latest in Cameroon's long list of obscure European managers. The Frenchman Roux, their first manager in 1960, was the local sales representative for Land Rover cars.

Nowadays, Cameroon's managers tend to be foisted on the country by embassies anxious for propaganda *coups*. The Soviets, who had run few successful projects in Cameroon (they once set up an agricultural university, but taught through interpreters) managed to place Valeri Nepomniachi in charge of the Lions for the 1990 World Cup. This was good news for world Communism, but not so good for Cameroon. "Nipo," or "the Russian" (the Cameroonians never mastered his name) came from the Soviet second division, spoke no French, and could talk to his players only through the driver at the Russian Embassy, who liked to improve Nipo's messages with his own ideas. Imagine what the Lions might have done in 1990 under Franz Beckenbauer.

I had come to Cameroon with a theory I wanted to test: that the 1990 World Cup boosted tourism to the country. For a start, the World Cup reminded people that Cameroon exists, a prerequisite for any tourist boom. Then, Cameroon got a good press. For a month we were told daily that this was a happy-go-lucky place with lots of voodoo, and the comparisons with Brazil cannot have hurt either. Tourism matters to Cameroon: the economy being what it is, a couple of hundred thousand extra visitors make a difference.

At the ministry of tourism I found the press officer reading *France Football* at his desk. I asked for an interview with the Minister, but was told that this was impossible: the minister had a lot on his mind because Biya, hoping to please the voters, was about to change his cabinet. Instead, I spoke to David Douala Diboti, the civil servant in charge of promoting tourism. Had soccer helped? "Enormously! You see, many people do not know where countries like Senegal, the Ivory Coast and the Congo are. Often they do not even know they are in Africa. The World Cup put Cameroon on the map." How had the ministry used the World Cup? He caved in. "I will be frank. We neglected to use it. We missed the opportunity. I regret that now." Had the ministry produced a single item of publicity, a poster for example, featuring the Lions? "Not one."

As we spoke, I felt that I had just given him an idea—that that day, for the first time, he had seen the potential of the World Cup—and when I left he suggested that the ministry might buy copies of my book and give them to European tour operators. It did not strike me as a brilliant plan. But imagine if after the World Cup, pictures of Roger Milla had appeared on the walls of European travel agencies: of Milla dancing by some corner flag, grinning his gap-toothed smile, and enjoining, "Visit Cameroon!"

* * *

A Cameroonian never calls himself a soccer fan: that he is speaks for itself. Charles was a fan too. One of the unemployed market sellers, he theoretically sold books, but as no one ever bought any he passed the time talking to passersby. He and I chatted about life and established that we were born in the same year, and I felt that if I had been a Cameroonian I would be selling books in Yaoundé market too. Charles failed to sell me anything, of course, but when he heard why I was in Yaoundé he lent me a book he would not sell, a monograph on Cameroonian soccer. He also invited me to the women's Cup final that Sunday. I had read that Cameroonian women's soccer was a popular sport that drew thousands of spectators.

On Sunday, I collected Charles on the way to the Omnisports. He had instructed me to wait in front of the bar in his *quartier*'s main street (its only street), and to tell anyone who tried to mug me that I was a friend of his. Thankfully he was waiting when I arrived. First we went to see his hut. Urine flowed in the ditches and children sat about. Charles lived in two tiny rooms, each a little bigger than a cupboard, which contained a stereo, records and books. I nodded and we walked to the Omnisports.

The stadium clock was broken, the toilets were locked, and the stands were uncovered, except the presidential terrace, which also had a canvas sunscreen. Thanks to the weather the Omnisports was a nicer place to be that November Sunday than a British stadium. The pitch, though battered, was the largest expanse of grass in that bare city, and in the heat it looked delicious. A military band played as the minister of youth and sports shook the players' hands. The finalists were Nifi Forestière of Yaoundé and Cosmos of Douala.

Five thousand spectators had turned up, more than any women's match in Europe can attract, but they were not real fans. This was a day out, an escape from men's soccer, where you care who wins and where you demand quality. The fans enjoyed this match as a parody of the real thing: when a Nifi forward attempted a bicycle kick and missed the ball, they had hysterics, and when the Nifi keeper headed the ball rather than catch it there was half a minute of applause and laughter. Whenever a player was injured three Red Cross men would sprint up, tuck her under their arms (they had no stretcher) and sprint off again, to suggestive cheers. The mood was sunny, and when Nifi scored with a fine header and everyone cheered, it felt like Africa at its best—until the military band struck up to celebrate the goal. Nifi won 1–0.

Once, in a game between PWD Bamenda and Tonnerre Yaoundé (a club secretly funded by the government), a Tonnerre striker rounded the keeper and patted the ball towards an empty net. Out of nowhere, a Bamenda fan leaped onto the pitch and cleared the ball from the line. Ten thousand fellow fans followed him, and the game was abandoned. Riots are common when a Francophone side visits Bamenda, capital of Northwestern Province, and the Army has shot soccer rioters on the streets. To Anglophones, PWD Bamenda is the pride of the Province; to Francophones, the "secessionist" club. Either way, Cameroonians agree that soccer is politics by other means.

One of the favorite stories of Anglophones in Cameroon concerns the soccer Cup final of 1979. Against all odds, PWD reached the final that year. However, on their way to Yaoundé for the match, the team and its president, Ni John Fru Ndi, the current SDF leader, were stopped at a checkpoint and thrown into jail by a policeman of the Bassa tribe. (Dynamo Douala, Bamenda's opponents in the final, was a largely Bassa club.) PWD eventually reached Yaoundé, but the night before the final, or so the story goes, a cook put a sedative in their food. PWD lost the match 3–1, and several fans killed themselves. Anglophones tell the story often, because it seems to them to express a moral of Cameroonian history: Francophones cheat Anglophones. For Northwesterners, the distinction between the club, PWD, and the party, SDF, is a fine one.

"The ordinary Francophone is corrupt," Barnabas Azeh told me. "Francophones believe in brutality." I had woken Azeh up, but when he heard my topic he spoke to me in his pyjamas. Hearing him attack Francophones, I pointed out that he wrote for the *Cameroon Tribune*, the paper that prints Biya's photograph on its front page. "I don't work for the government paper because I love the government," he answered morosely, "I do it because I need the money."

Just then a new scandal was breaking. A few days before I arrived, two sides fighting relegation, PWD and Colombe Sangmelima, had played the last match of the league season. It was a rescheduled match: originally, it was to have been played in Bamenda, but when the state of emergency was declared there it was cancelled and brought eastwards. PWD had had trouble training before the match, as the state of emergency forbade gatherings of more than three people in the Northwest.

Since Sangmelima was Biya's home town, the game struck many as a rerun of the elections. It was played behind closed doors, with even the press barred, and only soldiers present. Colombe won 1–0. I asked Azeh whether the match had gone off fairly, and he answered, logically, that no one knew.

The result left four sides, including Colombe and PWD, equal at the bottom of the first division on 22 points each. Which two of the four were to go down? The details were beyond me, but the question was whether their goal analysis over the whole season should determine the order, or just the goal analysis of the matches the four teams had played against each other. FECAFOOT, the Cameroonian FA, had to decide.

I am not sure which system they chose. All I know is that the relevant committee voted on the matter, and PWD and Diamant

Yaoundé were relegated. What is clear is that since a vote had to be held, the correct method of computing the table was plainly in doubt, and secondly, that the final table thus produced was predictable. Travelling through Europe, I had found many cases of FAs discriminating against certain teams—Nikolai Starostin could say a few words on the subject—but only cases from the past. Stalin and Beria are dead now, and European soccer is fair. In Cameroon, I saw the old tricks still being played.

As in England, the Cup final in Cameroon ends the soccer season and is its highlight. Perhaps the Cameroonian Cup final is an even bigger deal than ours, for whereas minor royals hand over the FA Cup, the Cup final in Cameroon is the one popular ritual that the president of the republic always attends. It is a tradition dating back to the first final, on Assumption Day, 1935, played before the French colonial governor, Repiquet. The president has to be there: in 1991, with the match previews already in the kiosks, Biya went on vacation to Europe and the game was postponed until his return.

This year there was a more serious problem. Biya had not appeared in public since the rigged elections, and it was feared that if he did show up he would be shot, or booed, or at best ignored. The president of FECAFOOT admitted to me that the authorities had considered calling off the final altogether. So there was general relief, two days before the match, when the first item on the radio evening news was that, "The Head of State, His Excellency Paul Biya, will on Sunday November 29th preside over the finals of the national soccer Challenge Cup." The report did not mention that this had ever been in doubt. The second item was that Biya had formed a new government.

The final that year was between Diamant Yaoundé, freshly relegated to the second division, and Olympique Mvolye, already in the second division. Mvolye was the richest and most bizarre club in Cameroon. Only three years old, they had been founded by a wealthy man named Damas Ombga. Ombga had earned his money buying arms for Biya and taking his cut. He was said to be the power behind Biya's throne (slip Ombga £50,000 and Biya gives you a seat in the cabinet), and he had modelled his club on Olympique Marseille. He had chosen the club's name to evoke the original "OM" and he dressed his team in a blue-and-white replica uniform of the French champions. As to the name "Mvolye," it is the village where he was born. "What do guys like that do when they become filthy rich?" Professor Nkwi asked rhetorically. "They are too uneducated to join the cabinet, so they build a tar road into their village and create a club overnight," and he drove me up the tar road through Mvolye, which took about three minutes. "Twenty years ago all this was bush," said Nkwi. Now Mvolye is a mini-suburb of Yaoundé, in part thanks to Ombga's road. On a grander scale than Ombga, though on the same principle, the late president of the Ivory Coast built the largest cathedral in the world in his village of birth.

Ombga had bought some of the stars of the 1990 World Cup side, including Stephen Tataw, the Lions' captain in Italy, and Bertin Ebwelle, and was thought to be paying them as much as $1,000 a month. This was unique: though some league matches draw crowds of 50,000, the receipts disappear before reaching the players, and all teams in Cameroon are semiprofessional. One problem is that as soon as a team does badly their backers pull out. "African entrepreneurs never invest on the long term," explained Nkwi.

Yet "OM" was still in the second division. If they could win the Cup, it would be the first prize in their history. They had lost the pre-match skirmishes: a couple of days before the final, four armed men had dragged Tataw from his car and beaten him up.

The Omnisports always sells out for the Cup final, and the atmosphere is renowned. "Get there early," various people had advised me, so there I was, nearly three hours before the match, in a virtually empty stadium. It was like finding Wembley deserted on Cup final day. I was not in the pressbox: since it is part of the presidential stand, everyone in it had to be vetted to make sure that they would not be shooting at Biya, and there was not time to check on me.

I had a personal interest in the first event of the afternoon, the parade of the national champions of other sports. I had met the volleyball champions of Cameroon, Amacam, since they were lodging at the *Mission Presbyterienne*. After they had crammed into the Mission's one guest room, I had to move to the proprietress's shack, where twice I woke up in the night to find her nephew urinating against my bedroom door. But the players were the most courteous people I had ever met, and never passed me without enquiring at length about my health. One evening, when they were brushing their teeth at the wash basin, they asked me how I was and I said I was well. Then I asked how they were. "very good," they replied. "We won our tournament today." "What tournament?" "The West African Championship." I murmured my congratulation. I had known from the first that they must be good, because they all had the same uniform. At the Omnisports, I waved as they passed.

The stadium was still almost empty, and Biya was due to arrive at 15:20 P.M.—the newspapers and radio news had given an elaborate protocol. But then, with only an hour to go before kickoff, tens of thousands of people materialized within a couple of minutes, as if they had fallen from the skies onto the concrete slabs. Why had they appeared so suddenly?

Waiting for Biya, I was as excited as anyone else. I did not suppose he was one of the great statesmen of our century, but when you see a man's poster everywhere for a week you are curious to see him in real life, particularly if he is a recluse. As his time approached, those on the front slabs fatuously stood to get a better view, and were berated by those behind. Then Biya was there, standing and waving in an open-topped limousine on the athletics track, followed by limos crammed with soldiers. But though I had seen his pictures hundreds of times, I did not at first recognize him. The person in the car was shorter and rounder than the Courage Man, Lion Man, and had a bald spot. Was he an imposter? The crowd was delighted and clapped and cheered as if he had been popularly elected. There were still large gaps in the stands, though, which was unheard of for a Cup final.

The teams warmed up with some breathtaking tricks. The Sports Minister at the women's Cup final had lost his job in the cabinet reshuffle, and this week his successor kicked off by whacking the ball 30 yards into touch.

I have never seen as neutral a crowd as the one at the Omnisports that day. Except for a few youths in Olympique Mvolye T-shirts, no one wore club colors, and all acts of skill were applauded impartially. An Olympique appeal for a penalty prompted scholarly debate.

The kickoff was the highlight of the first half. Directly after halftime Olympique's captain Tataw raced into the Diamant box, fell over, and won a penalty, which Ebwelle converted. Behind the Diamant goal, a train of boys and girls in identical Olympique shirts formed and danced the conga across the stand, while my two neighbors argued the penalty across me for ten minutes. It proved the only goal of the match, and Ombga had his first trophy. After the final whistle, acting on a hunch, I asked a fan in an Olympique shirt where I could buy one. He told me the street where they were being handed out for free. I understood: Ombga had created not only a team, but fans to go with it. Doubtless, the teenagers behind the goal were paid for their dance. It was all part of the Olympique Marseille fantasy.

The road past the Omnisports was cleared for dozens of military vehicles to rush past. While waiting for a taxi, I copied out the text of the T-shirt on the giant waiting beside me:

And World Cup 1990 will start in Italian soon!...

P'ong design for World Cup

When Speak to World Cup I'm sure you must be know?

That it is soccer game which excite

Every 4 years

They will find only one team to champion

And World Cup 1990 will start in Italian soon!...

And... I hope you must be exciting!

I'm sure...

When the giant spotted me writing, he kindly held out his shirt towards me.

Back at the Mission, I heard the radio news concede that the match had been "low-keyed." The prestigious Guinness Man of the Match Award had gone to Jang Sunday, the Anglophone captain of Diamant. "I was a bit surprised," Sunday admitted, and so, to be honest, was everyone else.

In the USSR, you could read the truth in *Pravda*, as long as you knew how to read between the lines. In Cameroon, the truth is not in newspapers, radio or TV, but is passed on from person to person, and gets distorted on the way. The trick is to have informed friends who stand at the beginning of the chain. I had questions to ask about the final.

On the day after the game, I first visited Fon Echekiye in the office he shares with Francophone colleagues at Cameroonian TV. (Apparently in 1990 they had renamed their studios after Milla.) We chatted vaguely for a while, and then he walked me to the elevator where no one could hear us, and told me that an hour before the final, with the stands still empty, soldiers had gone onto the streets and asked people in for free. It would not have done for the president to wave at empty seats. Why had people stayed away? First of all, Fon Echekiye explained, the finalists were mediocre teams, and the arms dealer had made himself unpopular by buying players from Canon and Tonnerre, Yaoundé's two big clubs. Then, people had no money. Thirdly, the opposition—and most of Yaoundé had voted against Biya—was boycotting the final. Jang Sunday, Fon Echekiye added, had been made Man of the Match purely to pacify the Anglophones. Certainly Azeh's paper that day was vocal in Sunday's favor, which suggested that something fishy had gone on.

There was other news: Diamant had not intended to play the final at all. Angry at FECAFOOT's decision to relegate them, the players had decided to shake hands with Biya and then return to the changing rooms. At the last minute they had changed their minds, or had had them changed.

I left the TV building and took a taxi to Bar Liberty, which has a collection box for PWD Bamenda on its counter. "Where is the office of the *Cameroon Post*?" I asked a customer. "Who are you?" he asked. I said I was an English journalist, and he walked me into the backyard of a private house. In the lounge were a dozen or so men sitting at typewriters or drinking beer, while women cooked in the kitchen. This was the *Cameroon Post*, a national newspaper, and the house was the home of its publisher. The staff had moved here after getting death threats and visits from the police at their offices. The *Post* is Anglophone—hence the PWD box at the Bar Liberty—and was by then the only opposition newspaper that had not been banned. The *Post*'s editor feared worse than a ban. "When these guys come to collect you, they are not gentle," he told me. Why had his paper survived so long? He cited the poor English of the state censors. In that week's edition, they had struck out a list of names of the detainees in Northwestern Province but had passed a two-page center spread detailing acts of violence. The editor found this very funny.

I was at the house to speak to Julius Wamey, *Post* writer, CNN correspondent, and, like every Cameroonian, expert on the politics of soccer. The low turnout at the final, he said, was "the first proof of

Biya's unpopularity since the elections." But, he sighed, "Biya is the kind of person who sees empty stands and thinks they're full. He's like a fat ugly person looking in the mirror in the morning and seeing a slim young man." And Wamey confirmed Fon Echekiye's view of Sunday's prize. We went on to the relegation issue. I said that I could see that FECAFOOT would like PWD to go down, but I still did not understand why they felt it was worth the trouble to arrange this, knowing what a fuss it would cause in the Northwest. In short, why did they *bother?* "Because they think in the end they can get away with it," Wamey answered. "Because they always have."

I took a final Toyota to Professor Nkwi, at Yaoundé University. He agreed that the stayaway at the final was probably due to a word-of-mouth boycott by the opposition. In the same way, he said, a boycott of French products was going on (France was still backing Biya) though no one had announced it. But when I mentioned Sunday's award he shook his head. He knew the rumor already. If an Anglophone had to win the prize, he asked, then why not Tataw, captain of the winning team, who played well? "People are trying to read meaning into everything now," he complained.

Two days later I was back at Douala airport, had met my porter of a fortnight ago, and had shaken him off. Then I was told that as I had not confirmed my seat I would not be on that day's flight. The next Aeroflot plane left in a fortnight. A friendly fixer advised me that other hopefuls were bidding for seats on my flight, and that to get on I would have to pay a bigger bribe than my competitors. I gave this man $100 and fretted for five hours in a lobby without air conditioning until he told me I had a seat. I ran onto the plane—there were more passengers than seats, and I did not want to strap hang to Moscow—and just 18 hours later, I was home.

Postscript: I had a twinge of nostalgia for Cameroon when I read months later how the Lions qualified for the World Cup. The deciding game was at home to Zimbabwe, on October 10, 1993. The opposition, still trying to unseat Biya, had called a general strike for the 11th. Biya responded by saying that if the Lions qualified on the 10th, the 11th would be a public holiday. Meanwhile the players, led by Bell, were threatening to throw the game unless they were paid their overdue bonuses. On the night before the match, the prime minister and my friend the FECAFOOT president brought them the money in cash. Cameroon won, and when the final whistle went the fans left the Omnisports immediately. They were furious with the players for missing the political point.

CHAPTER 14

MANDELA AT HELDERFONTEIN

HELDERFONTEIN. IT WAS THE journalist's event of the year, and I rang Mark Gleeson to ask if I should wear a jacket and tie. "Are you kidding?" he answered, "this is South Africa."

Whatever you read on African soccer, the chances are that Mark wrote it. He travels the continent and writes up its soccer for the Johannesburg *Star*, the BBC, *World Soccer, France Soccer,* the *Daily Telegraph* and *La Stampa,* to name but a few. If, say, an African Cup-winners' Cup semifinal is being played in Burundi, Mark flies in, hangs around for a week, and sells a dozen articles. He says his average is four pieces a day. He drove me to Swaziland once, knees to the steering wheel of his tiny car (Mark is 6' 8"), because there was an off chance that the Cameroon team might be landing at the airport. (They did not.) He knows the best prawn restaurant in Mozambique, and has been Roger Milla's tennis partner. In the players' tunnel at Botswana vs. Niger, the more senior Niger players went up to greet Mark, while their younger teammates looked on in awe. Being 6' 8" helps, he says, and so does being white. No one in Africa forgets Mark.

So he and I drove out of Johannesburg in shorts and T-shirts, through the bush to the Helderfontein country estate, where Nelson Mandela was to meet the South African national soccer team. The "Bafana Bafana" (Zulu for "The Boys") were due to play Nigeria two days later, in a game they had to win to have a chance of making South Africa's first ever World Cup. Mandela's visit had more to do with the nation's first ever multiracial elections, to be held a year later. Even by the standards of the rest of the world, black South Africans are soccer mad. "We need to be seen to be there," an ANC official told me, and of course the press was invited.

In 1992, to judge whether South Africa was ready to return to international soccer, Joâo Havelange and Sepp Blatter of FIFA visited Johannesburg. Solomon "Stix" Morewa, secretary-general of the South African FA, drove them in his Mercedes around the city's seven marvellous stadiums. Then he took them to a filling station in Soweto. It was his, and he wanted them to see it. Also, he had phone calls to make. So he told them to wait in his car, brought them soft drinks from the drinks machine and gave them a chance to ponder South African soccer's naïveté.

I visited the SAFA offices to arrange an interview with Morewa. In his office I found a woman, whom I asked, "Are you Mr Morewa's secretary?" She replied: "I don't know. I've only been here one day, so I don't know what his name is." I pointed out that her appointments book had Morewa's name on it, and I booked an interview. I turned up on the appointed day, and met Morewa, who showed me the appointments book. My name was not in it. He agreed to speak to me the next day. Mark drove me in, and as he had predicted Morewa was nowhere to be seen. "I think you're the fourth foreign journalist I've taken to meet Morewa and he's still not shown up yet," Mark consoled me.

Morewa managed to make it to the FIFA congress in Zurich, in June 1992. There, 16 new members were admitted to FIFA, but of these only South Africa raised an ovation from the hall. The world is happy to have South Africa back. People feel it is the land where gold and diamonds flow, where only human folly prevents greatness. Not only SAFA officials were going around Zurich saying that South Africa was about to win the World Cup, and the nation's fans joyously began to pick national teams.

It all went wrong. Even before South Africa played their first match, their manager, Jeff Butler, had to resign, when the news leaked that he had been creative with his c.v. His rather modest claim to have played for Notts County turned out to be false—though as his supporters pointed out, a cousin of his had done so. "We get people who say they've played for Liverpool and they haven't, or they've played two matches for Liverpool Reserves, and they'll have had ten clubs in South Africa without adding anything to the game here," John Perlman of the *Star* grumbled to me. Perlman liked to grumble.

Mark called South Africa's next manager, Stanley Tshabalala, a "coaching peasant." Poor Tshabalala was born in the wrong place at the wrong time. He grew up in the sanctions era, when South African teams never met foreign teams, and seldom even saw them on TV: the World Cup of 1990 was the first to be shown in South Africa. South Africa was less far removed from the world than, say, the moon or Pluto, but it was still a few light-years away. White South African soccer players tried to play like the English, but the blacks imitated the Harlem Globetrotters, and Tshabalala learned that soccer was about circus tricks. "Piano and shoeshine," he proudly called the South African style, and he fondly imagined that Brazil played the same way. After the Bafana Bafana lost 4–1 to Zimbabwe, his players revealed that he had given them no game plan at all. They had had to go out and ad-lib. Also, they complained, he was obsessed with *muti*. A 4–0 blackwash by Nigeria followed.

The journalists raged against Tshabalala, and he called them racists. Most South African soccer reporters are whites, and so are most managers. "Black players are scared of white coaches," Phil Nyamane, a rare black journalist, explained to me over breakfast at the *Star* one morning. "When the coach is a black man, they relax. Chiefs once brought over an Argentine manager, and when you spoke to him you realized: 'This guy knows nothing about soccer.' " But the funny thing was that Chiefs did well under him, because he impressed the players by being white." It is not just a matter of whiteness: South Africans tend to feel that any holder of a foreign passport is great and wise.

Eventually, Tshabalala slapped Sy Lerman of the *Sunday Times* in the face, and was sacked. (Lerman is known to other journalists as "Coach": they say he picks the team.) Tshabalala was succeeded by a caretaker, and then by Augusto Palacios, a Peruvian and a friend of Lerman's.

The Helderfontein receptionist was Miss South Africa 1982, and young men in tracksuits were swarming around her desk. "Any messages for me?" they would ask every two minutes. George Dearnaley, a white striker, found out that Sizwe Motaung, a black midfield player, was getting 50 phone calls from women a day. "Tell Sizwe's mother and sister not to ring so often," Dearnaley whooped, "because I know for sure that he hasn't got a girlfriend." Motaung didn't blink. Journalists had told me that white and black players hardly mixed, but four weeks in training camp seemed to be helping.

Mandela was due, and players were climbing out of the swimming pool and changing into tracksuits. I asked Roger De Sa, a bespectacled keeper, and one of three whites in the squad, whether the players were excited about the visit. "Not me," he said. "I won't be voting for him." While we waited for Mandela, De Sa and I chatted, and Innocent Mncwango, a black player, sat with us but said nothing.

De Sa is the son of Portuguese colonists and was born in Mozambique. His father played for Sporting Mozambique, a branch of Sporting Lisbon, and had a spell with the mother club until homesickness forced him back to Africa. Eusebio also started his career with Sporting Mozambique, and flew to Portugal to join Sporting Lisbon, but Benfica were quicker. "They caught him at the airport, offered him more money than he'd ever seen before, and he signed," claimed De Sa. De Sa supports Sporting—these things matter in South Africa. "When I was a boy everyone would come with their radios to the Portuguese Club at the weekend, to cheer on their team." Mncwango still said nothing.

We talked about Africa—South African whites discuss it as if they live in a different continent entirely. "The guys tell me that in Lagos they only got out of the stadium thanks to the Nigerian players. George Dearnaley says that when he was sitting in the bus, fans were shouting, 'De Klerk! Come here!' And I've got a bit of a temper, I'm worried that if I got into something like that I'd get angry." The Bafana Bafana had an away match coming up in Congo. "Is it worth it?" De Sa asked, without meaning it. "Who does Mandela support anyway?" he asked me. I knew, because the general manager of the Orlando Pirates had told me. "Mandela is a card-carrying Pirates supporter," Irvin Khoza had said, "and he has stayed at my house many times. Bishop Desmond Tutu is also a card-carrying Pirate." I told De Sa, who said, "Then I definitely won't be voting for him." De Sa plays for Moroka Swallows.

Half an hour late, and looking as ever like a Chinese giant, Mandela appeared. He chatted and joked, and when a terrified Steve Crowley, another white keeper, came racing up minutes late, he got a kindly headmaster's smile from Mandela. Palacios had reassuring words for the ANC President (*"No worry. We win."*) and then Mandela reached the journalists. He shook hands with the black reporters, and then, as these things still happen in South Africa, turned round to see us three white journalists standing together. Stricken with nerves, we had our hands by our sides, and he was thrown by finding nothing to shake.

All the time I was wondering whether I would dare ask a question. Even professional soccer players like De Sa scared me, and this was Nelson Mandela. Perhaps he was the most famous politician on earth, though Willem, my photographer, had said not. (We had debated the question.) He had certainly had his own Wembley concert. So when I asked, "Mr. Mandela, we hear that you are an Orlando Pirates supporter. Is that correct?" I was delighted. I had spoken fluently, he had heard me and the question had not annoyed him.

He said: "Noooo! I was asked this question many times during my long years in jail, and each time I answered, 'I support all the teams equally!' " It was an election-year reply.

I was passing the players' table when De Sa called me over. "So who does he support?" he asked, and the whole squad looked up eagerly. I said, "He supports all the teams equally." "I told you he was a Swallows fan," shouted De Sa.

Mandela then gave a speech. "Comrades!" he began, told some set-piece anecdotes that proved he was a regular guy, and moved on to soccer. "Tomorrow," he said, "the entire South Africa will be at the stadium." (This was surprising if true, for the match was scheduled for two days later.) He was not sure which side to support, he confessed, "because you will be playing against Nigeria, a country that has been highly supportive of the anti-apartheid struggle." This neutrality, noble in its way, must have disappointed Palacios, who had invited Mandela to Helderfontein. Palacios had played for Peru, and believed that politicians' visits inspired players.

"Soccer"—Mandela pronounced it "sucker"—"is one of the most unifying activities amongst us."

At Helderfontein that day, the claim rang particularly true. The players before him—blacks, whites, Coloreds, and Indians—had only soccer in common. Ten years before, the blacks among them could only have entered the estate as servants, and just three years before Mandela had been a prisoner on Robben Island. Quite near Helderfontein that day, other South Africans were enthusiastically shooting one another. "South Africans are sports-mad," Morewa has said. Apartheid aside, the country is a sleepy one-time colony at the bottom of the world, and besides sport there is not much else to do there. Johannesburg is built around golf courses, and in Soweto the crime rate dropped to unprecedented levels during the Italian World Cup. The idea that sport might help build the nation is less wishful than it sounds.

The cricket World Cup of 1992 had been a revelation. The 20-year sports boycott had ended just a couple of months before, and the nation—the *whole* nation—watched the tournament in rapture. When South Africa beat Australia by seven wickets, Steve Tshwete, the ANC man for sport and a former political prisoner, jumped into the arms of Kepler Wessels, captain of the team and an Afrikaner. "I never had tears on Robben Island, but I cried tonight," Tshwete said later. It was during that World Cup that South Africa's whites had to vote "Yes" or "No" to further reform of apartheid. The team let it be known that if the Nos won they would abandon the World Cup. The "Yes" vote was overwhelming, and the pundits said that you could do anything to white South Africans as long as you gave them international sport.

The doubters asked how sport could unite the nation when even in sport the races are separated. The Afrikaners play rugby, the English cricket, and the blacks most of the soccer. (We know South Africa for its rugby and cricket, but of course soccer is the most popular sport in the country.) I put this divide to the senior South African civil servant responsible for sport, a round man with glasses named Bodenstein. "Well, yes," he said. "But that's not really a result of ethnicity. I would rather say its preferences. Look, the black man is a ball player. He's got tremendous flair to play with the ball, and he grows up with a soccer ball in the back yard, and not so much with a rugby ball in the back yard." Many black South Africans live in back yards, and I suggested to Bodenstein that the "preferences" also had to do with income. You can only play rugby on grassy fields, and cricket requires perfect pitches and coaches who can teach complex techniques. "Yes, that is partly true," agreed Bodenstein, but he added that sports clubs were now open to all races.

But it would be wrong to be too gloomy: there is one sport that all the races at least like (only the local Chinese are not so keen) and that is soccer. South Africa is a country that could do with winning the World Cup, or at least qualifying for it, and the Nigeria match was crucial. President De Klerk thought so too, one of his advisers told me.

A few days before the Nigeria game, I was standing on a sidewalk in the center of Johannesburg reading the soccer news in the *Sowetan*, a black tabloid. A black stranger approached me. Was I going to the match? Who did I think would win? Did I not agree that the Bafana had improved? Whites and blacks would love to be able to talk to one another—almost everyone wants the new South Africa to work— but what else do they have to talk about? Soccer matters.

As you know," Mandela continued, "I have been on holiday for 27 years, but from that famous resort I have been able to watch the progress of the sucker game of this country. But there was a period when the standard began to drop, for reasons which we all know." I imagined the players hanging their heads: Mandela knew about their failure! By "reasons," he meant the sports boycott. But now Palacios, South Africa's fourth coach in six months in the world game, was promising better days.

"The African continent has come closer together," concluded Mandela, "because of this particular activity, in which you are our best ambassadors." It made me think back to Roger Milla in Cameroon: "Not just the success of Africa, but of the whole Third World."

Palacios handed Mandela a "present:" a baseball cap with the Kappa logo on it. A woman from the sponsor immediately jammed the cap on top of the ANC president, but Kappa had underestimated the size of the great man's head and the cap rode high above it. The photographers tried not to laugh, while Mandela showed the players the scars from the witch doctor's knife on his wrists and face. "You see, this *muti* is nothing new," he said. He posed for a team photograph, and the photographers begged him to shake hands with Doctor Khumalo, the second most famous man in South Africa, a master trickster who had had a trial with Aston Villa. Tall, light-skinned, and with the faintest moustache, Doctor looked more like a painter than a soccer player. Clasping his hand, Mandela boasted: "Now at last I can say to my grandchildren that for one day I was famous." Doctor blushed.

Later I had lunch with Palacios. The players sat at two long tables, but we ate alone. I was flattered by the attention, until I grasped that this man will hold forth to anyone. Nothing stops him, not even when my knife slipped and I scattered rice all over the table. (I had never dined with a national team manager before.) Palacios finished eating half an hour after me, and ended up drinking his ice cream.

Like his father and his two uncles before him, Palacios had played for Peru, though the number of caps he won depends on which interview you read. He claims that he missed the World Cup of 1978 through injury, but all coaches in South Africa who never played a World Cup tell the same story. Soon after that, an Argentine named Marcelo Houseman had turned his career into a whistle-stop tour of the world. Houseman had entered Palacios' life in 1979 in Costa Rica, where the Argentinian was a striker and the Peruvian a player-manager. Inflation hit Costa Rica, and Houseman moved to Hong Kong, from where he rang Palacios. " 'Negro,' said Marcelo—he does not mean it offensive, he calls me Negro for love—come to Hong Kong! I thought he was joking but then I came." From Hong Kong, Houseman took Palacios to Finland and later to Germany, and he once sent him to Australia when he himself could not take a job there. Then in 1985 Houseman rang his friend again to invite him to South Africa.

Palacios is a black man, and in South Africa he had to defy the law just to live with his white wife, but by his own account he prospered. He managed various clubs, and in 1992 he became manager of the Bafana Bafana. Houseman, now an agent in Johannesburg, told me he had got his friend the job. Palacios thought he deserved it. "There are too many English coaches here," he told me. "Maybe they are not the best English coaches. Sometimes the white coaches—because of apartheid—will swear and shout at the black players, so that the player thinks, 'I will do nothing.' "

When I managed to interrupt him I said, "Journalists tell me that the white and the black players in your squad don't mix much," and expected a flat denial. "A very good question," he replied. "When I started, you could see this everywhere. When we went to Durban, we went in four cars, and when the first one turned up all the whites climbed in. We ate at small tables and the whites would sit at one table. So I put them all at a long table, I made the room list to stop whites rooming with whites and blacks with blacks, and when the players form pairs to pass the ball, I stop two whites from pairing up." And did the whites and blacks play differently? "Yes, but the white players are learning."

Johannesburg. It was strange to watch a free Nelson Mandela meeting a mixed South African soccer team playing in the World Cup, and it was strange to visit the offices of the South African Communist Party in the business district of Johannesburg. The SACP was banned until recently, but is now probably the only growing Communist Party in the world.

The security guard unlocked the bars in front of the door, and I was admitted to meet Essop Pahad. Pahad is a member of the SACP central committee and of the ANC executive, and a soccer nut. He had just returned home from his years in exile at Sussex University and in Communist Prague. His elder brother, Aziz, is an even bigger fish in the SACP and the ANC, and the third brother, Ismail, runs a soccer club.

With South Africa changing day by day, I thought Essop might be busy, but three hours later it was I who had to end the conversation to get home. Mandela at Helderfontein was the end of the road; Pahad remembered the early days.

Pahad is an Indian (a very tall Indian) which in the 1950s meant that he played in the Indian league. "Everything was separate," he recalled, "the teams, the spectators. For example, next to Natalspruit, where the Indians played, separated from it only by a fence, was the Colored ground—they had a slightly bigger ground—and it was, 'Never the twain shall meet,' "

But there were impostors. A Turkish friend of Pahad's, registered as a Colored, had such light skin that he was signed by a white team. "He had to pretend to be white, and if you went to support him you didn't shout 'Mustapha!'—you called him by his nickname. Only in South Africa could this happen." Even then, the color bars were breaking down. Pahad and another Indian decided to move to the Colored league. First they had to go before the Colored league committee. "I gave my name as Gerald Francis, a beautiful Colored soccer player of the time, and the other guy said he was Baker Adams. The committee members laughed—a lot of them knew us—but they let us in no problem." He laughed too: "It sounds funny when we talk about it now, but I tell you, it was bloody tragic then."

Late in the 1950s, Pahad helped found the first ever mixed league—mixed that is, except for the whites. "It never even occurred to us to ask them," he admitted. "They were on the other side of the world."

Pretoria. The whites continued to play in their own league, until on February 18, 1977, in a match at the Caledonian Ground in Pretoria, the Arcadia Shepherds took the field with Vincent "Tanti"

Julius in their side. Julius was first a top-class goalkeeper, later a top-class striker, and always a black man.

Saul Sacks, a Pretoria businessman and no great radical, was the Arcadia chairman then, and still is today. I visited him at his home, where he gave me stacks of scrapbooks and told me: "Kai Johannsen, the former Glasgow Rangers player, was our manager. He and I decided to defy the law and field a black man, and we'd see if the sky fell down. On the day of the match, we hid Julius in the club office, and at seven-thirty that evening, half an hour before kickoff, I phoned Michael Rapp of the NFL." Rapp later moved to England and became a Spurs director. "I said, 'Listen Michael, as a matter of courtesy I would like to tell you that we will be fielding a black man this evening.' He said, 'That's fine,' but ten minutes later he phoned back and said, 'I've called around some other clubs and I have to warn you that if you go ahead and play him you'll be expelled from the league.' I said, 'So be it,' and that was that.

"Ten minutes before kickoff—it was the best-kept secret in South African soccer—we introduced Julius to the rest of the team and said, 'This is Vincent Julius, he's playing striker today.' When we ran onto the field the crowd rose as one man, even the whites—you see, the whites who came to soccer weren't like the Afrikaners." The next day the papers went wild, but the government did nothing. Other white clubs began to play blacks. Julius was the Arcs' leading scorer for three seasons running, though it was muttered that he never did his best against black teams. Later he joined the San Diego Sockers, on the fattest contract ever offered a black South African.

By playing for the Arcs, he made mixed soccer inevitable. When this became clear, the government acted. "The sports minister Piet Koornhof called me and one or two other white club chairmen to his office here in Pretoria and spoke to us for two hours without stopping," Sacks recounted. "Soccer to the government was an orphan, a black game with a few colonial whites involved. But

Koornhof knew everything about soccer: the players, the organization, foreign soccer. I don't know whether he'd read up on it for our meeting or whether he just knew."

Koornhof told the chairmen, "Merge with the blacks. The future of the country is with the blacks. Blacks and whites must learn to play together." It was an accurate vision of the future, but in the 1970s cabinet ministers never talked like that. "I was totally surprised," Sacks agreed. But Koornhof added, "Don't touch the Federation"—the league run by radical Indians and Coloreds. "Those people are Communists and politicians."

The chairmen took his advice. "Partly, I must admit, for commercial reasons," said Sacks, "because the blacks were crowd pullers, but for me it was also an idealistic step."

Today all teams are mixed, but some are still thought of as white and others as black. Wits University and Cape Town Hellenic have mostly white players and an almost all-white support, while the biggest clubs in the country, Orlando Pirates and Kaizer Chiefs, come from Soweto and have black fans.

When soccer went mixed South African whites were still going to matches. "There was a soccer culture like the one in England," I was told by Mark Gleeson, who at 30 is just old enough to remember. "My old lady and old man and us kids used to watch Arcadia, and we'd even take the bus to some away matches." Clubs like Highlands Park regularly drew 20,000, and even Kaizer Chiefs had lots of white fans.

As soon as soccer went mixed, black fans outnumbered the whites, even at white clubs like Arcadia. Roy Matthews, a former Charlton Athletic player who became manager of the Arcs, complained in 1979: "Even when we run onto the field, we get no support. I have even heard jeering, and that is no way to start a game. The only thing it does do is make the players play harder to show the crowd who is boss."

Later that year, the Chiefs visited the tiny Caledonian Ground, and around 30,000 fans were locked out. The "Callies" is in a white area, and the locals were unamused when the excluded fans threw stones and fought with police. The Pretoria city council immediately barred blacks from the ground, later banned soccer from it altogether, and Arcadia have never played at the Callies since. "Soccer had gone mixed," Lerman of the *Sunday Times* told me, "but it was mixed only in the sense that whites could play against blacks in stadium that were also segregated. So you would have 20,000 whites in one section facing 20,000 blacks in the other. It was virtually an invitation to have a race war. Naturally, there were incidents."

The white fans disappeared, never to return, even though by now, with armed madmen of all shades on the loose, soccer grounds are among the safest spots in the country. Barely a white fan will drive to a ground in a black township. I asked John Perlman if whites were right to be afraid. "Naaahhh," he said. "I remember, in the late 1970s, when there was no prospect of any political loosening, I went to Orlando Stadium, which was completely packed. People were hanging from the rafters, and everyone would beckon, 'White man! Come sit here!' 'Why have you come?' 'Who do you support?' "

At South African Breweries, the biggest sponsor of South African soccer, Adriaan Botha told me: "I always marvel that amid the turmoil of the townships the soccer stadium is an oasis of peace. In fact, we have more violence at our day-night cricket games." Why did he think that was? "I think the cricket fans go to matches all tanked up. These guys drink an enormous amount of beer. At the soccer, drinking is not allowed."

Even so, the only soccer most whites now watch is the FA Carling Premiership on cable TV. The big British teams have thriving supporters' clubs, and South Africans like Richard Gough and Roy Wegerle who play in Britain are heroes. Even the blacks watch the English game. "Many people said I was too short for the top level," says Bennett "Loverboy" Masinga, "but then I looked at players like Diego Maradona, Steve Hodge of Leeds or Ray Houghton of Aston Villa, and that gave me hope." Why Britain? "We have a colonial anglophile attitude," diagnosed Perlman. "I watch British soccer because that's what comes on TV," shrugged Mark Williams of Hellenic.

When I asked Mark Gleeson, he exploded: "The majority of our sports editors are Poms! They go in for the whole thing of 'Glory, glory, England Number One.' Take the *Star* today. The *Star*'s sports editor is Julian Kearns from Yeovil who'll never leave out an English soccer story, and there are two articles on English soccer: one on the recession, how Halifax Town and Stoke City are losing money, and there's a long preview of this weekend's matches. Sport at *Business Day* is run by a guy from Yorkshire called Terry Lofthouse. They don't even have a man on South African soccer!" Also, said Gleeson, the writers who cover the local game are mainly blacks, who are rarely pally with the white sports editor. "Nyamane doesn't stand up for his rights and he doesn't get his stories in. When I worked at the *Star*, it was easier for me to say to the editor, 'Why have you left my piece on South African soccer out? It's easier for me to be confident. Nyamane is lazy, but he says, 'If you'd been fighting as long as I have. . . .' "

Naturally, as soon as the sports boycott ended, South African clubs tried to bring over English teams on tour. When Everton seemed about to arrive, the *Weekly Mail* ran a piece entitled "Here Come The Whites!," pointing out the club's mysterious lack of black players. The first touring teams were Crystal Palace (complete with that friend of the black man, Ron Noades) and Sheffield Wednesday, and whites flocked to the matches. In Pretoria, they were spared the townships: for the match against Wednesday, the Pretoria city council let Sundowns use the Loftus Versfeld rugby ground, near the city center. I drove from Sacks' house to Loftus, which was deserted but for a dozen black workmen sprucing up the stands. It is a modern ground, with its own railway station, opposite a Dutch Reform church in a mansion suburb for whites, and as much an Afrikaner clubhouse as the government building in Cape Town. Sundowns vs. Wednesday was the first soccer game ever to be played there.

Behind the ground is the Pretoria Boys' High School, alma mater of Roy Wegerle. The parade of rugby and cricket fields outdoes any British public school, but there was not a soccer ground to be seen. "I battled for 16 years against a system in South Africa which was anti-soccer," complained Wegerle, in words strangely reminiscent of the political struggle. "As a white at high school I was supposed to play rugby and cricket. Soccer was for the black kids."

Johannesburg. The 1980s were the years of the soccer boom in South Africa: publicity, full grounds, and the construction of a dream stadium. The man behind the boom is now behind bars.

Abdul Bhamjee, an Indian, brother of Ismail Bhamjee of Botswana, and son of a poor Moslem preacher, left school at the age of 12. He rose to be public relations officer of the National Soccer League (NSL), and a public relations genius. Short, hyperactive, and very funny, he appeared on TV almost every night and fast became the most popular soccer official in the world. He promoted soccer as the "people's game," the sport the government ignored. He loved to taunt whites. When a charity soccer tournament packed 100,000 people into a stadium that officially could take 58,000, Bhamjee advised the rugby and cricket boards to hold charity competitions too. "I mean, they could get 20 or 30 people together, maybe 500 if they hyped it up."

His title of PR officer was misleading. It was felt, in true South African style, that a black league should have a black chairman, and so Bhamjee the Indian ran the league without the title. He pulled in the sponsors. Businesses liked to be seen helping the blacks, and by 1989 the NSL had built the FNB Stadium, also known as Soccer City, without a penny's help from the government. An all-seater stadium for 75,000, on the road from Soweto to Johannesburg, it is the finest ground in Africa. "The days when they can tell us how we can play and who we can play and when we can play are finally over," Bhamjee said when the stadium opened. He told Yorkshire TV: "They say, 'Give things to the blacks and they'll fuck them up.' We've proved them wrong." And he listed his three great qualities as "honesty, sincerity, and integrity."

"If there had been a one man, one vote election in South Africa, Bhamjee would have won it," Leon Hacker told me. Hacker, a thin man with a lined face, had sat on the NSL committee with Bhamjee. "Every black could hold his head up high thanks to the accomplishments of the NSL," Hacker said. "It was the biggest company in South Africa run by blacks, as well as the most high profile. Bhamjee said one season that we had had six million fans. If we say that we had four million that year, and if you add sponsorship income to that, the NSL dealt with enormous amounts of money."

"The moola is bulging in the pockets of the top brass," journalist Vusi Khumalo warned shortly before he died. When the Bhamjee scandal finally broke, the surprise was not so much the fact of fraud as the sums involved. Bhamjee was found guilty of 33 counts of theft involving nearly £2 million, and was given a 14-year jail sentence. He remained a PR officer to the last, telling the court as he left for prison, "I wish you a prosperous 1992." The stolen money is said to be in Botswana.

Fraud has become a South African custom, and most scandals are greeted with shrugs. When the owner of the Sundowns was found to have defrauded various banks, there was even public sympathy for him: he had endowed scholarships for poor children, he had built a good soccer team, and he had treated his players to a trip to London to watch the FA Cup final. That he and his mistress came along too was a mere detail. Freed from prison early, he tried to buy a new club, but failed. ("Prices have gone through the roof," he complained.)

But the NSL scandal reverberated, for the league had become a symbol of the new South Africa. The NSL committee had seemed an example to the country's politicians. Here was a body with a black chairman, Rodger Sishi, who supported Inkatha; a white liberal lawyer, Hacker, as vice chairman; and an Indian spokesman who supported the ANC. "Another white lawyer, President F. W. de Klerk, will be watching with interest to see if the cooperation works," I wrote in the *Berliner Tageszeitung* in 1991, when it seemed to be working. Gleeson grumbled to me that he had written the same thing, and even Bhamjee had concurred: "The NSL in my humble opinion is a model for a society."

Then the scandal broke, and suddenly it was the racists who were drawing the moral. The affair so upset Hacker that he withdrew from soccer. When I asked him whether he had ever thought of the NSL as a model for South Africa, he was honest: "That's what I thought. Even the police and defense-force teams were playing matches against black teams. There was then no contact in any way between blacks and whites, but there was on the field." In that case, did the scandal disillusion him about the new South Africa? "The scandal came at such an inopportune time—at a time when people were beginning to hold out hope that we could be governed successfully by blacks. Then the cynics could say, 'There, you see what happens when blacks get positions of authority.'" So what had Hacker learned? "Our system in this country has deprived the underprivileged for so many years that when they get control over large sums of money they're going to be tempted."

Then it turned out that most of the other members of the

committee were on Bhamjee's payroll. Hacker resigned, aghast. "I thought I was making a contribution to the sport, to the people, to the country, but really I was being made a fool of," he told me. "I didn't sleep for three months when this thing became known. I felt a sense of guilt that I had not protected the money of the people. I haven't been to a match since the scandal. It's very hard. I'll watch the Nigerian match on TV."

Cape Town. I took the bus south from Johannesburg to Cape Town (a 17-hour journey) and two days into 1993, I met a delegation from Cape Town Hellenic.

Cape Town has beaches, mountains and Dutch colonial architecture, but we met on an industrial estate outside town. The Hellenic chairman, George Hadjidakis, is a soft-drinks king, and assembled in the Seven-Up headquarters were Hadjidakis himself, the Bafana Bafana striker Mark Williams, and two Englishmen, Johnny "Budgie" Byrne and his son Mark. Budgie, who had been an England player in the 1960s, told me, "I could take the laces out of the ball." He had managed Hellenic for nearly 20 years. Mark was the club center-back.

Thanks to the end of sanctions, Hellenic was about to represent South Africa in the CAF Cup, Africa's version of the UEFA Cup. In the first round, they had drawn a club from Malawi. "Not only is it the first time in the history of the Cup that Hellenic is involved, not only is it the first time that a South African team is involved, It's the first time ever that a white team is involved," said Hadjidakis, a large Greek in a jersey and shorts. But Budgie, in shorts and a T-shirt, was worried about going into "Africa." "I saw grown men crying their eyes out in Ghana, Ron Greenwood included, when we went there with West Ham. And they were right, it was disgusting. But you've got a job to do." Hellenic had tried to sign Roger Milla. They had failed, but Milla's German agent had let them in on the tricks of

African soccer. Budgie explained: "It starts with the transport, the hotel, the chanting outside our hotel, the drugs they put in your food to give you diarrhea, It's terrible, and that's just what the blacks do among themselves." "I think as a white side we will be given more respect," Hadjidakis told him. "Also, there is a big Greek community in Malawi and I know the president." We all expressed surprise. "It's true," affirmed Hadjidakis. "Greeks being a nation of nomads, there is a Greek community in every nation. My wife is a third generation Greek from Zaire. I think the night before the game we should go for a big barbecue at some Greek house." "And maybe they'll let us pitch a tent in the garden so we won't have to sleep in the hotel," suggested Budgie. Hadjidakis reassured him again: "I have travelled in Africa a little, and I know that the Malawians are the most peaceful and loveable blacks in the whole of Africa."

How had Hellenic managed to finish second in the league with gates of just 3,000? The black teams lacked discipline, explained Budgie. "Blacks will always have that way with them—I've never been involved in coaching them—unless you can get them at an early age, like Peter Ndlovu. You have to mix in a couple of white players in the key positions, keeper, center-back, central midfield, striker, to keep the discipline. At Hellenic, we rely on discipline—we don't have their skill." He pointed to Williams, a man of color, who giggled. "He's the most indisciplined player you could ever meet. He's always late for training, he always annoys me. Some of his excuses are amazing. But maybe if I get him right I'll bugger him up. There are two professionals among us: him," pointing at his son, "and me. Mark kicks players in training! No one else does that here."

Mark Byrne drove me home in his van and explained on the way why the Bafana Bafana was in a four-week training camp. "Half of those guys live in tin shacks. Mark Williams has just moved into a proper house, but before he lived with eight people in a shack. That's why the black clubs move into hotels two or three days before a match." Budgie had arranged several trials for his son at English clubs. Once, at a Portsmouth practice, he had marked Paul Mariner and had ended up with four stitches in his forehead and three in his shin. "I asked Mariner, 'What was that all about?' and he just said, 'If you can't fucking take it, fucking fuck off.' There's nothing like that in South Africa."

Johannesburg. It is easy to sneer at Budgie Byrne. Granted, his language could do with a polish, but even sophisticated South Africans agree that whites and blacks tend to play soccer differently. After all, they learned it separately.

Phil Nyamane of the *Star* recalled for me a 1973 match between the South African Whites and the Blacks. "The whites played the offside trap, laid off the ball and ran into space, whereas our guys tried to walk the ball into the net, and we were beaten. The whites are taught tactics at a very young age, but when it comes to technique I think we've got it." Terry Paine, once of Southampton and now manager of Wits University, concurred in his own special language: "The black player basically has a very high skill factor. The blacks will tell you themselves that what they need is the discipline encroached on their makeup." Neil Tovey, a white ballwinner at the Chiefs, called his role "a white man's job in a black man's team." (Tovey was captain of the Bafana Bafana until he went on vacation instead of going to Helderfontein.)

So why did the blacks play "piano and shoeshine?" There was more to it than just the boycott, said Perlman. "If they're doing their tricks and sticking it to someone on the pitch, It's a glorious thing. It's saying, 'We do have something. Our community has something.' I really enjoyed it when a clever black player made an onrushing white player fall on his arse. That was me, as a white liberal, getting the thrill vicariously, so you can imagine how much it must have meant to the black player himself."

On days when they are feeling optimistic, South Africans like to say that their country has everything: gold, sunshine, and an ideal mix of white and black. They tell you that the new South Africa will be as rich as Switzerland, have no crime, and that it will win the 1998 World Cup. "If you mixed the skill of the black players and white efficiency, you could have the next Brazil," Gary Bailey has predicted. He elaborated: "The whites do the organizing and defending, the blacks do the creating and scoring. The blacks can't really defend because they don't realize that one mistake can cost you the match." Yet asked in the same interview to pick his South African team, he chose two black defenders, a black ball winner in midfield, and two white strikers. The notion that the blacks are stylish and the whites efficient is a little lazy.

Gaborone, Botswana. To prepare for Nigeria, the Bafana Bafana was playing a friendly against Botswana, so Gleeson, his co-journalist Peter Auf der Heyde and I crammed into Peter's father's Mercedes and drove north. I am now one of the few soccer writers in the world to have visited Gaborone twice.

At the border there was an hour-long line of fans, and in it were three shirt-sleeved politicians: Essop and Aziz Pahad, and the tiny Thabo Mbeki. Of course Mark knew them all. Mbeki had been the ANC representative in London during the years of exile, and was thought certain to become Foreign Minister in the first mixed cabinet, yet here he was, his shirt over his trousers, patiently lining up at the Botswanan border.

We saw the politicians again on the other side of the border. We were busy pumping up a flat tire on the Merc when they drove past us in a battered little vehicle. In South Africa, the political future is so uncertain that the locals are always on the lookout for omens, and this lack of side was a good one.

In Gabs, Mark went to strengthen some contacts at the National

Stadium, and Peter and I strolled to the Gaborone Sun, found two deck chairs away from the mêlée, and had a drink. Peter, a former semi-professional goalkeeper, *is* the soccer press in South Africa. Described by his friends as a madman, he edits and publishes the monthly *Soccer Arena* and the *South African Soccer Yearbook*, and he and Gleeson were then working on the first ever *African Soccer Yearbook*. They promised it would be "European standard," but it was tough going. In Africa, to find out how many caps a player has, or his weight, or date of birth, you have to ask him himself and hope he remembers.

Drowsing in the chair, I asked Peter how a man gets started in soccer publishing. He said he had been working for Chief Buthelezi's Inkatha Freedom Party until one day he was sacked. Inkatha paid him a settlement, and he used the money to set up his publications. "Why did they fire you?" I asked. "They said I was an ANC spy." "If you were a spy, why did they pay you a settlement?" "Their only evidence was that the government security forces had told them I was a spy. They could hardly say, 'We know, the government told us,' so they paid me a settlement." The story ended there: he never told me whether or not he really had been a spy. Thus a country acquires its soccer press.

But Peter had just started a second career. On his first venture as a soccer agent, he had found a German Bundesliga club willing to sign the South African captain Steve Komphela. Komphela was delighted, until Palacios called him in for a chat. The player was given to understand that unless he dropped Peter and took Marcelo Houseman as his agent, he would be out of the squad, captain or not.

We went back into the Sun, interviewed Fickert, and ran into Komphela, a thickset man—he played at center-back. He and Peter eyed each other tensely. "Don't worry about it now," Peter told him. "Just play." We popped into the *Sowetan* reporters' room, next door to Komphela's. On the bed lay an enormously fat young man, the reporter, while the photographer did something to his films. Peter pointed to the man in the bed and announced to me: "He's the one, he's responsible." It appeared that the man was responsible for coining the nickname "Bafana Bafana."

He stood in a great African tradition. Every team on the continent has its nickname: Cameroon is the Indomitable Lions, Botswana the Zebras, Nigeria the Super Eagles, the Kaizer Chiefs the Amakhosi, or the Phefeni Glamour Boys, and the Fairway Stars the Ya Wla Koto, a battle cry meaning, "The knobkerrie has fallen on the opponent's head."

South African players are known by their nicknames too: in black South Africa, as in Latin America, you become a real person only when you get a nickname. The Bafana Bafana that day included John "Shoes" Moshoeu, Fani "Saddam" Madida and Theophilius "Doctor" Khumalo. With a name like Theophilius, a nickname was pure necessity for Doctor, and Madida could be pleased with "Saddam" too: he had gained the nickname when he began to shatter defenses at the time of the Gulf War. He had since moved to Besiktas in Turkey, and heaven knew what they made of the tag there. Decades before, there had been a number of "Herr Hitler's on the South African pitches. "Jimmy Greaves" is a simple nickname to explain, but there must have been reasons for monikers like "Bob is a shilling," "Haleluya Sezeni," "Teachers" Meeting," and "Brrrr . . ." One unfortunate was known as "Baboon Shepherd," while "Hurry-hurry" Johanneson went to Leeds United and got himself picked for England, though one doubts that his nickname survived the move. Gary Bailey was "Sunshine" in South Africa but never in Manchester. Patrick "Terror" Lekota is a senior ANC politician, but is still known by the nickname he acquired as a player. Some players hate having nicknames. Walking into bars to shouts of, "Hey, Baboon Shepherd!," they feel they have lost some of their privacy. Pelé always used to say he was two men: Pelé as a public figure, Edson as a private person.

* * *

The National Stadium looked full of South Africans. It was hard to tell, since many Botswanans routinely go about in Kaizer Chiefs shirts. Certainly all the banners were for the Bafana Bafana, I saw as I walked around the athletics track. "Hey, white man! What are you doing here where you have no business of being?" one fan asked me. Thabo Mbeki was introduced to the teams, and the tiny man reached up and clasped each player's hand in a matey shake. Palacios' son sat beside his father on the South African bench. It was the Peruvian's first game in charge and he had vowed to teach the Bafana some discipline.

Maybe he had, but South Africa still played like a grotesque parody of Brazil: backheels, double and triple feints, all without point. Shoes tried to flick the ball over his head with his heel, failed, and was cheered by the crowd; but the worst offender was Doctor. After failing to walk a cross from Madida into the net, he turned and gave the stadium a massive grin. Later, he flicked the ball up and balanced it on his toe, showed it to a Botswanan defender and was rushed off his feet; then, as Botswana went off with the ball, he walked to the touch-line and asked the bench for water. Perhaps it was his good luck that Ron Atkinson had decided against bringing him to the Midlands, and the Zimbabwean team had rechristened him "Nurse," but the South African fans loved him. Roy Wegerle (who says he learned his tricks in South Africa) is a computer by comparison. Yet the joke was on the Gradgrinds as the Bafana won 2–0, the second goal stemming from an overhead volley from Doctor that set up a four-man move.

FNB Stadium, between Johannesburg and Soweto. In the 1950s, Essop Pahad had told me, when the South African team was all-white, two stands at every international match were reserved for non-whites. "They would be crammed full," Pahad reminisced, "with everyone supporting the visiting team. I can only recall one foolish Indian fellow supporting South Africa, only one foolish fellow, and he was always in trouble."

Before South Africa played Nigeria, the drums were going, the fans were toy-toying, and the *Sowetan*'s T-shirts were commanding, "Don't just stand There—Build the Nation!" On the field, Nigeria's Dutch manager Clemens Westerhof was gazing at the stands with Willem, my photographer and his compatriot. "There aren't many grounds as good as this in Europe," Westerhof assured him. Few all-seater stadium for 75,000 in Britain, certainly. Bhamjee could be proud in prison, though the NSL had never paid for the FNB Stadium and its construction had never been completed.

The crowd that day was 60,000. The pressbox was full to bursting. Those at the front could not see unless they stood up, and we at the back could not see if they did, so there were loud disputes. I was sitting at a desk marked "Foreign Correspondence," and my neighbor's place was designated "Sappa," an allusion to the South African Press Association, SAPA. The SAPA reporter had to file reports during the match: he wrote about six during the 90 minutes, and saw little of the game. I had to jolt his arm whenever there was a scoring chance, and I bear that in mind now when I read agency match reports.

Nigeria scored a psychological goal when the teams lined up for the anthems: every Super Eagle was eight feet tall. That made the psychological score 3–0, for they had whacked the Bafana in Lagos, and almost all of them played for European clubs. One Super Eagle was Swansea City's Reuben Agboola, which begged the question why a member of one of Africa's best teams could do no better.

It came as no surprise whatsoever when minutes after the kick-off, a particularly tall Super Eagle intercepted a South African back-pass and rammed the ball into the net. It was more surprising when the referee disallowed the goal for offside, for presumably he knew that there can be no offside from a backpass. The Bafana Bafana made halftime with the official score still 0–0. At halftime, Mark gave interviews on the pitch to black radio reporters. They all knew as much about soccer as he did, but they were black men and not confident enough to give their own views.

Early in the second half, George Dearnaley tapped a low cross into the net and the nation stood on its head. In the pressbox, the South Africans, black and white, leapt skywards, and the big white striker from Natal celebrated with 10,000 blacks in the stand behind the goal. Then the Botswanan in black gave a free kick for offside, and we were back in the Old South Africa.

The match ended scoreless, South Africa were out of the World Cup, and the nonstop drummers went home with headaches. But Westerhof (who had been predicting a Nigerian walkover) said, "All praise to South Africa," and Palacios told me, "For the next World Cup, I think we will be ready."

In the parking lot, with Perlman, I watched the two best South African players, Steve Crowley and Shoes, fight their way to their cars. I mentioned to Perlman how much at ease Crowley looked: he teased the fans and they him, and he knew the right clasps for their handshakes. It was the only place in South Africa where I had seen people forget their skin colors, I said. Perlman got angry again.

"That's the classic foreign correspondent's story on South African soccer! Look, when the crowd cheered Dearnaley they weren't even *aware* that he was white and they were black. South African soccer is past that kind of thing. There are other stories you should be writing!"

On the plane back to England I met a man I had already met in Cape Town. He was a white South African who supported Arsenal, perhaps because he had not seen them play since the 1970s. We arranged to go together to watch Arsenal play Leeds in the FA Cup later that week. It was a freezing night, and we stood at the Clock End. I saw almost nothing of the pitch, and nothing at all of the goal directly in front of us. Unfortunately all four goals were scored there. Leeds overran Arsenal in the first half, thanks to Gordon Strachan. "That Strachan. Dunno what they feed him on," said the man next to us, and he shouted at the Arsenal defense: "Go on, tackle him! What are you, the Gordon Strachan Appreciation Society?" David Hillier, the crowd's least favorite Gunner, made his umpteenth clumsy challenge and was booked. "Send him off, ref!" shouted one fan. "Ban him for life!" advised another. "Or longer if possible!" added a third. The game ended in a 2–2 draw. The soccer was dreadful, but five months later Arsenal had won the FA Cup.

CHAPTER 15

SHORT, DARK, AMERiCANS

THERE IS PROBABLY ONLY one city in the world where a
friendly game between El Salvador and Denmark can draw 30,000-
odd fans, and that city is not San Salvador, certainly not Copenhagen, but Los Angeles. On my way to the L.A. Coliseum I quite
forgot I was in the United States. All the fans on the streets were
small and dark, and few of the program sellers and beggars looked
Danish either. No one was waving gimmicky team symbols, all the
fans were men, and the only food on sale seemed to be unhygienic
burgers. It was all most un-American.

A *Boston Herald* columnist was the first person to see through the
1994 World Cup. Nix soccer festival or commercial bonanza, he
wrote: the World Cup was a scam set up by the immigration department. Get all the illegal aliens into one stadium and swoop, was the
idea. I sat in the Coliseum among what looked to be 30,000 Salvado-
rians, and if the organizers reported only 15,000 that may have been
because they had to pay the Coliseum owners a share of gate receipts.

Down below, I saw a man I had last seen in Latvia: Möller-
Nielsen was exercising the Danish substitutes. Less than three weeks
after the El Salvador game, both he and I arrived in Argentina (Denmark were playing there), so that in five months we were in the
same place three times. We coincided in three different continents.

The Salvadorian crowd was happy. It cheered the fireworks it
threw, the fan who was being led away, and the two policemen who
were leading him. It stayed happy even as the small, mediocre

Salvadorian side lost 2–0 to the big, mediocre Danes. In the final minutes, it succumbed to nostalgia for the civil war of yore, and stopped throwing fireworks onto the pitch and began to throw them into the stands instead. It chuckled at the explosions, but more and more people made for the exits, and when a bottle broke on the empty seat beside me I left too. The next morning at breakfast, the *Los Angeles Times*, in a 12-page sports section, carried not a word about the match. I was back in the United States.

"For me much easier to work here," the USA's coach, Bora Milutinovic, admitted to me later. "Here, you open the newspaper, not is soccer. Mexico every day you have something, something true, something the people write. Also this is Mexico." Milutinovic is a Serb who came to the States after two decades in Latin America.

Ana is a nanny from El Salvador. Leaving America again, I visited her family in South-Central L.A., where the L.A. riots took place. In the living room were a few cousins, Ana herself, her baby Diego, sleeping in a cot in the corner, and her husband, Hember, a soccer freak. Hember showed me Diego and explained: "Maradona is the best guy in the world for soccer. When Diego is two years older, I think I go to the park to find a team for him. When we see anything soccer on TV, I put him in front." Hember only watches the local Hispanic channel, which constantly shows Mexican league matches. But he had gone to the Coliseum for El Salvador vs. Denmark: "Denmark team had a lot of big people, hey?" I asked whether fireworks were common practice at matches in El Salvador. "In my country, they take you to jail."

He played himself, for a Sunday team—like going to church, he said. Were all the players in his team from Latin America? "All the players in my team are from Nueva Guadaloupe in El Salvador." In his league there were also black teams from Jamaica and Belize, and even a couple of black American teams. "When I came here, American people did not like soccer. But now American people are starting to like." Not all of them, though. Sometimes his team went to Rancho Park and found a softball game going on—Hember made as if to shield himself from flying balls. "They don't like, we don't like, they call the police, and they are Americans, so we have to go." But he liked to see the U.S. win, unless they were playing El Salvador. The United States' best player was Hugo Pérez, he thought. Pérez is from El Salvador.

The talk made Hember homesick, and he played me a promotional videotape of El Salvador. It appeared to show men kicking one another under water. "You see," he said. "Even on the beach, they play soccer."

When immigrants from Europe landed in the U.S., their children were teased on the street for their funny accents, clothes, and parents. The last thing these children were going to do was play a funny European game on the streets and be teased again, so they took up baseball. That is why Americans don't play soccer.

When we say that Americans don't play soccer, or that they celebrate Thanksgiving or come to Europe in tour groups, we are thinking of the big white people who live in American suburbs. Tens of millions of Hispanic Americans do play and watch and read about soccer. Yet even white suburban America plays soccer, in its way. I used to play soccer in America. I was ten when my family moved for a year to Stanford, a sunny Californian university town where all the boys and girls play soccer. Richer Americans tend to. Missionaries are trying to spread the word, but for the moment ghetto kids take the view that soccer is for softies.

Most of the coaches in Stanford had never played, so they took ideas from the sports they knew. One coach, when his team won a corner, would bellow code names like "Eagle!" or "Spiral!" at the child trying to lift the ball through the air as far as the goalposts.

Another coach, when his team was in attack, would place his two fullbacks exactly on the corners of the penalty box, and position his center-back in the semi-circle in front of the area. There they would stand, their hands folded behind their backs, until play returned to their half of the pitch. Then there was the right half who had orders to pass every ball he got five yards to his left. The theory was that the team's right back, overlapping, would get the ball straight into his feet. The ploy seldom worked.

Few of the children I knew minded much. They played soccer as European kids might play the oboe: because their parents thought it was good for them. It was fun too, sure, but nothing to get excited over. There were few good players. "OK, you have 15 million Americans playing the game, but for most of them it's just one form of recreation among many," Lynn Berling-Manuel, editor of *Soccer America*, admitted to me. "After Pelé, who hasn't played for a decade, most American soccer players can't name a single professional." None of my friends in Stanford ever watched soccer, even though George Best was playing for the local team, the San Jose Earthquakes. Someone must have gone to watch, however, for those were the days when it seemed that soccer had landed in America. The North American Soccer League drew large crowds, come to watch ancient Europeans finish their careers. "An elephant's graveyard," Gianni Rivera called the NASL, but what elephants! I remember, in 1981, seeing the Earthquakes play the New York Cosmos in a match that featured Best, Franz Beckenbauer, and Johan Neeskens. Months later, when we were watching the Earthquakes indoors, Best ran at a defender, *trod* on the ball, making it shoot over the man's head, and jogged round him to collect it. Of course he did nothing else all match.

Lawrie Calloway played for teams like Wolves, Blackburn, Shrewsbury, and Rochdale in England before coming to America in 1974, where his clubs included the Earthquakes. I do not remember him there. "We definitely became celebrities," he told me, in an accent that was a mix of Birmingham and California. "Coming from the English second division, which is where I spent most of my time, when all the attention went to the George Bests, the Charlie Georges, the Bobby Moores, to come here and have profiles written about you, to be on TV—it was very gratifying for me." As a journalist, I was touched.

But the NASL folded in 1985. The men who ran it tried to found too many clubs too soon, and they knew too little about soccer. "I only realized late on that about 100,000 people can pass themselves off as Polish internationals," the late Howard Samuels, chairman of the American League, confessed. The fans were no experts either. Calloway told me: "They cheered the cheerleaders, and when a guy booted it 60 yards or headed it 30 yards everyone was on their feet. The story I tell is that at San Jose we had a cheerleader named Crazy George, who became quite a celebrity, and who made the *Guinness Book of Records* for the longest cheer ever. He had the one side of the stadium shouting 'Earth' and the other 'Quakes,' and kept this going for thirteen and a half minutes—during which time the other team scored a goal."

Now Calloway is coach of the San Francisco Bay Blackhawks, and when we spoke they were trying to join the Mexican league. "It's a long shot," he confided. A very long shot, surely? "It's the same as Cardiff playing in the English league. Nothing's impossible." Even so, he admitted, the Blackhawks were praying for a new American pro league: "We don't really want to play in the Mexican league for the rest of our lives." San Francisco lies 475 miles to the northwest of the northwestern tip of Mexico.

Peter Bridgewater, another Englishman in California, is in charge of Stanford's World Cup. He is an angry man. I put it to him that while Rio, Rome, and Barcelona were natural World Cup sites, Stanford, California, was not. "Mr. Kuper, where do you live in

England? In London?! Highbury is a small town, *Wembley* is an even smaller town! Is Wembley a good place to have soccer?" And which teams did he hope would play in Stanford? "England!" But to tell it like it is, Stanford is like Leamington Spa.

Americans never found out that soccer is a man's game. Growing up in England and Holland, I had never suspected that girls could play soccer, but they did in Stanford. On our school playground we had kickarounds in which the whole year joined in. There are four-year-old girls in the United States playing league soccer, and nearly half the soccer players in the country are women.

I asked Lynn Berling-Manuel, female editor of the nation's largest soccer magazine ("I must say that I get a tremendous amount of mail addressed to Mr. Lynn Berling-Manuel") why America was different from the rest of the world. The key, she said, was that American women had come to soccer at the same time as American men. Unlike European women, they never felt like outsiders to the game.

How had she herself come to soccer? "My dad had never been to a soccer game in his life. I'm the oldest of six children, and with six kids you can't afford to go anywhere. So in 1967, our local soccer team, the Oakland Clippers, were offering a very cheap family package. For something like $20 you could take everyone *and* park the car, and Dad, being the big spender he was, thought this was just the thing. And so all my family became soccer fans, to some degree. I think this was a very common experience." The NASL tried to sell soccer to families, and it got women. "It was a unique marketing direction that other sports didn't have. At first they marketed soccer as a macho bang-'em-up, crash-'em-up game, and had a very tough time selling it. People came to the stadiums and said, 'This sure isn't NFL.' " The upshot was that in 1991 in China the U.S. won the first ever women's World Cup.

I had spoken to Calloway, Bridgwater, and Berling-Manuel over the phone. There are telephones all over the world, but Americans are the only people I found who use them to give frank interviews to people they have never met. After tramping the streets of Europe and Africa, I spent most of my days in L.A. in bed, on the phone. I reached April Heinrichs, the American captain who lifted the trophy in Beijing, at the University of Maryland. It is at colleges like this that the best women's soccer in the country is played. Heinrichs told me: "I'm a full-time women's coach here, That's my job, That's what I *am*, and I have a full-time assistant coach and a budget of over $80,000." I told her about the British TV series *The Manageress*: a soap about a woman who manages a male professional team, and who gains respect after a long struggle against sexism. Did Heinrichs identify with the struggle? "Absolutely not. I'm 29 years old. I belong to the first generation of female athletes in this country to be accepted. If you talk to women 10 or 15 years older than me, they have scars from their experiences." That dated acceptance to the early days of American feminism. Could the feminist movement take credit for America winning the World Cup? "Well . . ." said Heinrichs. I apologized: "Of course you still have to play well and score goals." "Apart from that," she replied, "absolutely, yes."

Had she played against England? "Yes. I get a sense that though it's a small country they have some really good players. I can't figure it: they don't train hard, they don't get together very often, and they don't take good care of themselves. I can only explain it because they have what we haven't got: every weekend they have some of the best men's soccer in the world on TV."

Did she agree that soccer in the U.S., and perhaps particularly women's soccer, was a middle class sport? "No." No? "No, I would say it was an upper middle-class sport. Unfortunately." Then she added: "But I'm quite pleased with that." Why? "I think it's important that education is stressed in this world."

* * *

Almost all the American players at the 1950 World Cup came from St Louis, Missouri. St Louis did have something distantly resembling a soccer culture, but the real reason for the lack of balance was that the American FA was based in the city and was too poor to scout around. As we know, the 1950 Americans beat England 1–0, but when they flew home it was in two separate planes, to save money. Their welcoming committee consisted of a player's wife, come to scold her husband for being back late.

A day after El Salvador vs. Denmark, I found the present American squad in a hotel overlooking the Pacific in Santa Barbara. The Red Lion hotel was far too expensive for me, so I found a room a couple of miles around the corner, in a hotel that was only somewhat too expensive. I walked to the Red Lion along the beachfront, where a few Hispanics were kicking a ball around. A small, subtropical campus town on the Pacific, whose inhabitants include Ronald Reagan, Santa Barbara looked far too nice to go wild over a soccer match.

I reached the Red Lion a full hour late for my appointment with Dean Linke, the American press chief. His deputy met me in the lobby. Dean was extremely sorry that he could not receive me in person; he had had to go to a soccer clinic; meanwhile, he hoped that this press pack would be of use—and the deputy gave me a file of documents as thick as a largish encyclopaedia. I knew the Brazilians said that playing the World Cup in the U.S. was like playing the baseball World Series in Brazil; I knew that American outdoor soccer had been run by a man who thought it a poor alternative to the indoor game; and Americans do go hunting for burgers when the referee gives a corner kick; but at that moment I thought they deserved the World Cup. The deputy even agreed with my judgment of Santa Barbara. "You'd sit in that stadium on the ocean, watching the match with maybe 300 other people, and if the game was bad you'd find yourself looking over the fence at the shore, at all the people sailing and lying on the sand." The local pro team had long since gone bankrupt.

Linke being away, I decided to meet the Rumanians first. They were also staying in the Red Lion, and I tracked down their handler, Julian Stanculescu, a chummy babyfaced Rumanian who lives in Chicago. On the floor of his room was a bag of soccer balls, used only hours before by real international soccer players, and while Julian talked I took a ball out and rolled it beneath my feet. Julian was pressing on me what looked like the brochure of a religious sect, and which had on its cover the photographs of two men who both looked like Julian except that one wore a beard. It turned out that the brochure described the aims of the American Soccer Academy, and that only one of the men was Julian (vice president). The bearded one was his father, Dr. Victor I. Stanculescu (president). Julian established their *bona fides* by assuring me that he and Dr. Victor were good friends of Bobby Robson's.

I juggled the soccer and Julian recounted substandard dirty jokes until two caterers came to ask what the Rumanians wanted for breakfast. The glamour of it all! What did the stars eat for breakfast? The Rumanians wanted omelettes and maybe cereal, except their doctor, who asked for a Bucharest dish of ham and eggs. The main thing, Julian emphasized, was that the drinking water must be in sealed bottles. The team had just flown in from South America, where several players had fallen ill from drinking unsealed water, and they were taking no more risks.

Then Julian took me to find the Rumanian coach, Cornel Dinu. Dinu was eating his dinner, and snapped at Julian without even turning round. I waited in the lobby for an hour and watched American and Rumanian internationals loaf about. One Rumanian, who looked to be still in his teens, and who, to judge from his rural haircut, had yet to make it big, sat alone on the sofa opposite me. I pitied him. Presumably he was an idol in Rumania, as big an idol, say, as Andy Sinton is in England, and Rumania after all is a decent soccering country, but here in Santa Barbara he was alone, and in some ways even lower on the social scale than me. At least I spoke the language and knew a couple of *Soccer America* writers, whereas he probably played for a small club and was a newcomer to the national side. I bet he wanted to go home.

Julian reappeared and said that Dinu was sorry and would speak to me now. By then it was already very late. I waited another hour. Journalists spend a lot of time waiting. Then Dinu appeared in the lobby, a tall man with a permanent rash on his face. He sat on the sofa and looked away from me. "This guy's a legend in Rumania," Julian, who was interpreting, assured me. Dinu had won 75 caps as a player, and after the fall of Ceaucescu had become minister of sport, a post from which he had since resigned to become manager of the national team. I asked him why he had done so. "Between politics and soccer, I chose soccer," he mumbled. He knew that life in the cabinet would have been more relaxed, but "stress is part of our life."

How was Rumanian soccer doing? He complained about brainless club directors. Gates had fallen too. "Before, soccer was the bread of everyone. Now people have other concerns." It was a soccer man's yearning for the good old days of Ceaucescu.

I asked about the trip through South America, and he frowned even more. "It was arranged by an agent who made all the arrangements to suit himself," he said. Rumania had flown endlessly, from Argentina to Paraguay, Ecuador, and Peru. "Once, we arrived a couple of hours before the match, after traveling for days. On our way to Los Angeles, we were flying in a plane that was headed for Los Angeles, but when we landed at Mexico City we had to get out and wait for the next flight!" Nothing of the sort ever happened in Rumania.

The next morning I went to watch the Americans train at a local college. I got there before them and waited with nervous students and a very nervous college coach, all armed with oranges. I was given one.

The Americans arrived and practiced. When practice ended, a few of them, including Milutinovic, the coach, mucked around in front of one goal, and let me retrieve the balls for them. I discovered that professional soccer players kick hard, and when I tried to catch a banana free kick from Milutinovic it spun straight out of my hands. I hoped he wasn't looking. Afterwards I asked Peter Vermes, a striker, how far the U.S. could go at the World Cup. He admitted: "I'd be kidding myself and you if I didn't say it: for me, I'd like to win the World Cup."

Back at the Red Lion, Milutinovic sprawled on a sofa in the lobby, my tape recorder under his nose and the American press at his feet on the floor. He has two nicknames: The Miracle Worker and Bora Ball. Unlike some miracle workers and most England managers, he is a funny man. He even likes journalists. Duncan Irving, an Englishman at *Soccer America*, told me of his first handshake with Milutinovic. Duncan gripped hard. Milutinovic gripped harder. Duncan gripped harder, Milutinovic gripped harder, and Duncan gripped harder. "Aha!" said Milutinovic. "Mafia!" He was no Dinu, and Graham Taylor might even still be England manager if he had sacked his PR man and hired the Serb.

Milutinovic had played in Yugoslavia, France, Switzerland and Mexico, and had managed Mexico and Costa Rica at the past two World Cups—it was under him that Costa Rica had beaten Scotland in Genoa in 1990. He talked to us about Latin American passion. *"Pasión,"* he said in Spanish. "Passion! You're not passionate," he told the press. Had he seen any passion growing among Americans yet? "This is the problem with these people: they don't have a problem." He meant that Americans were insufficiently torn to be passionate. A game of American soccer lasted three or four hours, and fans went off to eat, to go to the toilet. "But the people *like* this," he marvelled, "this is America. *Por* example, also, if you see this city of Santa Barbara, this hotel . . ." and he tailed off. "This is America, you understand? America is unique country in the world, we have everything."

I asked him whether it was a good time to be Serbian. "Why not? You know what, there's a problem, the English people is very proud to be English, I'm very proud to be Serbian. It's no good, but what we going to do?" And he added: "Maybe you from Zagreb?" I issued a hasty denial. "Was a joke!" he said just as quickly. He looked away from us for the first time, and I regretted the silly question. "My family is on the border with Bosnia," he continued. "Maybe a hundred yards. From here to ocean," he pointed out of the window. He changed the subject: "I'm very happy with the players. I speak Spanish, nobody understands me, I think people understand me, everyone is happy." How many languages did he speak? "I speak Spanish, Serbian, French, Italian, I understand Russian, Bulgarian is not a language and I try to speak English. I think four. English, if I'm hungry I ask to eat. Four." When we asked about players he answered with jokes.

The conference broke up, and Tony Meola, the American goalkeeper, came looking for me. Linke had sent him, he said. We sat down on Milutinovic's sofa, both of us 23, and he the star, and he told me what had made an American boy dream of playing in goal for the United States. Meola's father, Vincente, once a reserve with Avellino, had come to America to be a barber, and had landed up in Kearny, New Jersey. Kearny is not your average American small town. It is inhabited mostly by Irish and Scots families who came across in the 1920s, their passages paid, to work in the cotton mills, and they have clung to soccer. "All the dads of my teammates grew up somewhere in the U.K.," Meola told me. Also, as luck would have it, Kearny lies just three miles from Giants Stadium, and while Meola and I were growing up, in the great days of the NASL, the

New York Cosmos was drawing 80,000 at Giants Stadium, and the New York Giants, the American NFL team, were only getting 30,000. Though Kearny has just 38,000 inhabitants, it has produced three members of the present U.S. squad: Meola, Tab Ramos and Derby County's John Harkes. Meola and Harkes had played together for nearly 20 years, and Harkes' father had coached them.

It was not an all-American story, but it was one that many of the American players could tell. Linke's magnificent press pack told me that Hugo Pérez's father, grandfather and cousin had all played professional soccer in El Salvador; that Peter Vermes' father had been a pro in Hungary, Marcelo Balboa's in Argentina and Tab Ramos' in Uruguay. By contrast, Kasey Keller's father had been a softball pitcher, Eric Wynalda's an American soccer player at Princeton University, Bruce Murray's a golf pro, Chris Sullivan's a boxer and Chris Henderson's a semiprofessional baseball player.

Then there were players who had become Americans: Fernando Clavijo, a pro from Uruguay; Janusz Michallik, who had left Poland at 16, the son of a Polish international; Jean Harbour, who had come to the States to study biochemistry, son of a Nigerian international; Brian Quinn, a Gaelic soccer and hurling star from Belfast, who together with his wife had become an American citizen in a halftime ceremony at an indoor match; and the Pretorian Roy Wegerle, who got an American passport because he married Marie Gargallo of Miami. (The Midlands must be a nasty cold shock to both of them.) Two other players, Thomas Dooley (born in Germany) and Earnie Stewart (in Holland), are the offspring of European mothers and GI fathers. Dooley barely speaks English, but as he told *Sports Illustrated*, he has driven an American car for years. "That is not normal in Germany," he said. No, but it is normal in Germany to express your identity through your car. No doubt there should have been more Hispanics in the team, but Milutinovic could not send scouts to every Mexican semipro league in the country.

Next, a man from *Sports Illustrated* and I interviewed Eric Wynalda, who played for Saarbrücken in the Bundesliga, and who drove, I could not but notice, a car with the license plate "WYNALDA." Blond and tanned, he looked like everyone's idea of a Californian beachboy. This was accurate: he was a local, and had been shown surfing on German TV. "If he play soccer how he surfs," Milutinovic confided, "we're going to be world winners." Milutinovic and Wynalda liked practising their German on each other, and it was Milutinovic who insisted that Wynalda take his interviewers to the bar and treat us to drinks. We took the chance to ask the coach what he thought of Rumania. "Fuck Rumania! My problem is not to see if we win. My problem is to see if we make progress." Wynalda signed the tab in Milutinovic's name, and wrote on a generous tip.

He told us that he had been pushed into soccer by his father, Dave. Dave Wynalda is the son of Dutch parents, and he spent the World Cups of the 1970s jumping up and down in front of the TV. He called soccer "a thinking man's sport," though the way his son played it that was not always true. Eric Wynalda had been sent off against Czechoslovakia in the 1990 World Cup, and apparently Milutinovic had told him: "You need discipline, and the best place to learn discipline is Germany."

When we spoke, in the February of his first season in the Bundesliga, "the Big Mac on the Ball" (*Die Welt*'s phrase) was the third-highest scorer in the league. He had just sold 3,000 T-shirts of himself to FC Saarbrücken, his brother Brandt had come to Europe to work as his agent, and now *Sports Illustrated* was following him around. He returned to Germany after the Rumanian match, and as far as I know did not score another goal all season.

The man from *Sports Illustrated* asked him why soccer had failed to take off in the U.S. "You ask any of those U.S. Soccer Federation executives," Wynalda replied. "Any time they bid to buy time for soccer on TV, baseball, soccer or tennis buy them out for that time. That's the hot dog sports as I like to call them—meaning that you sit on your ass and eat hot dogs. Those guys see what's going on in Europe with soccer, and they all sit around in their smoky rooms and say, 'What can we do to stop that happening here?' What killed soccer last year was the rise of beach volleyball!"

"In Europe," he claimed, "the fans stand the whole time and they don't care, and they wave flags and they chant and they sing. At halftime everyone eats, and they go back into the stands. In Europe fandom goes much deeper than in America. When Brazil lost, people were jumping off buildings. I don't think anyone jumped off a building when Buffalo lost the Super Bowl."

He spoke to us some more on the morning of the Rumania match—Milutinovic led a relaxed camp—and when he went off to play, the *Sports Illustrated* man and I debated whether the English fans would fight at the World Cup. I said that if they so much as showed their faces in downtown Washington or L.A., let alone went about chucking stones, it would be the last we would hear of them, ever. Sadly, my prediction was never to be tested.

As Milutinovic had warned us, the people of Santa Barbara had no problem. In recent weeks I had seen South Africa vs. Nigeria, Arsenal vs. Leeds and El Salvador vs. Denmark. USA vs. Rumania was a lot quieter. In front of me in the stand was a family in deckchairs, and before kickoff the crowd politely applauded the four Rumanian fans who lapped the pitch carrying their national flag. This, plainly, was *pasión*. Among the spectators were many women and small children. It was a long way from Bucharest.

The game began, the USA scored almost immediately, and throughout the first half fans kept wandering into the stadium. Rumania's fantastic No. 8, Ilie Dumitrescu, made it 1–1. All through the second half, with scores still tied, fans strolled out again.

* * *

Organizing a World Cup keeps you busy. Scott Parks LeTellier, chief operating officer of the 1994 World Cup, presumably had lots to do, but he rang me back when I left him a message. I told him about the Santa Barbara fans, and asked if it worried him that they seemed to have no idea of what was going on. "That is a phenomenon of Southern California that is bewildering to me," he said. "You see people here streaming out of the Super Bowl midway through the third quarter, and it happens at our baseball games too. A columnist on the *LA Times*, in his coverage of the 1984 Olympics, said that the Southern Californians' penchant for leaving an event early reached its high point when a significant number of people left with two seconds to go in Carl Lewis' ten-second hundred-meter dash."

In Santa Barbara, on the pitch after the game, Dinu held court to the American press. He was in a good mood and glared only at the unhappy Julian, who was interpreting again. A local journalist asked what the American team had done best. Julian translated, "They're very nicely dressed. They'll need a hundred years to play soccer. The Americans only scare us if they bring aircraft carriers. I respect their coach. Yugoslavia has produced many great coaches. I know, because I'm Yugoslav myself, on my mother's side." The journalists looked hurt. "I do have great respect for the American people, civilization and democracy," the ex-minister consoled them. What prospects did this young Rumanian side have? "All the Latins have great trust in the next generation. We've always thought that what will come in future will be better than us. That's what has always fooled us."

Then as all the other journalists watched, Dinu strode over to me, followed by Julian, and presented me with his card. "He thinks you're very professional, you're very good," Julian explained. Three months later, Dinu was fired.

CHAPTER 16

ARGENTiNA, CAMPEON!

ARGENTINA PLAYED BRAZIL TWO days after I arrived in Buenos Aires. Officially the match celebrated the centenary of Argentinian soccer, but the real cause for joy was the return of Diego Maradona, playing his first match for his country since his ban for taking cocaine. "They all take drugs. Everyone takes drugs," one fan explained to me.

It was a pleasant walk to the River Plate stadium, for the area around the ground is unlike the rest of Buenos Aires. Whereas my lasting impression of the city is of broken paving stones and sewer smells, the streets around the River Plate stadium are broad, and even quite clean. The neighborhood looks like Maidstone, and River, once the club of the English, are now known as *los Millionarios*.

My friends parked in the shooting club opposite the ground, a few hundred yards away from the old Marine School of Mechanics, EMSA. In the 1970s EMSA was the Argentine Navy's torture camp and was known as the Auschwitz of Argentina, but when Argentina staged the World Cup of 1978, it was used to accommodate players. The 1978 final had been played in the River Plate stadium.

The ground was noisy for the game against Brazil. At times, in response to the chant, "If you don't jump you're an Englishman," half the crowd leaped into the air, but most of the time, I was told, they just sang:

Maradona's an Argentinian

Brazilians, Brazilians,

How bitter you look,

Maradona's an Argentinian

And he's better than Pelé.

The Argentine President, Carlos Menem, was missing, but 500 journalists from around the world had come. I was able to identify the ones from Brazil because they were wearing their national team shirts. The word "Press" on the back of the shirts proved their objectivity.

Soccer does not get any bigger than Argentina vs. Brazil, even without a hundredth birthday to celebrate, and with both teams calling on their players in Europe, the combined salaries of the 22 starters came to $60 million. These two sides were probably the best in the world, and yet all attention was on one little man. He announced that he felt "peaceful." Anyone else would have taken the money and run years ago, but Maradona is not like that. He was going up in the elevator in a grand hotel once when, to the astonishment of the patrons, he suddenly rattled on the elevator doors and screamed, at the top of his voice, *"Argentinaaaaa!!!"* The man is what they call a winner. He has taken so many painkilling injections that he might end up in a wheelchair, and he has won everything, but he keeps playing. That night he warmed up amid hundreds of photographers. They snapped and snapped, and the match started ten minutes late, disrupting TV schedules all over the world.

From the kickoff, the scene was instantly familiar. The yellow-blue-and-white of Brazil, the blue-and-white stripes of Argentina, the white confetti streaming down, the smoke bombs, the incessant noise—long before you see Argentina vs. Brazil you know what it looks like. This meant that actually to be in the stadium was disappointing, like watching a film for the tenth time. It was impossible to see things afresh—unless you were an American. "I've never seen home side advantage like this," murmured my neighbor, the *New York Times* correspondent. The crowd protested whenever the Brazilians strung two passes together, and each time the culprits would quickly return the ball to its rightful owners. The first half was all Argentina.

It has been said before, but Maradona can play. He had lost weight since I had seen him wander about for Sevilla against Español, four months before to the day, and he broke open the Brazilian defense at will. Several times he chipped passes onto his strikers' right feet, but each time they fluffed them. Even so, Argentina scored first. Mancuso aimed a weak shot at goalkeeper Taffarel, and the ball bounced through his hands into the net. Despite the setting, a common-or-garden blunder.

Maradona continued to play with concentration. The referee, Filippi, had to cope without his advice, he mishit barely a pass, and in the 26th minute, he gently nudged a 25-yard free kick onto the Brazilian crossbar.

Yet he had changed. He was an older, wiser, fatter man now, without the strength to dribble through half a team, and he limited himself to hitting passes from midfield. His teammates had to walk the ball into his feet, and the next day's *Buenos Aires Herald* had the audacity to note that Leo Rodriguez, the man he had replaced, was quicker.

By the second half Maradona was finished, so he just walked around and gesticulated at Filippi when Filippi was not looking. At one point he even kicked a clod of mud the referee's way, though he did not mean to hit him, proof of which is that the clod missed. It was ungrateful behavior nonetheless, for Filippi had entered into the spirit of the evening by giving a free kick every time the great man overturned. With Maradona only present in body, Brazil soon equalized. The match degenerated in the final minutes, with the Argentine Ruggeri and the Brazilian Valdo living up to the centennial slogan "100 Years with the Same Passion," and being sent off for fighting.

A few hundred journalists and I waited outside the changing rooms for the players to emerge. Hanging about for inane quotes is the dark side of journalism. We stood there for nearly an hour, until, with deadlines looming, the men at the front began to bang on the doors. These stayed shut, and I left. Two hours later, at one in the morning, I was still wandering around the stadium looking for a bus.

The oracles must eventually have appeared, or else the journalists made up the quotes themselves, for the papers were full the next day. The Argentine substitute Alberto Acosta was quoted as saying, "Maradona? I have seen him speaking with such emotion that I have no doubt he will soon return to his greatest form." The Brazilian manager, Carlos Alberto Parreira, called Maradona "a player from another planet," a phrase his striker Careca modified to "a player from another world."

Whether or not Maradona turns out to be from another planet or world, he has a weird life. On the day before the match he had attended an Argentine FA banquet at which he was named the country's player of the century. (His response was to say that Alfredo Di Stefano was better.) The match against Brazil was on a Thursday, and on the following Saturday he flew to Spain, to play for Sevilla against Logrones on Sunday. On Monday, he flew back home, to play against Denmark on Wednesday, and in between he made time to insult the Sevilla board and to apologize again. No wonder he ended up on cocaine.

"Soccer and politics! What an original theme!" General Enciso explained, when I told him the subject of my book. The General was very kind. In Argentina at least, it is an unoriginal theme. There, soccer and politics is a respected academic field, almost like particle physics or neurology. A particular focus of research is the World Cup of 1978.

Argentina, the host nation, won the trophy that year. General Enciso is no fan, and during the final against Holland he found himself the sole passenger on a Buenos Aires bus, but he remembers that night. "There was an explosion of ecstasy and hysteria. All the country was on the streets. Radicals embraced with Peronists, Catholics with Protestants and with Jews, and all had only one flag: the flag of Argentina!" Would he compare it to the Falklands War, when the crowds filled the streets of Buenos Aires again? "Exactly! It was exactly the same!" The General beamed with delight—he is a charming man. I suggested that since soccer was such a great healer, it would be nice if every country could stage a World Cup every year. He laughed: "It would be very costly."

FIFA awarded Argentina the World Cup of 1978 at the start of the 1970s. In 1976, the Argentine army seized power in a coup.

Coups were regular events in Argentina. A favorite local joke was to declaim, when passing the Military Academy: "Look! There, our future presidents are being trained." (The same joke is made in Africa.) But the new bunch of generals was not funny. They set up a new organizing body for the World Cup, the Ente Autarquico Mundial, but its chief, General Actis, was shot dead as he travelled to his first press conference. The generals began to fight a "dirty war" against their own people. Eleven thousand "subversives" (a term the *militares* interpreted broadly) "disappeared," were held in camps and secretly killed. A favorite method was to drop them from airplanes into the River Plate.

One Sunday morning in Buenos Aires, I discussed the deaths with Osvaldo Bayer, historian and film director, who spent these years in exile in Germany, the land of his fathers. Bayer opened a bottle of champagne and told me, "I would never have thought that in my country, this Roman Catholic country, there could be such brutality. General Pinochet of Chile was an angel by comparison, because he only *executed* the people." Bayer's work includes a film and a book called *Fútbol argentino*.

I also spoke to Hebe Bonafini, a maternal woman who echoed

General Enciso: "The World Cup was like the *Malvinas*. The flags, the drinking, the crowds, the '*Argentina, Argentina.*' For the crowds it was a *fiesta*—for the families of the disappeared, a *tragedia*." Mrs. Bonafini is president of the Mothers of the Plaza de Mayo, a group of women whose children "disappeared." Argentina became a democracy again in 1983, but to this day, every Thursday, the mothers and grandmothers of the disappeared demonstrate on the Plaza de Mayo square in Buenos Aires. They want the full story of the murders and they want to see the generals punished. On other days, a dozen *Madres* assemble in a small office in central Buenos Aires, ostensibly to file press articles about their cause, in truth for the company. To most Argentinians, the women are a disquieting image of the past. People wish they would, somehow, disappear.

Mrs. Bonafini, wife of a factory worker, had lost both her sons. One was tortured in her own house before being taken away, and she had found blood and water on the bathroom floor. I was at first ashamed to ask her about soccer, but she found the topic quite natural. In the 1970s, as the world began to notice the murders, the generals ferociously planned the World Cup. A smashing *Mundial* won by Argentina, they reasoned, would make up for the occasional death at home. It was their chance to reunite the nation.

They made sure the World Cup would not fail for lack of money. From nothing, concrete stadiums arose that could accommodate more spectators than the cities in which they stood could provide. The generals built new roads to link World Cup sites, improved communications and introduced color TV to Argentina.

Argentina had no money to spare, so it was found elsewhere. Vital projects that did not serve the World Cup were cut. As *The Times* reported in February 1978, the popular phrase in Argentina was changing from, "It will be done *mañana*," to "It will be done after the *Mundial*." Of course it was not the World Cup by itself that ruined Argentina: during the rule of the generals inflation fell, from 600 percent in 1976 to 138 percent in 1982—but that was still the highest rate in the world.

The *junta*'s slogan, "25 Million Argentinians Will Play in the World Cup," was soon popularized to "25 Million Argentinians Will Pay for the World Cup." How much they paid is one of the secrets of the military era. Four months before the tournament, in February 1978, the finance secretary of the military government, Juan Alemann, admitted that the final bill would probably come to $700 million, against an original estimate of $70 to $100 million. Had the *junta* known this beforehand, Alemann added, it would never have staged the Cup.

If we accept the figure of $700 million, the 1978 World Cup cost several times more than any previous World Cup, and almost three times as much as the tournament in Spain, four years later. However, the true figure may be far higher than $700 million. Firstly, it is notoriously hard to assess the cost of corruption. The usual estimate of the informal extra bill for the Argentine World Cup is $300 to $400 million, but perhaps it should be higher. Admiral Carlos Lacoste, for one, who succeeded Actis as organizer of the World Cup, and who was vice president of FIFA at the same time, is now growing old in some style in Uruguay. (He organized the World Cup badly. The grass at the River Plate stadium was foolishly sprinkled with seawater, and died. A new pitch was hurriedly laid, but its bounce was odd.)

Then there was the cost of bribing Peru. Argentina met Peru in a second round group match, and had to beat them by at least 4–0 to reach the final. This appeared to be out of the question, Peru being a decent team, as Ally MacLeod's Scotland had already found out. But Argentina *had* to win the World Cup, and the Peruvian generals were short of cash and happy to help a fellow *junta*. Lacoste made the arrangements. Argentina shipped 35,000 tons of free grain to Peru, and probably arms too, while the Argentine central bank unfroze $50 million in credits for Peru. Argentina's manager, Cesar Luis Menotti, barred the goalkeeper and all the substitutes from his team talk, and Argentina beat Peru 6–0 to reach the final. It may be the only World Cup match so far to have been won with a bribe.

We cannot be certain that bribes were paid. The story was told in the *Sunday Times* in 1986 (on the day that England played Argentina) but the newspapers' main sources, a senior civil servant of the *junta* and two soccer officials, understandably chose to remain anonymous. The author of the article, Maria Laura Avignolo, was put on trial for "moral turpitude" and other crimes, but was acquitted. In Lima, the Peruvian Manzo, the reserve goalkeeper at the World Cup, got drunk once and said his team had taken dollars to throw the game; but the next day he denied it. As for the game itself, no soccer match can provide incontrovertible proof of foul play. Peru played in white shirts instead of their usual strip, missed several simple chances, and their goalkeeper, Quiroga, a naturalized Argentine known as *El Loco*, played more eccentrically than usual. The Peruvian lineup included four inexperienced reserves, while one defender was used up front. But Graham Taylor came up with bizarre teams all the time, and no one was shipping him grain.

Every *Madre* we spoke to brought up the match and recited the evidence of foul play. "The soccer fanatics don't believe this," added Mrs. Bonafini. "Soccer fanatics, religious fanatics, political fanatics —fanatics are always dangerous."

The generals staged the World Cup to impress their own people and the world. The World Cup would bring thousands of journalists to a nation whose very coups had seldom earned more than a few paragraphs abroad. "If it were necessary to make some correction in the image of us which exists abroad, the World Cup will be just the occasion to show the Argentine's real way of life," said General Merlo.

The generals hired a New York public relations firm, and the country was prettified. How to make Argentina look rich? Destroy its slums. Bulldozers were sent in to *villas miserias*, and their inhabitants were banished to provinces not lucky enough to stage World Cup matches, or into the desert of Catamarca. Along the main road into Rosario, the generals built a wall, painted with the façades of nice houses, to hide the city's slums from the view of passing foreigners. The "Misery Wall" was shortlived: at night the slum dwellers would steal the slabs of concrete for their own houses.

The Misery Wall is a particular obsession of Adolfo Pérez Esquivel, perhaps because he is a sculptor and a former professor of architecture. "They produced a grand piece of stage scenery to hide the misery and oppression of the Argentine people," he told me in his house. A rail-thin man with glasses, he won the Nobel Peace Prize in 1980. He was an enemy of the *junta*, and was arrested in 1977 when he went to a police station to renew his passport. He stayed in jail until one day before the World Cup final. "He is a totally discredited man in Argentina," General Enciso warned me.

Before the World Cup, said Pérez Esquivel, the *militares* carried out Operation *El Barrido*, raiding flats and "disappearing" up to 200 people a day. They did not want the politically suspect to be around to meet foreign journalists. As the *Mundial* drew nearer, many prisoners were killed, to prevent discovery, and some secret camps were moved to remote spots where journalists would not find them, or were relocated onto barges. It is unclear whether these measures were recommended by the public relations firm.

Soldiers patrolled the streets, guarding against *Montonero* attacks, and some foreign journalists were fooled by the peace and quiet. David Miller of the *Times* reported that most Argentinians were "transparently neither unhappy nor, any longer, repressed." Andrew Graham-Yooll, an Anglo-Argentine journalist who fled the country in 1976, remembers British journalists coming home and telling him what a beautiful country he had. "There was the bolshie press and the tame press," he says.

There were enough bolshies. Amnesty International had taught a lot of sports journalists the rudiments of Argentine politics, and ignoring the danger, many told the truth. Hundreds of articles invoked Hitler's Berlin Olympics; two German TV commentators spent the opening ceremony of the World Cup educating their viewers about the "disappeared"; and TV crews from around the world filmed the photogenic *Madres* at their weekly protest. One Frenchman, hearing distant gunfire during the World Cup opening ceremony, reported that people were being shot on the streets outside. He was not to know about the shooting club beside the River Plate stadium, and he paid for his mistake: Argentine journalists beat him up at the press center. Few of them liked the regime (many Argentine journalists had "disappeared"), but this affront to their nation was too much to bear. They themselves had been *ordered* not to criticize the Argentine team or its manager.

The generals would have treated these foreign subversives as they had the local press, except that they feared giving the world's newspapers more material. But they were outraged. They had fed these foreigners, they had taken them to Mendoza to taste wine, they had shown them real Argentine hospitality, and this was their thanks! As for the expected tourists, they had failed to materialize. There were only a few hundred Scots, for instance, when at one point half the nation had vowed to go.

All in all, the World Cup was no coup for the generals. Rather, it helped the rest of the world to see what a nasty lot the *militares* were.

Every Spectator at the World Cup,
Every Spectator at the World Cup,
A Witness of the real Argentina

as the *Montonero* slogan had it. Europeans suddenly found themselves reading about Latin American politics and society over breakfast, and they saw or even bought a World Cup bumper sticker that depicted a soccer covered by barbed wire. "It's thanks to the *Mundial* that we became known in the world," the *Madres* told us. (And they added, "That was the only good thing about the *Mundial*.") Thanks to foreign publicity, Pérez Esquivel and a few other prisoners were freed from prison on the day before the final. "I was able to watch the final against Holland here in my home," he recalled happily. (Admittedly, he spent the next 14 months under house arrest.) The World Cup was bad for investment and tourism in Argentina, and good for human rights.

Yet when the hopeless referee Gonella blew his whistle to end the final of the last World Cup ever staged in South America, the generals were happy men. For there the people of Argentina were, all together, and undeniably dancing in the streets. Buenos Aires was packed all night. "To see all those people cheering on the streets without anything being done to stop them—it was quite a shock," Daniel Rodriguez Sierra, a teenager in 1978, told me. "It was very painful, very terrible, to watch the euphoria on television," said Mrs Bonafini, "and to us it seemed very dangerous." Not to celebrate was to be for Holland, and the *Madres* were made to feel like strangers in their own country.

The *junta* tried to capitalize on the joy. "The day that 25 million Argentinians aim for the same goal, Argentina will be a winner not once, but a thousand times over," the Finance Minister Dr. Martínez de Hoy, an Old Etonian, told a lunch for meatpacking executives. The head of state, General Videla, drew the same moral in a televised speech. It seemed that soccer was the new opium of the people: give your subjects a World Cup and they will love you.

So it seemed, but it was not so. *"Argentina, campeón,"* Bayer writes in *Fútbol Argentino*, "but the joy is not joy. It is a kind of explosion of a society which has been obliged to keep silent." The Argentine poet, academic and journalist Carlos Ferreira, in his poem *"Mundial,"* recalls the days after the celebrations:

> and singing the song of forgetting.
> . . . the bad part was the end,
> undignified and muddled,
> those cadavers returning
> to the riverbeds,
> to the mass graves,
> shaking their heads,
> and singing the song of forgetting.
> And we are there,
> with those drums,
> with those crazy sweating flags,
> with the world upside-down . . .

Only the generals had forgotten the cadavers. People can think. If they are poor, and frightened, and champions of the world, they are pleased to be champions of the world and upset to be poor and frightened. Maybe bread and games are all the people want, but as Bayer points out, in 1978 they had lots of games and little bread. The fans made no mental connection between the national team and the *junta*. They cheered the players and (some of them at least) whistled at General Videla when he appeared in a stadium. Five years after the World Cup, the generals gave way to a civilian government. If they had thought they could save their jobs by spending Argentina's money on soccer, they were naïve. Their use of the World Cup shows not how Machiavellian they were, but how stupid. They were the bullies at the back of the classroom who had taken over the lesson.

The generals had a simple, fascist view of society. A country must be strong and united. If all the people are cheering as one—if, to quote General Enciso, "there is only one flag, the flag of Argentina"—the country is strong and united. The way to bring about this happy state of things is through triumphs. Triumphs are not boring achievements like providing work, housing, and a stable currency. No! Triumphs are military victories or great patriotic occasions. A triumph is whatever brings people onto the streets cheering *"Argentina! Argentina!"* Stringing together triumphs was the generals' one policy. The biggest triumphs they scheduled were the hosting and winning of the World Cup, and the invasion of the Falkland Islands. This was all the same thing, so much so that the World Cup song, *"Vamos Argentina, Vamos a Ganar"* ("Go on Argentina, Go and Win") was cranked out again during the Falklands War. (There is an exact parallel with Brazil here: the marching tune, *"Pra Frente, Brasil"*—"Forward, Brazil"—written for the 1970 World Cup, became the theme tune of the Brazilian military regime.)

"These generals were kids," agreed Graham-Yooll. "In 1982 they launched a military invasion and thought the world would applaud them!" Why were they so naïve? "Our military never had to play politics. They have been brought up from the 1920s to believe, 'You bark an order and everyone does as they're told.' At the World Cup, they said, 'Now you bloody well enjoy yourselves!' and they thought everyone would."

The generals had planned another triumph for 1978, but it never came off. Since 1977, they had been arguing with Chile over three islands in the Beagle Channel. (You will be stunned to hear that each country claimed the islands as theirs.) An international court of arbitration ruled in favour of Chile. Argentina rejected its decision. Tension grew; and then, in June 1978, in the middle of the World Cup, the Argentine defense minister said Argentina would "take action" to recover the islands.

The idea was to translate the patriotism created by the World

Cup into an immediate war. Fascist governments aim for perpetual motion—the crowds must always be on the streets—and so the *junta* bought body bags, and told hospitals to keep beds free.

The war was aborted at the last minute. It seems that the *junta* voted to start fighting but was vetoed by Videla. By then the Catholic church was mediating, and in Latin America it is not done to defy the Vatican. By the end of 1978 it had forced a settlement. The *junta* began to look out for other triumphs, and in 1982 it sent the body bags and arms for the Chilean war that never was on to the Falklands. In a sense, the Falklands War belongs to the aftermath of the World Cup. And it is said that one reason why the regime surrendered to Britain when it did, in May 1982, was because Argentina might otherwise have had to miss the Spanish World Cup.

The generals silenced public debate, the *Madres* apart, but as in all dictatorships there was coded protest. If we believe Cesar Luis Menotti, manager of Argentina in 1978, he protested in the language of soccer.

Menotti is a thin, big-nosed, chain-smoker who grew up in Rosario, birthplace of the Peruvian keeper Quiroga. It is a town with traditions of radical politics and stylish soccer, and Menotti inherited both creeds. For Menotti, soccer is a form of art, and he won the 1978 World Cup with Rosarian soccer played by men like Ricardo Villa, Osvaldo Ardiles and Mario Kempes—though not by Diego Maradona, much to the 17-year-old's sorrow. "It is a homage to the old, beloved Argentine game," said Menotti after the final. It was a coded protest.

By beating Holland, the radical appeared to have saved the generals, but as soon as it was safe to do so, Menotti argued otherwise. He was often attacked, he writes in *Fútbol sin trampa* ("Soccer without Tricks") for coaching Argentina under a tyranny that "contradicted my way of life." But what should he have done? "To coach teams that played badly, that based everything on tricks, that betrayed the feelings of the people? No, of course not." Defensive soccer, like dictatorship, imprisons the free spirit. Instead, writes Menotti (or rather Carlos Ferreira, his ghost), by playing free, creative soccer, his team evoked not only Argentine soccer as it once had been, but also the memory of a free, creative Argentina.

It is easy to scoff at this. For a start, Menotti sounds like a man desperate to excuse himself for winning the World Cup: he will not accept that he won it for the generals. Also, Ardiles has praised him precisely for teaching the players discipline. "Many Argentinians, South Americans, don't care about bread, but only about the honey you put on it," the Spurs manager explained. And the Argentinians still played "tricks." Menotti's squad included a few traditional butchers, and even a couple of players called Killer; Peru was bought; and it seems that under orders from the *junta*, the players had drug injections. One source says that Mario Kempes and Alberto Tarantini were still so "high" after the Peru match that they had to keep running for another hour before they came down again, and that Ocampo, the team's waterboy, came up with most of the post-match urine samples; though there must have been other suppliers too, for after the final, one sample showed a player to be pregnant. The Dutch left saying that Argentina could only have won the World Cup in Argentina.

The final argument against Menotti is that the generals themselves had asked him to play open soccer. It helped public relations, and his talk of a traditional Argentine style suited their quarrel with "the influence of foreign ideas and Communism." Argentina was the greatest country in the world, and the World Cup proved it.

And yet Menotti is in earnest: evil, for him, is dictatorial rule and the style of play propagated by Carlos Bilardo. *Menottismo* and *Bilardismo* are two opposing attitudes to life.

Bilardo has a big nose too, and he also won a World Cup for

Argentina, in 1986, but there his kinship with Menotti ends. A boy of good family and, like Crippen, a qualified doctor, Bilardo played his soccer for Estudiantes, a team legendary for a certain lack of nobility. "We tried to find out everything possible about our rivals individually, their habits, their characters, their weaknesses and even about their private lives, so that we could goad them on the field, get them to react and risk being sent off," Juan Ramon Veron, another Estudiantes player of the 1960s, has explained. The fame of Estudiantes spread to Europe too, because from 1968 to 1970 the gang were champions of South America, and they played horrifying World Club Cup finals against AC Milan, Manchester United and Feyenoord. The Argentine team of the 1966 World Cup, who struck Alf Ramsey as "animals," were part of the same wave.

"He was very clever," Wim van Hanegem of Feyenoord says of Bilardo. "A skinny little guy, but he was very skillful. Mean? Yes, That's true, but I didn't mind that so much. What was less pleasant was that he used to spit. I can't stand that—I'd rather be kicked." Against Feyenoord, Bilardo snapped the spectacles of Joop van Daele. Today he says, "I can't remember that," and he probably can't.

Dr. Bilardo became manager of Argentina, and built a manly team. Argentina won the World Cup in 1986, and reached the final in 1990, but to the untrained eye they looked like a street gang. Perhaps the defining act of that side was Maradona's "Hand of God" goal: a classic Estudiantes ploy, except that no Estudiantes player would have bothered to offer an excuse. It was *Bilardista* soccer, though Bilardo refuses to see styles of play as philosophies. He thinks soccer is just soccer, and that in soccer only winning matters.

"I am ashamed as an Argentinian," pronounced Menotti in 1990, "because what I see of my country at this World Cup has nothing to do with our true character. Everywhere," he continued, "in literature, in art, in soccer, you can roughly identify two schools.

One that treasures aesthetics, and another that tramples on beauty. This Argentina looks like a dead end street in China."

Menotti is becoming a café philosopher, and with the generals safely back in the military academy, Argentine soccer is no longer politics by other means; but in January 1993, when Tenerife met Sevilla in the Spanish league, there was a final episode of *Menottismo* vs. *Bilardismo*.

Bilardo was by then at Sevilla, where he had built another team from a horror movie. They stacked up fouls, and during one game, in full view of the TV cameras, Bilardo abused his team's physiotherapist for treating an injured opponent. The Sevilla squad included two Argentinians: Maradona and Simeone.

The new Menotti was the Tenerife manager, Jorge Valdano. A columnist for the Spanish quality newspaper *El País*, Valdano likes soccer even though he played for Bilardo at the 1986 World Cup. In his team at Tenerife were three Argentinians: Redondo, Pizzi and Dertycia.

When the two teams met, the Buenos Aires press corps dropped everything and flew over. Everyone was ready for the dirtiest match since the Battle of Highbury, and Maradona failed to defuse matters. He told the press that he could never forgive Redondo. Why not? Once, years before, that Satan had dropped out of a friendly international to sit an exam.

Came the day, and it was not so much *Menottismo* vs. *Bilardismo* as *Bilardismo* on both sides. Tenerife won 3–0, thanks to two penalties, both scored by Pizzi; there were 13 yellow cards, and three red cards, one for Pizzi, and one for Maradona, who tried to get Redondo sent off; a brawl involving Bilardo; and an encounter between Simeone and police officers that prompted the civil governor of Tenerife to order an investigation. Bilardo called Valdano "a thief with white gloves on." Valdano said: "It is a significant fact that despite leading his country to two World Cup finals Bilardo is regarded as Public Enemy Number One in Argentine soccer."

* * *

Independiente vs. Huracán was the first match of the 1993 Argentine league season. The players took the pitch to a volley of fireworks, some of which were thrown straight at them—the Independiente stadium is compact, and the fans are bonkers. The match started, and the teams aimlessly kicked the ball back and forth, until in the eighth minute Independiente's Hugo Perez hit a 35-yarder which went in off the post, prompting more fireworks. Not long after, Huracán's left half hit a pass with the outside of his right boot to his center-forward, who lobbed the ball over the Independiente goalkeeper on the volley. It was a marvelous goal, and quite fair, but neither player bothered to protest when the referee disallowed it. Minutes later, however, half the side raced up to threaten the linesman after an eccentric offside call.

Independiente went 2–0 up, but the game was briefly halted while their fans threw missiles at their own goalkeeper, Luis Islas. After a couple of minutes, the referee returned Islas to his goal, and the match went on, though the shelling did too. Then Huracán's Cruz fouled Independiente's Guillermo Lopez, and with admirable openness, punched him in the stomach. A free-for-all followed, after which Cruz, and Moas of Independiente, received red cards. Independiente won 3–1.

I asked Lopez, victim of Cruz's foul, why the match had been so violent. He explained that Huracán were poor losers: "In the first half, five violent tackles were committed on me: two on my ankles, three on my left knee, two of these five with the score at 2–0. In the second half, I was tackled with violence twice more." He added that the referee should not have sent off Cruz and Moas.

A statue was to be unveiled, in a Buenos Aires park, to celebrate the centenary of Argentine soccer. Though the newspapers had announced the event, the spectators were two old men, two small girls, myself and two English friends. At seven o'clock a few dozen old men in suits toddled up from the Argentine FA's building and began to greet each other. "They see one another every day," one of the small girls explained, "but they like to make a big show of hugging and kissing." The sight of old men embracing in front of a figure covered in a sheet attracted only three more people. Argentinians are used to ceremonies: in front of an adjacent tree stood a plaque in praise of trees.

The *bobos* (Ruud Gullit's word seemed to apply) untangled themselves after a while, and unveiled the monument. It was a straightforward, life-size, metal soccer on a pedestal. "My son is the sculptor!" one *bobo* shouted, and they all photographed each other for approximately 20 minutes. I asked the girl whether any of them were famous ex-players, but she said not.

One elderly spectator pointed at us and shouted, "You taught us soccer in 1893!," meaning that the British had. This is true of almost every country in the world, but the Argentinians know it better than most. At times Argentina can seem like a former British colony, a Spanish-speaking version of Australia or India. When Argentina first beat England, by 3–1 in 1953, a politician exclaimed, "We have nationalized the railways, and now we have nationalized soccer!" Long before the Falklands, England was the country Argentinians most wanted to beat, and when the war came the generals had an easy job of mobilizing feeling. One bumper sticker printed for the conflict showed the little Gauchito, mascot of the 1978 World Cup, posing with his foot on a hapless British lion. And in 1986, most Argentinians felt that the Hand of God goal was exactly what England deserved.

On the other side is colonial Anglophilia. I met one woman who had briefly lived in Rickmansworth in the 1970s, and who had spent the years since thinking about it. What she missed most, she said, were the gentle people and the nice English weather. Had she ever been back to visit? She sighed: "I cannot go back and visit, because then I would never be able to come back and live here."

Once there were tens of thousands of Britons here. Many stayed and became Anglo-Argentinians. The past is preserved in the names of soccer players like José-Luis Brown, and possibly of Daniel Killer, while at Argentinos Juniors I saw one Carlos Patricio McAllister, the red-haired grandson of an Irishman, playing poorly on the wing.

That is one end of the social scale. At the other, in shabby, smoggy Buenos Aires, Edwardian Britain lives on. The smartest club in town is the Jockey Club; the tearoom in the Calle Florida is the Richmond; and you can find the Anglo-Argentinians and their out-of-date accents in the *Club Inglés*. They play polo, rugby, cricket and lawn tennis (on South America's only grass courts) in the suburb of Hurlingham.

The British ambassador's residence, steaming in the February heat, is part of Anglo-Argentina. The entrance hall is one of those British rooms that are so grand they have no seats, and for 15 minutes I stood there waiting with a British diplomat. Apart from me there was only one thing in the hall that jarred: the last entry in the ambassador's guestbook, open on the table, which read, "Charlton, Bobby and Norma, Manchester." We were waiting for Bobby Charlton to arrive.

Charlton had come to Argentina to promote Manchester's Olympic bid, and the night before, at a country house just outside Buenos Aires, a Bobby Charlton XI, in "Manchester 2000" T-shirts, had taken on a team captained by President Menem. In the Yorkshire Television series *The Greatest Game*, there is a scene in which the YTV film crew catches up with Menem, who is waiting at Ezeiza airport for the president of Israel to arrive. As the plane lands he tells YTV: "Soccer is the thing that formed me physically and it has given me a great deal of spirituality." He is asked whether he had dreamed of playing for Argentina. "All children have a dream.

That was my dream when I was a child." Only as president had he realized the dream, captaining Argentina in a charity match in front of 55,000 fans.

My diplomatic source had played for Charlton against Menem. He told me about it gleefully. The president, resolved not to lose, had roped in a couple of ex-professionals. "And we were just a few beery guys who hadn't played soccer in years!" I wished I had heard of the game in time to wangle a place in the team. At first Menem's XI had walked all over Charlton's, but in the second half they had given the Englishmen their best player, who began to score lots of goals. "This guy who had no connection with the embassy and spoke not a word of English," lamented the diplomat. "When we started catching up with them, Menem got very worried and began shouting at everyone. He took it very seriously." Who won? "They won, about 14–7." What was Menem like as a player? "Hopeless. Actually, I suppose that for a 62-year-old he wasn't that bad. He doesn't move at all. He just stands in the center of the field and his teammates bring him the ball and he gives these really easy safe passes to the guys standing next to him."

While we were waiting Charlton was dashing around town, giving interviews and meeting Menem again. The diplomat complained, "It's madness. Douglas Hurd, the foreign secretary, was here a few weeks ago and he got 40 minutes with Menem. Then Bobby Charlton turns up and he gets a soccer match, a dinner afterwards, and then another hour this morning. It shows you where priorities lie in this town." Perhaps we should appoint Charlton foreign secretary, or maybe Gazza.

The Argentine soccer press had been almost as keen as the president to meet Charlton. The day after Argentina vs. Brazil, Charlton had given a press conference at which he had complained about players talking to the referee. "I've been playing soccer since before Maradona was born," he said, "and I've yet to see a referee change his decision because of protests." The papers ignored this attack on local custom, but they all carried Charlton's line on the player of the century question: he thought Di Stefano was better than Maradona. It was an inane debate.

Charlton arrived, exhausted, but prepared to chat on the veranda. He jogged up the stairs in his sports jacket and flannels, a stocky man, a soccer player in civvies. A steward brought us drinks. Out of courtesy, I first asked Charlton about Manchester's Olympic bid, but he was too tired and bored to put together sentences, and instead answered with a string of phrases: "My home for forty years . . . Weather is very nice in summer . . . Airport . . . Forefront in railways, computers."

I asked him about Menem and he became more animated. "He's a very intelligent soccer player. You play a lot with players who maybe haven't got the quality of professionals and they try to do things they can't do. Menem wasn't like that—he kept it simple. He never got caught in possession, and he laid the ball off when he needed to. In context—taking into account that he's president of a country with probably a lot of other things to do besides play soccer—I was very impressed." He denied that this was a diplomatic answer, and I believed him: Charlton takes soccer too seriously for that.

Had he met other heads of state who liked soccer? "A lot of the African heads of state love their soccer—in many cases it's the only sport that goes on in those countries. The president of Ghana did, the president of Kenya, the heads of state of some of the North African states, the Pope . . ." "Your brother Jack met the Pope," I giggled, "and said he was smaller than he had expected." Charlton nodded solemn confirmation—I had got the facts right.

I asked him about the tour he had led to South Africa during the apartheid era. "We played Kaizer Chiefs in Soweto, and it was one of the nicest days I've ever had. They beat us 2–1, but it was a very close game and we nearly drew it. We were just made to feel so welcome! There were only, say, 20 white people in Soweto that day, and the people were so pleased to see us. In fact, at the end they took us on their shoulders and tried to carry us off home with them. We had to fight to get our lot back on the bus."

What had he and Menem discussed that morning? "Sport generally, and he asked me who was the best of Maradona and Di Stefano." In the sight of God, even the leader of men is a mere soccer fan. And Charlton had nominated Di Stefano? "For his brain. He was the brainiest player I ever saw." Menem had shown knowledge of British sport, and Charlton had invited him to Manchester, "to play golf and do the other things he likes to do. Time went very quickly. I feel we overstepped our allotted time." In Whitehall they were green with envy.

Menem is a fan, but he is also a politician. In matters of sport he follows the lead of Chairman Mao.

One day in 1966, the China News Agency reported that Chairman Mao Tse Tung "was relaxed and easy after a swim in the Yangtse River on July 16th when he covered a distance of nine miles." This suggested that Mao, contrary to rumor, was neither paralysed nor dead. Also, the times given implied that at the age of 75 he had broken the world record for the distance. Even while breaking it Mao had helped the Chinese people. "As he advanced through the waves," the agency reported, "he chatted with those around and when he discovered that a young woman close to him knew only one swimming stroke he taught her the backstroke."

This is a case of a ruler acting as a sportsman to prove that he was not dead. Normally, rulers play sport in public for another reason: to prove that they are regular guys. Campaigning for the American presidency, Bill Clinton and Al Gore had themselves photographed tossing an American soccer back and forth. In Brazil, politicians have been known to campaign in the shirts of popular soccer teams.

British prime minister John Major was often shown spectating at Lords or Stamford Bridge. One theory is that he only pretended to support Chelsea, but is in fact an Arsenal supporter. He certainly fits the Arsenal profile—Major is lower-middle class, lives in Hertfordshire, and seems to enjoy dullness—but no politician can be seen to support Arsenal. In England, as long as a man supports a soccer club he is accepted as one of the lads—unless he supports Arsenal. According to this theory, Major's advisors therefore told him to find another club. Chelsea was the obvious choice, David Mellor being a fan already (and the proud owner of a Chelsea kit) and prepared to take Major to matches.

It could just be that the pictures of Major at the bridge have made him more popular than he might otherwise have been, but it hardly won him the 1992 election. British voters vote on other issues (namely income tax). In Argentina, however, soccer matters more, and when General Videla revealed that he did not like the game he was showing his lack of political savvy. By popular demand, Argentine politicians are machos of the people, and the great name in this tradition is Juan Domingo Perón, president of Argentina from 1946 to 1955, and again from 1973 to 1974, and founder of a political movement called Peronism.

A big, strong man, Perón was champion fencer of the army and a respected boxer and skier. As president, he restricted freedom and tried to help the poor, but Peronism is a style rather than a set of policies. Both the far left *Montoneros* and the Thatcherite Menem called themselves Peronists. Peronism is a popular, manly style, whose focus is the leader—Perón was known simply as *El Líder*. Perón, says Bayer, was "the absolute demagogue about soccer," and he often went to matches. He had no team: considering himself leader of all the people, he claimed to support all the teams equally.

Menem is a Peronist of the right, but he tries to appeal to the poor much as Perón did. Meeting Bobby Charlton was probably a thrill, but it also made sound political sense. When I asked the doorman of the *Club Inglés* (an unrepresentative sample, no doubt) what he thought of Menem, he replied enthusiastically: "He plays tennis, he plays soccer." At 63, he has recently had to give up boxing and motorcar racing. "Menem receives Sabatini, or some world boxing champion," grumbled Pérez Esquivel. "He not only receives these people, but eats or goes out with them. But I have never been received by Menem!"

Unlike Perón, Menem has a team. River Plate ("Reeber," the Argentinians say) are a risky choice as the so-called club of the rich. The masses support Boca Juniors. An Argentine saying has it that 50% of the population plus one supports Boca, or as Menotti once put it, the club's fans are "semi-criminals." They hate him too. (As I correct the manuscript, Menotti has just been made coach of Boca again.)

Bayer admits that Menem's open support for River is principled. In fact, says Bayer, "it is the only thing in which Menem is not a demagogue." However, Bayer suggests that to make up for his own folly, Menem has ordered his daughter to be a Boca fan. Certainly, everyone seems to know that she supports Boca.

The fact that a President likes soccer can have great consequences for a society. Marcelo Houseman knows. I spoke to him in Johannesburg, where he has a big house and a maid who calls him "Master."

As a soccer player, Marcelo was the journeyman to end all journeymen. After growing up poor in Buenos Aires, he travelled the world with Augusto Palacios. Marcelo was a mediocre player, but his brother René was special. René "Hueso" Houseman, a winger with a big moustache and his socks round his ankles, came on as a substitute in the 1978 World Cup final and, some say, swung the match. Today, the two brothers are soccer agents. They run the grandly named World Sports International, and try to sell South American and South African soccer players to European clubs.

Marcelo took me around his mansion. His greatest treasure is a framed photograph in his front room that shows him with Carlos Menem. He got in with the Menem family by meeting Menem's son at a party, and these days he goes to matches with Menem's daughter.

Now, Marcelo grew up poor. When I told him, in Johannesburg, that I was going to Buenos Aires a month later, he said he would be in Argentina then too and would look after me. "You get anything stolen," he assured me, "we'll get it back for you. It's no problem. We know all the crooks—we grew up with them." No doubt he meant it, though when I arrived in Argentina I found that he was still in South Africa.

The point is that he grew up poor. Normally, the only way a poor boy would meet one of the plutocrat Menem family is as a valet. Marcelo met the Menems thanks to soccer, and he understands this perfectly well. He told me: "Thanks to soccer, I've met politicians, millionaires, pop stars. I've met Mick Jagger. When Rod Stewart came to Argentina for the World Cup, I showed him around."

Marcel drove me home, at a hundred miles an hour, overtaking right and left, in Palacios' Mercedes. I complimented him on his wealth. He was honest: "You've got to remember that in the last couple of years we've done a lot of deals with the Argentinian government. Menem came in in 1989, and since then we've done very well." It was a glimpse of the way a country like Argentina—most of the world, in fact—operates. The way to get on is to be friends with politicians or big businessmen. The way to be their friend is either to be a politician or a big businessman yourself, or someone else they want to meet: a great soccer player, or failing that, the brother of one. "That's the cousin economy of Menem," nodded Bayer, when I told him.

With patrons like Menem, there is no need for bright soccer stars to finish in the gutter, and there are bonuses besides. The day I left Argentina, a minor scandal broke over a man named Hector "Bambino" Veira. He had been charged with raping a minor, but suddenly the charge was reduced and he was released. It happened that Veira had been manager of River Plate (and a great San Lorenzo player) and Menem had told the Supreme Court judges that his case should be reconsidered. "Under him," the President argued, "we won everything."

Amílcar Romero, whose works include *Muerte en la Cancha*—"Death in the Stadium"—is a specialist on Argentine soccer murders. A small, cheerful man, who looks no match for his subject, Romero took his little daughter along to our meeting, and let her draw pictures while he lectured me on violence.

In Argentina, he explained, there are two kinds of soccer crime. "Firstly, the most spectacular kind, the violence in the stadium on Sundays with flags, gangs, and knives." The second type of crime is unique to Argentina and happens during the week: violence and blackmail, ordered by the club directors and carried out by the gangs. The victims of this second type are usually the players.

When the directors have a problem, the gangs—the *barras bravas*—fix it, for a fee. Maybe a club president wants an opposition goalkeeper to throw a match; his manager to resign; a star player, lured by European clubs, to sign a new contract. He calls in the *barra*, and the player is threatened with blackmail or worse. "There are three important factors in soccer," Romero enumerated. "Violence, information, and money. The gangs have violence and information. The directors have money."

The *barras* are a kind of Argentine KGB. They control the players' lives. Blackmail is easy. Not only do they know which soccer players use drugs, but often they even supply the drugs themselves. They also know about players' women. Romero cited the case of the San Lorenzo player who wanted a fat new contract. Too fat, the club felt. Over to the *barras*. The player had a girlfriend, but he was picking up women in clubs, and the *barras* let the girlfriend know. Not only that, but San Lorenzo refused him any kind of contract. "Don't haggle," was the message to his teammates.

Sometimes the *barras* destroy a player in the stadium. They stand behind the goal, pretending to be ordinary louts, and whistle every time he touches the ball. Either he is negotiating a new contract, in which case the abuse lowers his price, or, if the club has had enough of him, he agrees to leave. The chants during an Argentine match often have little to do with events on the pitch. As club directors need the hooligans, many clubs pay their transport to away matches and give them free tickets to home games. The *barras* sell these tickets: they get into matches by storming the turnstiles. Gatekeepers tend to step aside.

Sometimes the gangs threaten players with violence or just beat them up. A few days before I arrived in Argentina, Daniel Passarella, captain of the 1978 World Cup team and now manager of River Plate, was duffed up in Mar del Plata. The cause was a complicated fight on the River board, between a pro- and an anti-Passarella director. "Part of business, a *guerre de boutique*," Romero explained.

It happens all the time, but Passarella broke with protocol and made a scene. Two hooligans were arrested, but a judge decided to let them go. "But," a journalist told me, "they must have found one honest judge in Mar del Plata, because this man arrested them again." The thugs were easy to find, since they had stayed on in Mar del Plata, and they were shocked at being arrested. The police seldom trouble the *barras*, and some gangs are even led by police officers. Once, when Boca Juniors were given a penalty in the last minute of the match, it was the police who opened the gates so that the opposition's fans could storm the pitch. The president of one Buenos Aires first division club, when negotiating a contract with a player, fills the room with policemen. "The player knows his job is to sign," grinned Romero. And there is a famous photo of a city chief of police, swathed in club colors, standing in the middle of a *barra* and waving a club flag—"like a policeman wearing a Liverpool shirt!" Romero said.

The *barras* work for themselves as well as for the directors. "There isn't a single player who doesn't give the gangs money," said Romero. "Maradona is the first in everything: he is the best player in the world, and he pays the gangs the most. After the World Cup in Mexico he wrote them a check for $30,000, for practical reasons making it out to Air Peru. For the players, the underworld is simply a tax."

Gangs are useful things. The *barras* are multifunctional, and they often work in fields other than soccer, sometimes for politicians. A prominent member of parliament organizes the Boca Juniors *barra*, but the gangs also do freelance work. If there is a demonstration against a politician or his policies, he might send a *barra* to create havoc in the crowd, so that he can say afterwards, "These demonstrators, look what they have done." On occasion, the *barras* carry out assassinations.

"Organized violence here spread from soccer to the rest of society, whereas in Europe, it was the other way around," said Romero. That is what happens in a poor country with rich soccer clubs. In Argentina, the big clubs are the Microsofts and Fords of the nation's economy. The Dynamo Kiev mafia in Ukraine is another example of a big team in a backward state. "The president of River Plate," Osvaldo Ardiles has said, "is more important than the governor of a small province."

Romero put it more strongly: "I am 50 years old, so I was born in 1943, the year of a coup. The soccer regime has been a more constant political presence in my life than our *juntas*. 'Politics passes, soccer remains,' " he quoted an Argentine sage. "It is as eternal as the armed forces, or the Church."

Soccer is a shortcut to power. The biggest soccer clubs have tens of thousands of members, who come to the club every day for all sorts of activities. For example, clubs run kindergartens, primary schools and high schools, most of them with long waiting lists, and River Plate are even planning to set up a university. I tried to picture the University of Oxford United. "The University of Reeber!" laughed Romero. "Where is the state?" Is soccer a state within the state? "Yes, but the soccering state is more convenient, more direct"— there a man can act without worrying about democracy.

It was noisy in the war room. A window was slightly ajar, and the ancient cars of Buenos Aires frequently drowned out General Sanchez. Maybe, I pondered, the window had not been closed properly during the Falklands War, and the generals had not been able to hear one another. I was in the building of the Supreme Council of the Argentine Armed Forces, the highest military organ in Argentina, and the setting was classic South America. The Supreme Council building is shrouded by palm trees, guarded by soldiers with moustaches and machine guns, and stands directly beneath a large advertising board. At reception I handed in my British passport.

An aide ushered in Sanchez, a member of the Supreme Council, and we shook hands solemnly. Sanchez is not his name, but I recently received a letter from him begging me not to mention him or the Supreme Council in my book, and I decided to grant at least half of his request.

Sanchez is a tall thin man with a military moustache—no surprises there—who looks like Enoch Powell. He had primed himself for our meeting. He was carrying two files, one containing his incidental writings on soccer, and the other his book on soccer tactics. Written in 1951, it had never been published, and what he had in the file was the original, yellowed, typed manuscript. He looked nervous: he had walked around with his ideas in these dusty files for 40 years, and here was someone who wanted to know. It was why he had overcome his natural caution to speak to me.

He began by telling me about the "Superteam" he describes in his book. "It plays total soccer—you know that Holland played total soccer, Johan Cruyff. When a team attacks, it must attack with all; when it defends, it defends with all. Because with all together, it is easier to fight." He was keen to make clear that his Superteam played 4–3–3, not 4–4–2, and that though he was convinced of his system, "I don't believe I have the absolute truth." It was the phrase of a man who takes his views seriously. After all, he is a man with power. Soccer managers hate listening to laymen: Brian Clough, for instance, grew short with a club director, a pork butcher who tried to tell him his business. But would a manager consider a general with battlefield experience to be a layman? Would it be safe to do so in Argentina? I asked Sanchez whether he had ever talked tactics with any of Argentina's managers. He said not, but took from his file a letter he had written to Menotti in 1982, before the World Cup in Spain. "Soccer is a spiritual support to the nation," read the General. "That is its value. We support you in your endeavor."

Early on, a tension developed in the conversation. General Sanchez wanted to talk about tactics. I wanted to talk about soccer and politics, soccer and national culture, and soccer and military strategy. "If my team is concentrated on this small piece of paper," Sanchez would gesticulate, "and the opposition is spread out over that big file, then I will have superior numbers in the crucial areas. You must have a force that is compact, organized and moving forward." I suggested that his ideas on soccer rang somewhat military. "No, It's not military," he snapped, before adding: "The principles of war can be applied to anything." I suspected that he had done things the other way around: that he had applied his theories on soccer to military strategy, rather than vice versa. It was chilling to listen to: old men all around the world expound half-baked coaching-manual wisdoms, but here was one who might use them on a battlefield.

I asked why the general loved soccer so. "In soccer is the force of a people. Rugby is also about the body, but it does not have the penetration to the public. Soccer is the great passion of the Argentinian people, just as American football is the all-consuming love of the American people," he said, revealing a sketchy knowledge of the USA. And he admitted: "For myself, I cannot see the skill or the interest in American soccer. It is a brute sport."

How important was it for a country to have a great soccer team? It was "important for the spiritual state of the population. I am not speaking so much of Argentina, but particularly of the African peoples, of nations who in general have no great culture."

I quoted General Enciso: "Argentina is known in the world for the quality of its meat, of its soccer, for the singer Carlos Gardel, for its Formula 1 drivers—but especially for polo and soccer." "We Argentinians will not tolerate that we are only spoken of for our soccer," Sanchez replied sternly. "Argentina has its own values, not just soccer." What were they then? His list included courage, modernity, technology and medical care. We argued. I insisted that if General Sanchez were to step into an English pub and ask the clientèle to associate with "Argentina," the response would be, "Diego Maradona," and not "medical care." This was just not true, said Sanchez.

I broached the topic of the Falklands. Did General Sanchez agree with General Enciso, that the popular euphoria around the 1978 World Cup was similar to the euphoria around the Malvinas? He looked blank. I had to explain the question three times before he said that yes, he more or less did see it that way. It was something he had never considered before: General Sanchez is just not interested in political culture. "Are you more interested in the game itself, or in the social aspects?" he asked. He looked hurt.

The conversation tailed off, and Sanchez gave me a brief guided tour of the building, built centuries before by a Spanish merchant, as he told me proudly. There was no one else around, and when the telephone rang in a room we were viewing the general answered it himself. We said goodbye at the front door. "I am worried that I have not answered your questions," he fretted. "You will have to rearrange my answers."

CHAPTER 17

PELÉ THE MALANDRO

ARMANDO NOGUEIRA, BRAZIL'S MOST famous soccer writer, lives in a penthouse flat overlooking a blue lake in southern Rio. We had been talking for two hours, and he had presented me with four of his books, when he suddenly had a new thought. He ran out of the room to fetch a frame that contained a letter and a photograph.

The photograph showed a scene from the World Cup of 1970, from the quarterfinal in Guadalajara between Brazil and England. More precisely, it showed Pelé and Bobby Moore. Pelé is tweaking Moore's shirt between two fingers, while Moore is poking his foot precisely between Pelé's legs at the ball. Both men are frowning with concentration, yet neither is so much as touching the other. The mutual courtesy is the astonishing fact. Moore had died of cancer while I was in Argentina, and he had been given long obituaries in the South American press.

The letter beside the photograph will be a Nogueira family treasure until the line dies out. It is from Pelé.

Athenaeum Hotel, Piccadilly, London.

> My brother Armando,
>
> If you ever describe this action with "Bob Moore" in your book Bola de Cristal, *you could say that we were being too courteous for a World Cup game. But* that *is sport.*
>
> *Your friend,*
>
> *Pelé.*

This sums up Brazilian soccer. Instead of noting that Brazil beat England and went on to win the World Cup, Pelé merely remarks on the beauty of an irrelevant incident. Consider also his reaction to Banks' legendary save in the same match: "At that moment I hated Gordon Banks more than any man in soccer. But when I cooled down I had to applaud him with my heart."

When we think of Brazil, we think of Pelé's team. This Brazil first appeared in 1958, at the World Cup in Sweden, when Pelé was 17. Brazil beat the host nation 5–2 in the final, during which Brazilian fans chanted, *"Samba, samba,"* and after which the team ran a lap of honor first with their own flag, then with the flag of Sweden. That Brazil won the World Cup again in 1962, lost it in 1966, when Pelé was kicked out of the tournament, and won it again in 1970. The Brazilian style fleetingly reappeared in 1982, but nowadays is as likely to be found in Dutch or French colors as in the yellow and blue. As Brazil, it barely exists anymore. I was in Rio to find out why the Brazilians used to play that way, and why they no longer do.

Rio de Janeiro is really two cities: the one Johannesburg, the other Soweto. The rich, light-skinned people live along the beachfronts, and the poor, dark-skinned ones in the *favelas* on the mountains. The *favelas* are painted in pastel shades, and look like pretty summer houses from below, which is the angle from which the rich always see them. The rich never go up the mountains. The murder rate in the *favelas* is high, and the *favela* dwellers can sniff a rich man a mile away. The air-conditioned metro does not venture there, and there is no running water nor lighting nor beaches nor anything else. In the great days of Brazilian soccer, the *favelas* were the home of the *Malandro.*

We feel when we see Brazil play that the Brazilian style comes naturally to Brazilian people. The Brazilians think so too, and when you ask them to explain they talk about the *Malandro.*

The *Malandro* is a figure from Brazilian folklore. His ancestors were slaves—Brazil abolished slavery as late as 1888—and he is resolved to be completely free. He thinks discipline is a good thing for the mediocre, but not for the *Malandro*. He is a con man, a trickster. He works alone and obeys no rules. Though poor, he manages to dress well, to eat in the best places, and to charm beautiful women. The point is that Brazilians see themselves as *Malandros*: he stands for the national character. Or at least, he did.

Professor Muniz Sodre gestured upwards from his window. "Let me draw you a picture," he said. "If you go to a *favela*," and I would have been mad to do so, "you will see a woman—there is no man in the house—who takes care of her five or six boys. The smartest of these boys, who can flee from police if he needs to, who can put up a fight, is a good soccer player. He can dribble past life's difficulties. He can provide food for his mother. There is a deep connection between tricking defenders on the soccer field and being a smart boy in real life. This boy is a *Malandro*."

Classically, the *Malandro* is a black man, and he excels at the ancient sport of Brazilian blacks, the *capoeira*. The *capoeira* is a cross between a dance and a martial art. The dancer wears knives on his heels and dances around his opponent trying to cut him. The *Malandro* wears a silk scarf not just for style—it protects his neck in the *capoeira*. "You find the *capoeira* where you least expect it," said Professor Sodre. "For example," he grinned, "I am a *capoerista*. I am a master with the knife."

I was surprised to hear it, as Sodre is also a 50-year-old professor of communications at the Federal University of Rio de Janeiro. The air-conditioned lecture room in which we spoke was an outpost of Europe, far removed from black con-men with knives on their feet. Sodre explained: he was a mulatto, who had learned his *capoeira* from a black master in Bahia. The master had known all about *Malandros*. One day, a black foreigner had visited the master's *capoeira* school, and Sodre had spoken to the man in French. Later, the master asked Sodre where the visitor came from.

"From French Guyana," Sodre told him.

"Nonsense," replied the master. "I know about guys like that. He's a black man from Rio. He probably worked in the docks and picked up a few words of French there. He's a *Malandro!*"

Sodre protested that the man had spoken perfect French.

"You're too young to understand. But he can't fool a *Malandro* like me," the master told him. A *Malandro*, the master knew, is so clever that he can speak French without knowing any.

"To understand our soccer," said Sodre, "you have to understand the *capoeira*. *Capoeira* is a way of tricking your opponent—not like boxing where if you are stronger you win. It is a body philosophy."

The *capoeira* is a dance, but also a sport, and so is great Brazilian soccer. For years after the British brought soccer to Brazil, blacks were barred from Brazilian clubs, and mulattos who wanted to play powdered their faces to look whiter—echoes of South Africa. The great age of Brazilian soccer arrived when the blacks were allowed to play. The first great black soccer player was Leonidas, highest scorer in the World Cup of 1938, and Brazil's three World Cups were won mainly by black men: Pelé, Didi, Garrincha, Jairzinho and so on. So "black" were these teams that when Didi married a white woman, he was nearly left out of the squad for the Swedish World Cup.

These players were not themselves *capoeiristas*, but they came from a culture that admired grace and trickery. They were soccering *Malandros*. Sodre said: "The greatest soccer idols were the great dribblers, players like Garrincha and Pelé, who used to invent movements—the Dry Leaf, The Bicycle—just as the great *capoeiristas* did." The archetypal *Malandro* soccer player was Garrincha, a tiny mulatto winger from the *favelas*. In a popular anecdote, the Brazilian manager is outlining the opposition's game to his players, and when at last he finishes Garrincha asks him: "Have you told the other team all this? Then how do they know what they are supposed to do?" For the *Malandro*, the con man on the pitch, it was madness to plan how to play. You simply did what came to you. Garrincha could destroy systems, even though his one leg was longer than the other. The "Little Bird" played in three World Cups for Brazil and earned two winners' medals, and on retiring found himself living with his wife and eight children in a slum very like the one he had come from. He drank himself to death, but a million people lined the streets of Rio for his funeral, and *Garrincha: The Joy of the People* is a famous Brazilian film. "Brazilian soccer is not only a sport," said Sodre. "It's a kind of stage play, a theatrical movement."

They were staging a theatrical movement at the Maracaña that Sunday. A stand had collapsed the year before, killing three people, and the ground had been shut for months. The disaster was quite predictable, Brian Homewood, a British journalist working for Reuters in Rio told me. "Brazilian politicians like to build new things, rather than spend money on maintenance which nobody sees. Eventually something fell down."

That day, the biggest stadium in the world looked in good shape, and the soccer was still as Sodre had described it. Vasco da Gama beat Botafogo 2–0 in what was probably the best game I saw all year—though hundreds of the best Brazilian players have gone abroad, neither of these teams were the best in Brazil, and not one player on the pitch was a regular international. The moment of the match was the first goal: a Vasco free kick hit the top of the Botafogo wall and rebounded to a Vasco forward who, from 25 yards out, volleyed it into the net. You can see goals like that at all levels of soccer, but most are flukes. This player swivelled his body to place the ball in the far right corner, where the keeper was not, to score a quite deliberate goal. The game was gloriously attacking.

"These are our roots," Carlos Alberto Parreira, the manager of Brazil, told me a few days later, in the João Havelange building in central Rio. Carlos Alberto captained Brazil in 1970; Carlos Alberto Silva managed them briefly in the 1980s; and Carlos Alberto Parreira, a dapper man in a tailored sports jacket, is a different person altogether. I was speaking to him at a press conference he gave to announce his squad for a friendly game against Poland. (It was then not even known where in the country the game would be played.) Parreira and the Brazilian press sat around a horseshoe table, the list of names was handed out, and then, instead of the manager explaining his choices to the gathering, the journalists came to his desk one by one for exclusive interviews. After he had given 20 or so "exclusives!" in an hour, it was my turn. Parreira still looked unruffled.

I asked whether his Brazil would be more attractive than the dreary side of 1990. He replied in perfect English: "When we played in England all the journalists asked me this. Yes, that is what we want. We want to go back to our roots: to the flat back four, to zonal marking and attacking soccer. That is how our players have played since they were boys." His view is that even if he wanted to he could not change the way Brazil plays. He says the only manager he knows who changed a nation's style and prospered was Carlos Bilardo, who won Argentina a World Cup by turning Menotti's side into a gang of thugs. Parreira told me, "You cannot put Brazilians into a—," and unable to think of the word, he tried to mime a straitjacket.

But Brazilians are changing. Take the fortunes of Brazil at the last six World Cups.

The manager who prepared the 1970 team, João Saldanha, best known as a sports commentator, put his faith in *Malandros*. "Brazilian soccer is a thing played to music," he said. Told that Pelé, Gerson, Rivelino and Tostao could not possibly play in one midfield, he replied, "I don't care if they are all the same type of player, or if Rivelino and Gerson are both left-footed. They're the best, they're geniuses, let's trust them. They'll know what to do." But Saldanha never made it to the World Cup.

Theories abound as to why he was sacked after taking Brazil through the qualifiers. Some say he was too bad-tempered and got into too many fistfights, and that Pelé disliked him. (Saldanha had considered dropping Pelé.) Others point out that Brazilian managers get sacked: it is a fact of life that requires no further explanation. The most interesting theory is that President Emilio Garrastazu Médici, Brazil's military dictator, wanted Saldanha out. As president of Brazil from 1969 to 1973, Médici tortured lots of people, but he was also a soccer fan.

As a young man Saldanha had been a Communist, but when he was appointed manager of Brazil, Médici invited him and his team round to lunch. Saldanha declined on the grounds that the training schedule would not permit it. Not long after, an Argentine journalist asked why Dario was not in the team, and Saldanha explained that Roberto and Tostao were better players. But Dario was Médici's favourite player, said the journalist. "I don't choose the president's ministry, and he can't choose my forward line," Saldanha replied.

He was fired just three months before the World Cup. The first two men who were asked to replace him refused: they feared that if they failed, the fans might not rest content with burning them in effigy. Finally Mario Zagalo, the "Little Ant," took the job, recalled Dario, and led Brazil to glory in Mexico. It was the last time they won the World Cup.

While Brazil gets knocked out of World Cups, a debate rages in which the whole nation takes part. (As one Brazilian manager lamented, in an echo of Golda Meir: "I have a nation of soccer managers!") The debate is between traditionalists and modernizers. The traditionalists, men like Saldanha, argue that great players make their own rules. The modernizers insist that Brazil has to change, and that the team of 1970 was, above all, organized. They point to Pelé's defeat by European force in 1966, and say that the Brazilian way is charming and out of date.

Zagalo had had no time to impose his ideas in 1970. The Little Ant was a quiet man, a churchgoer, more of a Swede than a Brazilian, and at the World Cup of 1974 he revealed himself as a modern thinker. "Don't concede goals, don't let the other team play, and only attack when certain," he commanded. Brazil was knocked out, and his house was stoned.

Claudio Coutinho was physical trainer of the team of 1970. Two World Cups later, in 1978, he was manager. He did not enjoy sole control. Admiral Heleno Nunes, in charge of Brazilian sport, was a prominent Rio member of ARENA, the government party, and Nunes believed that "a win in Argentina will be very important for ARENA." To win votes in Rio, Nunes made Coutinho pick Roberto of Vasco da Gama, the city's number one team. Coutinho agreed—he was a military man himself. A former volleyball player and army captain, he had studied the physical training of American astronauts in order to revamp P.E. teaching in the Brazilian army. Being an educated man with perfect English, he was an instinctive modernizer, who dismissed the dribble as "a waste of time and a proof of our weakness." When he went on to praise the European tactic of overlapping, one ex-manager retorted: "Overlapping is what Garrincha does by himself." Saldanha watched Coutinho aghast, but never lost hope: "No, no, no, I believe these guys, Zico, Rivelino, and the rest, said yes to Coutinho. In training they will run back like defenders, but on the field, in the play, I don't believe they will obey. I hope they don't."

They did, of course. So dull was Brazil at the World Cup that on the very day they reached the second round, Coutinho was burned in effigy by Brazilian fans at the team's base in Mar del Plata. Then Argentina bought Peru, Brazil went out, and the suicides rained from Rio apartments.

* * *

At every World Cup we read about Brazilian suicides and African witch doctors. The press seems to believe that when Brazil is knocked out, devoted fans jump off apartment blocks. The truth is probably different.

In the early days of a World Cup, while the Brazilian team are still winning, life in Brazil is a party. Cars honk on the streets, and everyone sings and dances. Then Brazil loses and is knocked out. The mood suddenly changes, and the people who suffer most are the nation's manic-depressives. Carried along by the general euphoria, they cannot bear its end. Their "high" becomes a "low," and they commit suicide.

Coutinho died in a skin diving accident before the next World Cup. Tele Santana managed Brazil in 1982 and he reproduced the beautiful game of old. To general dismay, his team lost 3–2 to Paolo Rossi's Italy in an unforgettable match. Two years after the World Cup, Socrates, one of Brazil's stars, remade Santana's point: he turned down £1 million contracts with Roma and Juventus because of clauses that forbade him to make love for three days before a match. He joined Fiorentina instead. "Now we all know why Brazilian soccer is a game of beauty and passion while its Italian counterpart bores everyone to tears," wrote that propagandist of excess, the *Daily Express*.

At the next World Cup, Santana's team went down with honor again, and then the modernizers took control. The Brazilian manager in 1990, Sebastiao Lazaroni, was the sternest of all.

A mediocre goalkeeper, Lazaroni quit the game early and read a lot of soccer books. "The national team must become less playful," he warned, and in Italy he fielded players who looked like Brazilians and wore Brazilian uniform but who played like the dourest of

Eastern Europeans. With seven defenders, Brazil beat Sweden and Costa Rica by 1–0 each and Scotland by 2–1. At one point the Italian police had to step in to stop the Brazilian press from tearing Lazaroni into little bits. "This is the great danger of Lazaroni's logic: he will only be right if Brazil win the World Cup. If we are eliminated early, only the memory of a bad team will survive," warned Pelé. "Pelé is a sad old man," responded the Brazilian players.

Brazil was eliminated early. Against Argentina, they played magically and all but broke down the woodwork, but the Argentines scored in the 83rd minute and won 1–0. It was a victory with a whiff of sulphur and *Bilardismo*: during the match, the Brazilian player Branco had called to the sidelines for water, and someone on the Argentine bench had sportingly thrown him a flask. From that moment on Branco played groggily, and he later declared that he had been slipped a Mickey Finn.

Overnight Lazaroni became Brazil's public enemy number one. He was lucky he had a job waiting at Fiorentina, for there was no way he could go home. The nation demanded a return to old ways. "There is a sense that the way we played in 1990, that that is not Brazil," Parreira told me. Of course he did. Parreira is an educated man, but after Lazaroni he can hardly preach "modern" soccer. Parreira's Brazil will be more traditional than Lazaroni's, and more modern than Pelé's.

Soccer is never just soccer. In debating soccer, the Brazilians also debate the kind of country Brazil should be. "Maybe it's the same for Englishmen too," Luis Eduardo Soares, an anthropologist, suggested to me. "When our national team plays, we feel that the identity of our country is being played out on the field. Our values are being shown to the world." Brazilians feel this more strongly than we do. To them, Coutinho, Zagalo and Lazaroni, proponents of dull soccer, were not just losers but traitors. The issue, in politics as in soccer, is whether Brazil should imitate Europe, or whether it should try to return to its own past. Brazil today is backward (try making an appointment in Rio) but it is creative: great soccer, great samba, and great cinema. The greatest foreign debt in the world, too. The modernizers, in politics as in soccer, want to turn Brazil into a second Germany.

Fernando Collor de Mello, a fluent English speaker, was elected president in 1990, with a brief to "civilize" Brazil. His mission failed. Collor championed discipline, but not for himself, and having been elected to destroy corruption, he became the most corrupt president the country could remember. In 1992, he avoided impeachment by resigning.

Collor was a *Malandro*. There are only a few left now, sang Chico Buarque in his *Opera of the Malandro*, and they are all politicians. Brazil is changing. The *Malandro* has left the *favelas*, where he has given way to the killer, and he has disappeared from soccer, which is growing ever duller. The black dribblers are gone. There is less space to play in the cities, and so the clubs draw more players from schools and sports clubs, which means more rich kids. The stars of the 1980s, Zico, Falcao and Socrates, were white and middle class. Even *capoeira* is becoming a white sport, taught in fashionable Rio schools where often only the master is a black man. So greatly has Brazil changed that at the 1990 World Cup, Pelé singled out a German, Lothar Matthäus, as the one man who was playing like a Brazilian. The Brazilians are getting it the wrong way around: modern soccer, backward politics.

CHAPTER 18

CELTiC AND RANGERS, OR RANGERS AND CELTiC

CELTIC WAS PLAYING RANGERS in Glasgow, and I travelled there by way of Northern Ireland.

I spent months preparing for the game. On a train in France, I met a rare Protestant Celtic fan, who assured me that the ancient Glaswegian custom of asking passersby if their religion had fallen into disuse. He said: "Nowadays they don't ask, 'Prod or Catholic?', or 'Billy or Dan?', they just ask, 'Which team do you support?' " I always say, 'Partick Thistle,' and they laugh and go away." But if I were to go about in team colors, said this man, "they'll just back stab you without even talking to you." I decided not to go about in team colors.

I also prepared by reading Celtic and Rangers fanzines. I read them in Moscow, in Cameroon, in the bath of the house I stayed in in Cape Town. From the bathtub you looked out onto Table Mountain. You also looked out onto the patio, from where your housemates looked back at you, so it was not the most soothing place to read fanzines. Reading them tended to remind me of the Yugoslav war anyway. The following is taken from *Follow, Follow*, a Rangers fanzine. Bear in mind that Rangers are Protestant, that Celtic are Catholic, that a "Prod" is a Protestant, and a "Tim" a Celtic fan, or simply any Roman Catholic.

> Only one of Hitler's main henchmen was a Prod, the foreign minister von Ribbentrop. . . . The three most distinguished non-Jewish anti-Nazi resisters, Raoul Wallenberg, Dietrich Bonnhoffer and Pastor Niemoller were all Prods. And let's not forget that Hitler was a Tim!

Follow, Follow has a circulation of 10,000, and is quite a force in Glasgow.

Possibly Rangers and Celtic fans are the only people who live in the real world. Certainly they live in a world rather different from ours, and ours only matters to them when it connects with their rivalry. And it never matters all that much, for even as World War II raged several of their games ended in riots. An Old Firm game in 1975 inspired two attempted murders, two cleaver attacks, one axe attack, nine stabbings and 35 common assaults. On the other hand, the clubs also inspire great love. Rangers no longer allow the ashes of dead fans to be scattered on the Ibrox pitch, because, in the words of John Greig, former Rangers player and manager, "we were doing so many that we were ending up with big bald patches—even in the middle of summer." Scarcely a Glaswegian novel fails to touch on the Old Firm game, and it is in the main thanks to Rangers and Celtic fans that Scots watch more soccer matches than do any other Europeans except Albanians. This suggests that there is less to do in Albania than in Scotland.

I say that Celtic are Catholic and Rangers are Protestant. This has to be qualified. Celtic have always fielded Protestants, and players like Bertie Peacock were even rumored to be Orangemen—members of the extreme Protestant Orange Order. It was different at Rangers.

The punk group Pope Paul and the Romans (also known as The Bollock Brothers) once sang "Why Don't Rangers Sign a Catholic?," and sometimes Rangers directors would reply honestly. "It is part of our tradition," said Matt Taylor in Canada in 1967. "We were founded in 1873 as a Presbyterian Boys' Club. To change now would lose us considerable support." The *Bush*, a Presbyterian Church newspaper, raised the issue in 1978 and saw its circulation fall from 13,000 to 8,000. The paper soon folded. Today, the table tennis and snooker tables at Ibrox are still painted blue, but in 1989 the club signed the Roman Catholic striker Maurice Johnston.

Not the View, a Celtic fanzine, scooped with the news that "Rangers are to break with a 100-year tradition and in a shock move sign a good looking player." In fact, Johnston was not the first Catholic to play for Rangers: rather, he was the first Catholic the club had knowingly signed since World War I (even if his stepfather was a Protestant and a Rangers fan). To Rangers fans, Mo Johnston was the worst Catholic of them all. He had head-butted Stuart Munro of Rangers in the 1986 Skol Cup final, and while being sent off had made the sign of the cross "at" the Rangers fans. Just before joining Rangers he had seemed on the point of signing for Celtic. When he chose otherwise, the Shankill, Belfast branch of the Rangers Supporters Club folded in protest. Meanwhile, Celtic fans nicknamed him *La petite merde*, in honor of his spell in France. *Scotland on Sunday* called Johnston "the Salman Rushdie of Scottish soccer," for offending two sets of fundamentalists at once, and the player took Rushdie-like measures. Fearing Glasgow, he took a house in Edinburgh. It was a gasoline-bombed by Celtic fans. He hired a 24-hour bodyguard. Celtic fans attacked his father.

During his time at Rangers, *Follow, Follow* writers debated whether he was trying his best for the team. He was certainly trying his best to please. It was soon reported that he had sung The Sash, a Protestant song, at a supporters' dance, and also that years before he had spat on a Celtic crest. The Govan R.S.C. voted him Player of the Year after his first season, but a year after that he was gone. He never transformed Rangers into a Catholic club. "Rangers could sign Pope John Paul himself and I don't think it would make any difference," as William English told me.

English is a young Royal Mail worker and Ibrox regular who finds some of his fellow fans hard to explain. When I placed an advertisement in *Follow, Follow* he phoned me, eager to talk, and we met in a Glasgow café. He told me: "There were guys who, when Mo scored, didn't count that goal, so if the result was 1–0 they'd count it as a 0–0 draw. I've seen guys almost get into fights at matches for encouraging Mo Johnston. The strange thing is that once the booing stopped, Mo got *worse*." Johnston is an eccentric.

Now Mark Hateley, the Rangers center-forward, is rumored to be a Catholic. English said: "When Hateley plays, you get guys shouting, 'Come on the Queen's Ten!' They won't say 'Queen's Eleven' because they don't count Hateley." Before, there had been doubts about Trevor Francis (said to have sent his children to a Catholic school) and Mark Falco (a Protestant with a habit of crossing himself), while even Terry Butcher ("Celtic, you hate 'em so much") finally had to deny publicly that he was Catholic.

Hateley was accepted most of the time, said English. "But if he misses a couple of chances, they go: 'He's a Fenian, isn't he?' " I asked, "So he can't have three bad matches in a row?," and English said, "I wouldn't recommend it." I asked how anyone *knew* that Hateley was a Catholic. "They say Hateley's *wife* is a Catholic. I don't know how *anyone* knows that." Did English think Hateley was a Catholic? "It's a terrible thing to say, but he doesn't *look* like it." What? "Well, Catholics, I'd say, are more likely to have jet black hair, with no tan at all, or else tight orange hair." He pointed at a group at the other end of the café: "For instance, I don't think those four guys are Catholics."

"I paid for my season-ticket one week," Danny Houston recounted to me mournfully, "and they signed Mo Johnston the next." Houston, an honorary deputy grand master of the Orange Lodge in Glasgow and Scotland, boycotted Rangers during the Johnston era. I visited him at his house. He was dressed in a tracksuit.

The Orange Order is an Irish Protestant society founded in 1795 and is strongest in Scotland and Ulster. Every summer the

Order holds Orange Marches, which often end in brawls with Catholics. "We're working-class people who are Loyal and Royal," as Houston defined it. "Orangemen support all sorts of teams. You get Airdrie supporters, Falkirk supporters . . ." But few of them are Parkhead regulars, and most just support Rangers. One man who walked up to an Orange March while dressed in a Celtic shirt was arrested for breach of the peace.

Houston insisted he had no objection to Rangers signing a foreign Catholic, but "Roman Catholicism in the West of Scotland is synonymous with Irish Republicanism." That was his catchphrase. Real Sociedad, he said, signed only Basques, and in the German league before the war there had been a Jewish team called Maccabi, which the Nazis had banned. "So why should anyone act like the Nazis? Why does Scotland have this hang-up about Rangers being a Protestant team? There's not a *Scottish* Protestant in the current Celtic team. Does anyone ever say that?"

Graeme Souness, the Rangers manager who signed Johnston, was making a point to fans like Houston. Before capturing Johnston, Souness had done his best to buy the Welsh Catholic Ian Rush from Juventus (the living person Rush would most like to meet is the Pope), and had bid for the Catholics Ray Houghton and John Sheridan. Yet the change in policy was also down to David Murray, the Rangers chairman.

Matt Taylor in 1967 was afraid of losing fans, but Murray in 1989 was more interested in luring sponsors. "Soccer is no longer a pie-and-Bovril game," he liked to say. Fans (or some of them) want Rangers to be a Protestant club, but sponsors do not. Murray has gone for sponsors, and they have responded.

Max Weber, the German sociologist, famously observed that where Protestants and Catholics live together, the Protestants tend to be richer. There used to be a wealth divide of this kind in

Glasgow, but today Rangers fans like to insist that they are just as poor as Celtic fans. That is the accepted wisdom—and yet Rangers F.C. are rich and Celtic F.C. are poor, and Bluenoses at Old Firm games chant, "You haven't got any money." The Kelly and White families run Celtic far more laxly than Murray does Rangers, yet it would be wrong to give Murray all the credit. He could never have done at Celtic what he did at Rangers: for most businessmen in Glasgow are Protestants, who would not buy executive boxes or pay £75 for a five-course meal at Parkhead.

Colin Glass is a prominent Glasgow insurance agent and a Rangers fan. He grew up in Dundee, but moved to Glasgow at the age of 18 to be near his team. Now he owns a house in Florida, and says that but for Rangers he would have moved there. "I didn't become a Rangers fan because of religion. I did it because I liked the colors, the red, white and blue," he assured me.

"And Rangers get the image in the press of being the religious bigots! You know these stories about thousands of Rangers fans returning their season tickets when Johnston signed? Well, I happen to know the Rangers director in charge of season tickets. Do you know how many tickets were returned? One!" Yes, but other fans burned their season tickets in front of Ibrox. "A media stunt."

I said that Celtic fans were quite as convinced that the press was biased against them. "But they have got a *general* paranoia that there is discrimination against Catholics." Then he said: "There is discrimination against Catholics, but not so much in the media. There is discrimination in jobs, by a lot of businesses in Western Scotland. So when, say, a referee's decision goes against them for perfectly legitimate reasons, they get paranoid. A Catholic friend of mine told me that he walked out of chapel recently when the priest started on about how everyone was against Catholics, right down to soccer referees."

When it comes to job discrimination, Glass, given his position, is a strong witness. I asked for his evidence. "If you take a look and see the number of Masonic handshakes at places like the chamber of commerce. The police too. I remember once, at a police retirement do, the chief inspector talking about Catholics. He said, 'I promoted two of them, and you know, one of them turned out not bad!' This man had no idea what he was saying!"

Glass told me that three of his four assistant managers were Celtic fans. But: "If someone called Patrick O'Leary applied, I wouldn't put him in a job approaching normal executive businessmen, because when he phones up and gives his name, they'll say 'No.' " Catholics should dissemble more, he said. "They call their kids Bridget Teresa or names like that. My view is, why do they give their children that handicap when neither they nor I have the power to change people's prejudices?" Could he tell a Catholic from a Protestant? "Catholics speak slightly differently. The police here will ask, 'What *exactly* did the suspect say?' Take 'stair': we say 'steer,' they say 'stayer.' "

"But it works on both sides: the Labor council of Glasgow is totally dominated by Catholics. There was a firm called Lafferty's Construction, now bust. Every single tender from the district council that Frank Lafferty went for, he was *just* under the next bid. He used to sit in the directors' box at Celtic Park."

"The worst club match in the world, without a doubt," said Jim Craig, a well-coiffed, gray-haired Glaswegian dentist about the Old Firm game. What was it like to play in? "I loved it! I'm of the warrior class, and a warrior is trained to fight. Sometimes I went through the whole game without ever doing anything constructive, and got praised at the end."

Craig used to be Celtic's right back, and he once scored an own goal against the Rangers. "Twenty-three years ago—people still tell me about it—and it wasn't even a very good one," he lamented. "I tried to glance it beside the post. It hit the inside of the post and went in. A few years ago Terry Butcher scored an absolute smasher in the game for Celtic: the ball came across and he threw himself at it and it *screamed* into the corner. I wrote to him, 'I scored a mediocre own goal in the Old Firm match back in 1970 and I'm still reminded of it. You'll be remembered for all time for that one!' "

"The tribal supporters don't want the game to change. It's a great day for them, to go out there and hate the opposition. If you played behind closed doors, they'd stand outside at either end and shout. It's hard for me because I'm not a passionate person. It's hard for the players, because very often your whole season is judged on how you do in the Old Firm games." We shook our heads and deplored the fans. Then Craig said: "Don't forget, though: you'll get a summer holiday, I'll get a summer holiday, but they won't get a summer holiday." In Ulster in the 1970s, he had met a man whose father was dying of cancer. "The son asked me to come round and see the guy, who was a Celtic fan, and I did, I brought along some pennants and badges, and then I went back to Scotland and, I must admit, clean forgot about it. That November I got a letter from the son. His dad had lived much longer than anyone had expected him to, and all he talked about for the last six months of his life was that a Celtic player had been to see to him. Not 'Jim Craig,' but a Celtic player. It's hard for players: you're fighting with the manager, you're injured, you're carrying an injury, you're coming back from injury, and it's very much a job. You forget that that other side of soccer is a tremendous thing."

The most famous Celts in history are Jock Stein's "Lisbon Lions." In 1967 they became the first British team to win the European Cup, beating Helenio Herrera's Inter Milan 2–1 in the final in Lisbon. Craig is a Lisbon Lion, and I asked what he remembered of the game. "I'm still always asked about it, and I still don't think it was a penalty. I was determined he wasn't going to turn past me, and I thought, 'If

I bump into him the referee isn't going to give a penalty, not at this stage of the game.' How wrong I was." But later he set up Tommy Gemmell's equalizer, and then Chalmers scored the winner. The post-match banquet was the one at which the Celtic coaches abused Herrera. "We had Scotsmen falling out of closets for weeks afterwards," said a British diplomat in Lisbon. Three years later, Craig was on the bench when Celtic lost its second European Cup final to Feyenoord. What had gone wrong? He thought it might have had to do with the biorhythms of the two teams.

Few soccer players go on to become dentists, I said. "Nowadays there are a lot of Catholic lawyers, doctors and so on. You didn't have that forty years ago. These people were fighting a system. That's why when Jock came and the team suddenly picked up, it was wonderful for these people."

I told him about my book. He shook his head. "It's hard for someone from beyond Glasgow to understand the place. This is a strange city. I'll give you an example. The other night, I was walking down the street, past this building that's just been bought by the ministry of defense, and I saw a light on inside, so I climbed up on the ledge to see what was in there. This guy comes past, looks at me and says: 'You're a nosy bastard!' Then he says: 'What's up there anyway?' "

The Old Firm divides Scots all over the world, from the USA to South Africa, but the region it affects most is Ulster. The province, after all, is like an Old Firm game got out of hand, and when the Old Firm meet it grows tenser than usual. A week before Celtic vs. Rangers at Parkhead, I went to Ulster.

I started from Dublin, capital of the republic. "I'm Irish aren't I," one Dubliner wrote to me, explaining why he supported Celtic. "From a very early age in Ireland your father embeds the words Glasgow Celtic into your system. You will be very grateful for this introduction to the world's finest club, and it will probably be the only time in your childhood that you will obey your father's orders most willingly."

From Dublin I took the bus up to Derry, in Ulster. Recently, a Derry family scattered a relative's ashes over the running track at the Rangers ground only to watch groundsmen sweep up the ex-fan seconds later. From Derry I took another bus to the small town of Limavady. On its deserted main street, David Brewster has a solicitor's office. I asked him whether I could leave my backpack at the reception desk. "Better take it with you," he said. Politicians in Ulster are careful people.

Brewster, who was wearing a blue pullover, is tipped as a future MP. He is an Ulster Unionist, and so, naturally, is a Rangers fan. He was the first of many lucid Old Firm fans I met. "This," he said, indicating a scar around his eye, "is, as a matter of fact, a souvenir of Glasgow. But in Glasgow, 99% of the time you can be as bigoted as you want and the worst you'll get is punched. All the stuff that you've bottled up for months in Ulster, you can let go there in 90 minutes. Things get very intense over there, but you won't get shot." In Ulster itself, he said, Old Firm fans kept quiet. Celtic and Rangers shirts were read as simple sectarian symbols. "Pat Rice, a Roman Catholic, was killed in about 1971. He was educationally subnormal, and he used to walk around in his neighborhood, one of the toughest areas of Belfast, wearing a Rangers scarf. He had been warned—he got on people's nerves—and in the end he got murdered. So the Old Firm is not that tribal."

In other words, there was no street rivalry between Celtic and Rangers fans in Ulster? No teasing, no fistfights? "In Belfast, Catholics and Protestants who do work together avoid religious topics. The phrase is, 'Whatever you say, say nothing.' If you ever ask the folk here anything, by way of an opinion poll for example, they'll be very guarded about expressing an opinion. Yet they know the religious affiliation, or the *perceived* religious affiliation, of virtually every club in England and Scotland." I went straight back to Derry, and caught a bus to Belfast, arriving there late on Thursday evening.

Belfast used to have its own Old Firm games. Belfast Celtic, a clone of Glasgow Celtic, was founded in 1891, and their matches against Protestant clubs were always hairy affairs. There was gunfire at games against Linfield in the 1930s and 1940s, and finally, after fans invaded the pitch and broke a player's leg in 1949, Belfast Celtic folded.

Later, the tiny Belfast club Cliftonville began to attract Catholics, simply because their ground, Solitude, lies near a Catholic area. Matches between Cliftonville and Protestant teams can produce quite spectacular violence. Graham Walker, a Rangers fan and a Queen's University lecturer in politics, has even seen Protestant fans throw a grenade: "It went off at the back of the Spion Kop, where the Cliftonville fans were. The back of the Spion Kop is where the Falls Road is, so the fans started cheering and singing, 'We've Got Another One'—they thought the bomb was one of theirs." But Cliftonville is a very small club. Belfast Catholics look to Glasgow for most of their soccer.

I stayed at Queen's University, which has a Celtic Supporters' Club and a Rangers one. All the committee members of the Queen's R.S.C. that year were also members of the Unionist Party. On Friday morning I found Lee Reynolds, the R.S.C. chairman, waking up under a Union Jack in his room. "You probably can't go into a Protestant house in Ulster where there isn't a Rangers scarf, or a mug, or something," he told me. I mentioned that I also wanted to speak to the chairman of the Celtic Supporters' Club. "Oh yes, D.J. We'll go and find him." We met Thomas "D.J." McCormick, draped in Celtic scarf, outside the student union, and Lee introduced us. The two were overly polite to one another, like diplomats of warring states at a UN meeting. D.J. told me he would take me to the match the next day. He decided that instead of sitting in the pressbox I would stand on the terrace with the Celtic fans.

Later that Friday I went to see Michael Fearon, another solicitor, but a Catholic who works on a lone Catholic street in the Protestant part of the city. Walking through Belfast you think of bombs. As you walk through Fearon's door you are, to the casual eye, identifying yourself as a Catholic, and you hope that no one watching minds. Happily the street seemed deserted, but I decided not to get lost on the way back to Queen's.

I asked Fearon how popular Rangers and Celtic were in Ulster. "It's *Celtic and Rangers*," he corrected. "The most fanatical Celtic and Rangers fans come from here, from the six counties." He was one of them: "I wrap a Tricolor around my shoulders, put on a scarf with a picture of the pope and sing, 'Fuck the Queen.' And there's thousands like me." Why? "I'm a downtrodden nationalist, and when you stand on the terraces at Parkhead and look across, you can see the people who keep us down here." And yet going to Glasgow meant a holiday from Ulster: "Politics in this country, on both sides, is intransigent, and totally, totally predictable. There's no such thing as that weird animal, the floating voter, here." At an Old Firm game, I suggested, there is the possibility of beating the Protestants for a day? He agreed, and gave me an article on Maurice Johnston that he kept in his drawer. I asked him for his stereotype of the Rangers fan. "It would have to be the potbelly with the McEwans shirt over it. Every time at night before the TV goes off, he stands up for the British national anthem. The reality is, he's just like me."

D.J. and I took the train to his parents' house in Larne, the port for the Stranraer ferry, and the next day, rather early on a very cold morning, we walked to the boat. I was staying on in Glasgow after the match, but D.J. was making a 22-hour round trip that would cost him at least £70. Ulster Old Firm fans are almost quantifiably the most loyal supporters in Britain. The Glasgow academic Raymond Boyle surveyed Belfast fans of Celtic and found that:

- LESS THAN 50 PERCENT OF THEM HAD FULL-TIME WORK.
- 80 PERCENT MADE ALL 16 ORGANIZED TRIPS TO PARKHEAD EACH SEASON.
- 49 PERCENT SPENT MORE THAN £500 A YEAR ON CELTIC. SOME TOLD BOYLE HE SHOULD HAVE ALLOWED A CATEGORY FOR OVER £1000.
- 80 PERCENT OF THOSE WHO FILLED IN THE POLITICAL SECTION OF THE QUESTIONNAIRE VOTED SINN FEIN. HOWEVER, 40 PERCENT OF THE SAMPLE LEFT THE SECTION BLANK.

Ours was an all-Celtic boat—Rangers and Celtic fans travel best separately—and on it was a rubber-faced man the others called "Reeva." He was probably the one person in the world who could jump on a table in front of a ferryload of Celtic fans and shout, "Can You Hear the Rangers Sing?," without getting a response. Reeva was the Larne village idiot, and he gave me a barrage that he insisted I quote verbatim in my book. He never made the match that day: he was arrested in Glasgow before kickoff for talking to a policeman's horse. "In Northern Ireland you belong to one side or the other," Paul Hamill, head of the Larne C.S.C., told me. "Either you are, or else you aren't. If I miss the boat tonight, I'll be given a bed, be given money. It's happened before. Celtic is a big family: It's essentially an Irish club, an Irish club playing in a foreign league." Many Rangers fans agree, and think that Celtic players never try their best for Scotland because they feel Irish. "He'd rather be wearing a green shirt than a blue one," is the terrace phrase.

Our coach finally reached the East End of Glasgow and D.J. gave me a Celtic scarf, for safety's sake. When we passed Rangers fans we looked away, and so did they.

It was still cold, I was still sleepy, and I found it hard to feel partisan. No one else did: Parkhead was full, *Follow, Follow* had called for a flag day, and the Rangers end looked like a crowd at a Royal Wedding. Their Union Jacks are considered so provocative in Glasgow that the police regularly confiscate them, which, as *Follow, Follow* points out, is peculiar: "After all, it is the national flag."

The most devoted foreign fans admire British fan culture. People from all over Europe come to Glasgow for the Old Firm game, and there is even a Rangers fanzine published in Switzerland called *Strangers on Rangers*. Some of the foreigners try to imitate the British, which explains the Union Jacks on terraces all over Europe (especially Eastern Europe) and the songs borrowed from Britain. "Here We Go," which Auberon Waugh called the national anthem of the working classes, is rapidly becoming the new Internationale. The British fan's repertoire is limitless. Though there are soccer fans all over the world, I doubt that *Dicks Out!*, the recent collection of terrace songs, could have been published anywhere but in Britain. Perhaps in Argentina.

British fans are unique. In Britain, soccer itself is almost incidental to fan culture. More than any other supporters in the world, British fans are aware of themselves *as fans*. They think a lot about their own numbers, their visibility, their group character. Man City fans say they were the first to wave inflatable bananas; Liverpool fans think they have a famous sense of humor; Leeds fans are racist. The British fan's main virtue is devotion, which is why the Rangers fanzine *Aye Ready* writes that "Celtic fans are about as loyal to their team as Philby, Burgess and Maclean were to the British Empire."

Every British man (at least) has his team. Nothing else in soccer matters nearly as much to him. A Rochdale fan wants to read about Gazza and David Platt, but most of all he wants to read about

Rochdale. My friends in Holland and Germany liked some teams more than others, but these sympathies were slight and changeable. For years I thought I was a neutral myself, until I noticed a mild pang whenever Ajax lost. Coming to England, I met people who had not the slightest desire to kick a ball themselves but who were devoted to teams which they knew to play poor soccer and which they went to see play every week.

Of course some foreign fans *are* devoted to one team, but even they are unlike British fans. In Holland, or in Italy or Cameroon, being a fan is a rather passive affair. Perhaps you love your team, and maybe you sing and shout in the stadium, and if you are particularly devoted you spend much of your spare time with other fans of your team, but you hardly ever think about being a fan. In other words, you want your team to win, but you do not care if the opposition's fans outflag you. *Follow, Follow* did care. So did D.J., who muttered to me when he saw the flags, "When we go to Ibrox we fill the stand with Tricolors."

British fans are historians. When two British teams play each other, their histories play each other too. This is especially true in Glasgow. Every Celtic fan of any age can talk to you for days about the Lisbon Lions, and every Old Firm fan knows that in 1931 the Rangers forward Sam English accidentally kicked the Celtic goal-keeper John Thomson in the head, whereupon Thomson, the "Bonnie Lad from Fife" died. The Celtic anthem sums it up:

It's enough to make your heart go oh oh oh
It's a grand old team to play for,
It's a grand old team to see,
And if you know your history,
It's enough to make your heart go oh oh oh

("And all you've got is your history," the Rangers fans retort.)

Other countries have no history. German fans can hardly reminisce about great matches of the 1930s, not with the old photos showing swastikas and Hitler salutes. In Russia, many clubs changed their names after the Bolshevik revolution, and Stalin once even disbanded CSKA Moscow—by accident, but that is another story. Some countries just have no time for tradition. Ajax, the club with the most glorious past in Holland, is to move to a new stadium outside Amsterdam later in the 1990s, and none of their fans seems to mind. The British bent for the past extends even beyond soccer. Take our Parliament: when the Conservative Party broke its election promise and levied VAT on fuel in 1993, Michael Heseltine pointed out that Harold Wilson had once raised VAT after vowing not to. What happened 30 years ago seemed relevant still, because like Celtic, the Labor Party is a unit with a history. When Labour plays the Tories, their histories play each other too. Margaret Thatcher liked to invoke Winston Churchill; the Tories never tire of discussing 1979; and on the Labor side, Tony Benn and Peter Shore complain that Labor is drifting away from its traditions. When John Motson tells us that "these two sides last met in the Cup in 1954, Rovers winning 1–0 thanks to a 31st minute own goal," he is making a very British point.

British fans enjoy fan culture, and most of all they enjoy hating their rivals. Celtic and Rangers fans need each other. Perhaps their rivalry is still based on real religious divides in Glasgow, but I question whether these divides alone are strong enough to make the Old Firm such a phenomenon. After all, more than 40 percent of Catholics who marry now marry Protestants. And if Celtic and Rangers really do stand for two poles in the city, then this is not reflected in Glaswegian politics: Celtic and Rangers fans alike vote Labor. Yet perhaps that is because the political divide in Glasgow—Labor, Conservatives and Scottish Nationalists—is a Westminster divide.

Had Labor won the 1992 elections, it would have created a Scottish assembly. Soon, truly Scottish parties would probably have replaced the Labor and Tory Parties. How to know what kind of new parties these would have been? By using the Old Firm rivalry as a guide to feeling, in the West of Scotland at least. By this guide, it would appear that in an independent Scotland, a left wing, republican, Catholic party would oppose a center-left, Unionist, Protestant party.

Unless, that is, the Old Firm rivalry has outlived religious hatred. I suggest that that is the case, and that the Old Firm has survived as a phenomenon because the fans enjoy it so much. They are not about to give up their ancient traditions just because they no longer believe in God.

That day's *Celtic View* (known to fans as *Pravda*) had an Old Firm quiz that started with an easy one: "True or False—it took Rangers nearly five years to beat Celtic for the first time?"

Our end sang for the IRA hunger-striker,

> Will you swear to bear allegiance to the flag of Ireland
> Bobby Sands MP
> Bobby Sands MP
> Will you swear to bear allegiance to the flag of Ireland?
> Will you wear the black beret?
> Will you serve the IRA?
> If you can,
> You're a man,
> BOBBY SANDS!

and, "Get the Brits, get the Brits, get the Brits out NOW!," and, even more simply, in praise of the IRA, "Ooh aah up the Ra, say ooh aah up the Ra!" That very afternoon, an IRA bomb killed two children in Warrington.

The Rangers fans were singing,

Surrender and you'll die, die, die,

The cry was no surrender,

Surrender and you'll die, die, die

With heart in hand . . .

We'll guard old Derry's walls

and "Nooooo Pope of Rome!"

As for me, I was just freezing. Being a neutral among fanatics is tiring. Had I really left Ulster that morning? Was this really part of the country I lived in?

The Ninety Minutes' Hate kicked off, and the man leaning into my ear became the ten millionth person in history to shout "Fuck off, you Orange bastards!" during an Old Firm game. Celtic scored, and a few dozen people hurled themselves down the stands at my back while Rangers nearly equalized. As the Celtic board later noted, Rangers kicked off while Celtic players were still celebrating, and Stuart McCall's shot came just 12 seconds after Celtic's goal hit the net: the referee's an Orange bastard. Then Celtic scored again.

The match was poor—Old Firm games tend to be. As the Glaswegian joke goes, "And in the middle of it all, a soccer match breaks out!" Tradition is that Celtic have a more refined style than Rangers, but all I could see was two teams running around much too fast. Half the players are fans in jerseys, and they play in a frenzy of rage. Peter Grant of Celtic is known to Rangers fans as "Rasputin," "The Mad Monk," or "The Mad Priest," and according to Gary Lineker, Terry Butcher used to sing Rangers songs in the England changing room.

The match ended at last, Celtic winning 2–1, though since Hateley had scored the Rangers goal many would consider it 2–0. I returned my scarf to D.J., turned left into the London Road and realized my mistake. No one else was coming my way, and Rangers fans were walking down the road towards me: on Old Firm days, the fans of the two clubs use separate routes. The first few fans to pass gave me uncharitable glances, and then one man carrying a banner threw me a fake head butt (a "Glaswegian kiss") as he went by. I say it was fake, but I only knew that when his nose stopped moving an inch from mine. I pretended not to notice and walked on.

My room in the B & B was freezing, so I went to write up my notes in the TV room, where the temperature was nearly bearable as long as you wore two coats. Two men, one wearing a ponytail, the other a military moustache, were drinking whisky from bottles. They offered me some. I refused. The ponytailed one pulled a newspaper clipping from his coat and handed it to me.

The story—from the *Sun*, and about a year old—certified that he had been arrested for driving a horse and carriage down a highway. The man's picture beamed from the page. "That's what I do," he told me. "I'm a gypsy." Every few seconds he would repeat the offer of whisky, and each time I would refuse. I asked the man with the military moustache what he did. "Ask me! I'm his boss," the man with the ponytail said. The man with the moustache was silent. "What does he do?" I asked. "He works for me." I asked them who they supported, Rangers or Celtic, but they said they didn't care.

By now my temperance was offending the man with the ponytail, and he said that he was going to break the whisky bottle over my head. I got up to leave. He looked at me and said, with disdain: "You're ignorant, do you know that? You're an ignorant cunt." I went to bed.

CHAPTER 19

FROM BOSTON TO BANGLADESH: AT THE 1994 WORLD CUP

MY JOB AT THE World Cup was identifying players for American TV. I sat in the commentary box for the Boston matches and when a player scored, or otherwise attracted notice, I had to say who he was. The technical people then flashed his name up on screen.

Five minutes into my first game, Argentina vs. Greece, a big, dark haired, rather Argentine-looking Argentinian collapsed in midfield. "Tell me who it is, brother!" the assistant producer demanded over the headphones.

I had no idea. "Balbo, number 15," I said. And as the name "Balbo" appeared on screen, clarifying matters for millions of Americans, the player stood up. It was Chamot.

"You cannot do this to me, brother!," came the voice over the headphones, and foreign journalists wrote more articles about know-nothing Americans. I spent most games wishing they were over.

So I visited the Nigerian training camp to find out what the players looked like. Emmanuel Amunike was little, Peter Rufai was easy to spot because he always wore a keeper's jersey during matches, and Daniel Amokachi had a strangely shaped head.

One Italian woman journalist stood a foot away from Amokachi, stared into his eyes and asked: "Are you Daniel Amokachi?"

"No," said Amokachi, and pointed at his Nigerian teammate Sunday Oliseh. "He's Daniel Amokachi." The woman went off to tug at Oliseh's shirt and Amokachi returned to his room.

I sympathized with him. Every newspaper in Italy had to fill ten pages a day on the upcoming game against Nigeria. Most of the *paparazzi* were sticking with Arrigo Sacchi's team in New Jersey, where they could ask players things like, "Who is better, Signori or Yekini?" (the answer went, "Signori is a great player, and Yekini is a great player too."), but a few dozen had come to the Holiday Inn near Boston where the Nigerians were staying. Every journalist had to produce a world exclusive every day. The woman who had addressed Amokachi wanted to know whether the Nigerian players roomed together. They did. And (this with raised eyebrows) did they enjoy it?

Worried that I would not be able to identify the South Korean players, I visited their camp too. It was an hour outside Boston, in a small town called Boxborough, where England had stayed before losing to the U.S. the year before. The South Koreans were bored witless. When I arrived with a Boston journalist named Frank, we were the first foreigners to drop by and were given an interview with the South Korean manager, Kim Ho, in the hotel bar. Players and journalists crowded round, and the next day our photos were all over the Seoul newspapers.

The Greek journalists had to cover a terrible team. At practices, an outfield player stood in goal while others blammed shots over the bar. Then they would form pairs and pass the ball over each other's heads or into the bushes. Soon the Greek papers were printing photos of Athenians in bars making obscene gestures at TV sets. The players complained that the coach, Alkis Panagoulias, a Greek American, made them travel to receptions all the time to meet other Greek Americans. Panagoulias replied that the World Cup was about culture, too.

The foreign journalists got most of their stories on Greece from Minas Hantzidis, a midfield player and the only man in the squad who spoke English. It was astonishing to see how often he was profiled.

For Argentina, Maradona was in a great mood. He spent most practice sessions hanging around the touchline, granting audiences and bantering with three old men in the stands dressed in togas. They hosted the Argentine version of Fantasy Soccer League.

Later, when he was banned, 20,000 Bangladeshis marched through Dhaka chanting, "Dhaka will burn unless Maradona is allowed to play." Few people threatened to burn down London's West End for him. Maradona, the little man, friend of Fidel Castro, conqueror of England, appeals more to poor nations than to rich ones.

But in those days before ephedrine, all ran as smoothly as if Maradona were a relatively normal human being. An Argentine radio journalist named Roberto, who had come to Boston a month before the World Cup just to be prepared, complained to me: "Nothing ever goes wrong in America. The organization is perfect. I prefer England, which is more like Argentina."

Not totally like. "The year after the Malvinas War British journalists voted Maradona the best player in the world," he said. "That's the difference. Argentine journalists would never have done that."

Roberto also told a story about Antonio Rattin, the Argentine captain sent off against England in the 1966 World Cup. Rattin, said Roberto, had been arguing with the referee, holding his arm across his chest and pointing at his captain's armband to indicate his right to talk. But the referee, thinking Rattin was making a "short arm" at him, sent him off.

Many of the American journalists knew everything about soccer. They had spent years telling their sports editors how important the World Cup was, pronouncing it "*World* Cup" as if to emphasise its significance. Their sports editors just didn't understand them. One Boston journalist told me he was descended from the great Arsenal manager Herbert Chapman. This man, who owned 0.3 percent of the shares in Charlton Athletic, talked about the state of the Albion Rovers ground, and was an expert on the Taylor Report. I avoided him whenever possible.

I met a Mexican who hoped Americans would go back to ignoring soccer. "Whenever the Americans like something, they take it over," he explained. In fact, the World Cup conquered the USA rather than vice versa. People stopped thinking soccer was posh and boring, even though George Bush went to the matches in Boston. The murder of Andres Escobar, the Colombian who scored an own goal, helped persuade Americans that this thing really mattered—this was the *World* Cup. In Britain, I was often told, fans care so much they even kill each other.

The more desolate the country, the more the World Cup mattered. The competition changed little in Norway or Switzerland, but in Rwanda it briefly stopped the killing. Rwandans of all tribes supported Nigeria, and during the World Cup whole armies powered up generators and clustered around TV sets.

However, the World Cup always inflames conflict and causes more deaths than goals. In Ulster only Catholics supported Ireland. On June 18, Protestant gunmen stormed into a Catholic pub in the village of Loughinisland, where the patrons were watching the Republic beat Italy, and shot dead six Catholics.

When the Irish lost their second game, to Mexico, the text "Viva Mexico" appeared on a wall off the Shankill. And when they drew their third game, against Norway, to reach the second round, young Catholics in West Belfast chanted at British Army patrols, "It'll shut the Brits up when we win the Cup."

At the Shorts aircraft factory in Belfast, a Catholic was suspended for wearing an Ireland shirt to work. Shorts said it was trying to create a neutral workplace. Elsewhere in Ulster, Protestants wore Glasgow Rangers shirts to work when Ireland were playing.

In South America, three presidents went on TV to criticize their teams' lineups. "Perhaps if we had strengthened the attack after

Luis Garcia was sent off, we would have had more opportunities," commented the Mexican president, Salinas, after his team were knocked out by Bulgaria.

President Menem of Argentina offered views too, but though he was in Boston, he watched Argentina's matches on TV in his hotel suite. Famously, he had attended Argentina's 0–5 defeat to Colombia in 1993. "If I get to Boston and we lose, I will get the blame," a senior diplomat quoted the president as saying.

The Bolivian president did watch his team live. Asked whether he shouldn't be attending to domestic priorities, the answer came: "In Bolivia, the World Cup is the top domestic priority."

The Brazilian president, Itamar Franco, went on TV during the tournament to beg his coach, Carlos Alberto Parreira, to pick the 17-year-old striker Ronaldo. Parreira paid no attention. Franco cared. Presidential elections, due in October, set his finance minister, Fernando Henrique Cardoso, against the radical socialist "Lula."

A quarter of all Brazilians said they would decide who to vote for only after they knew who had won the World Cup. No Brazilian does anything until Brazil is knocked out, and each competition costs the country more than £2 billion in lost production.

What would sway the floating voters? A London stockbroker specializing in Latin American markets explained: "The feeling is that if Brazil wins, people would think things in the country are not so bad after all, and that would benefit Fernando Henrique."

Brazil won, and so did Cardoso, who made Pelé his sports minister. Romario, who scored five times for Brazil, had supported "Lula."

On the streets of Haiti, the way to get applauded was to wear a Brazilian soccer shirt. Haiti missed the World Cup—they were kept out by Bermuda—so the whole country supported Brazil.

Meanwhile the Americans were trying to force Haiti's ruling *junta* to step down. President Clinton considered sending in the army, but first he tried imposing economic sanctions. TV-watching

Haitians ignored these. Indeed, everyone was so busy that talks between the generals and the opposition could not take place. At match halftimes the *junta* broadcast bloody videos of the U.S. invasion of Panama, with texts like "No to Intervention" superimposed. The Americans did nothing.

When Rumania beat Argentina, Rumanians of all ethnic groups embraced. President Iliescu said the team, led by the ethnic Macedonian Gheorge Hagi, had created a "national consensus." That was before the ethnic Serb Belodedici missed the deciding penalty in the quarter-final against Sweden.

This book argues that soccer affects politics, and that it always has. Yet it makes sense to think that the World Cup matters more today than it did even in 1990.

For a start, there are far more TV sets in the world now than there were then. The average human (a Chinese peasant, John Travolta, Essex Man) watched six World Cup matches in 1994. In 1950, Britain learned by telegram that the USA had beaten England in Belo Horizonte. Few telegrams send thousands of people out onto the street. Haitians, Rwandans and Bangladeshis saw the games on TV in 1994.

Thanks to TV, the World Cup is the best way we have of ranking the nations of the world. Many people understand life as a constant struggle for status between 200-odd nations. That is how they read the Gulf War (Americans annihilate Arabs in longstanding grudge match), the Maastricht Treaty talks ("Game, set and match to Britain," said John Major), or international trade (Japan beats America, again and again). But the World Cup is the ideal stage. It is hard to compare GDPs in a way that is quite as visually appealing, and in the World Cup the USA does not dominate and little countries have a chance.

For Rumania, the World Cup meant sudden status. To prove it, Rumanian newspapers reprinted stories about the team that had appeared abroad.

"In the World Cup, all we lost is two games. We didn't lose our national honor," a Colombian state governor tried to argue. But he was standing beside Andres Escobar's coffin. In the World Cup you do lose your national honor. The soccer team *is* the nation. "Mexico always attacks. That's what Mexico is," said the Mexican goalkeeper Jorge Campos.

Along with TV sets, democracy is spreading across the world. More and more politicians have to worry about voters, and they turn to soccer. The South Americans are desperate; President Clinton appeared on prime-time TV telephoning the American team; and General Abacha, the Nigerian military ruler, addressed his team almost daily during the World Cup. I put it to the Nigerian sweeper, Chidi Nwanu, that here was a politician trying to steal a bit of glory. Nwanu disagreed. He said the World Cup meant a lot to Nigeria, and it was the head of state's job to acknowledge this.

Cameroon, still under President Biya, was still running short of cash, and Henri Michel, the Lions' French coach, had to pay for soccerballs out of his own pocket. There was no money to send the team to the USA, so the government organized *Action Coup de Coeur*, theoretically to solicit donations from fans. Instead, civil servants, who seldom got paid anyway, were forced to make "voluntary" donations.

Most of the money disappeared and the campaign became known as *Action Coup de Peur*, or *Cri de Coeur*. The players, led by goalkeeper Joseph-Antoine Bell, spent most of the World Cup discussing whether or not to go on strike.

The government officials accompanying the team put pressure on Michel to drop Bell, and to calm things down. Bell retired before the final match against Russia. Russia won 6–1, and *Coup de Coeur* became a big political issue.

Cameroon's goal against Russia was scored by Roger Milla, recalled to the team by President Biya as he had been in 1990. Perhaps Biya will do the same again in 1998, when Milla will be 46.

Silvio Berlusconi, the Italian Prime Minister in 1994, did well out of soccer. Voters deserted the corrupt old parties to elect his new one, Forza Italia, in April 1994. ("Would you vote for a party named after a soccer chant?," I asked a political scientist friend. He thought for a bit. "Yeah, probably," he said.) It was Berlusconi's work as president of AC Milan that persuaded many Italians to vote for him.

He took over Milan in 1986, when they had returned to Serie A after a 1979 bribery scandal. At Milan, Berlusconi created a cosmopolitan, organized, rich team that beat all comers from the rest of Europe. This was exactly what voters wanted him to do for the Italian state, stuck in the European second division after its own bribery scandal. One article on the elections described a bar in which upstairs 40 people were attending a Forza Italia meeting; downstairs, 80 were watching a Milan game. Probably all 120 of them voted for Berlusconi.

But the Brazilians beat the Italians, because their defense was soundest. Brazil's coach, Carlos Alberto Parreira, had ignored the instructions of his mother, President Franco and Pelé, the troika leading those Brazilians who wanted the team to attack more. Parreira pointed out that Brazil had done that before, and lost. His Brazil was more Brazilian than Lazaroni's team of 1990, but more European than Santana's of 1982. Parreira found the synthesis.

"You are asking which is more important—Brazil or a U.S. invasion?," one Haitian fan asked an American reporter in 1994. "We are hungry every day. We have problems every day. The Americans talk about invading every day. But we only have the World Cup every four years."

CHAPTER 20

THE PRESIDENT AND THE BAD BLUE BOYS

IMAGINE IF BRITAIN WERE occupied by Austrians and Serbs. Britons would grumble for a few years, but after a while they would start forgetting they had ever been free, and they would bumble along, falling a little further behind the Germans each year.

But if after hundreds of years they were suddenly freed, they would be pleased. They would say that Britain would now again become a glorious nation, just as it had been when it was led by John Major. They would build a statue of Major sitting on a horse in a main square, and Manchester United, renamed Rapid Manchester by the Austrians, would be given back their old name. For a couple of years Union Jacks would fly from every office. But after a while people would start forgetting that they had ever been occupied, and they would bumble along again, falling a little further behind the Germans each year.

Croatia fought a war and left Yugoslavia in 1992 to become an independent country, after being ruled by Austrians and Serbs for hundreds of years. Walking around Zagreb you see red-and-white checkered flags everywhere, and now, in the main square, as in most central European towns, there is a statue of a local hero sitting on a horse. One tourist brochure told a long story about a Zagreb man "of Czech-Polish origin" who had invented something called a mechanical pencil, which the brochure said had changed the life "of the entire human population." A Zagreb square had just been named after him.

The city is full of people in pork-pie hats walking around shopping for things they can't quite afford, and only at the Dynamo Zagreb ground—for no one calls the club by its new name, Croatia Zagreb—are you reminded that until very recently this country was at war.

A statue of a group of soldiers stands in front of the ground, and the text beneath them says: "To the fans of this club, who started the war with Serbia at this ground on May 13, 1990." No one yet believes that the Yugoslav war really did start at Dynamo Zagreb, but before too long they probably will. "You don't need a century for this to become myth," Zvarko Puhovski, a philosophy professor and basketball fan, grumbled to me.

On May 13, 1990, Dynamo met Red Star Belgrade. The Croats who supported Dynamo and the Serbian fans of Red star fought a battle so fierce that many Yugoslav TV viewers realised then that it was all up with their country—that the quarrels between Serbia and Croatia would lead to war. Westerners tend to have heard about the Cantona-style karate kick that Zvonimir Boban, the great Croat player, deployed on a policeman at the game. However, Boban left Croatia soon after the match to join AC Milan. The Bad Blue Boys, the Dynamo fans, went to war instead.

The Bad Blue Boys named themselves after the Sean Penn movie *Bad Boy*, which they all saw several times. They come from Zagreb suburbs so depressing that the blocks of flats daily surprise you by not falling down. When Yugoslavia was still one country, the BBB—as they are usually called—would follow Dynamo Zagreb to Sarajevo or Belgrade to fight Bosnian or Serbian fans. When war broke out, they put on army uniforms and went to fight Serbian fans in uniform.

The original Croatian army was very largely staffed by the BBB. Many Croats in those days did not feel all that Croatian—after all, they had been living in Yugoslavia for nearly 50 years. Tomoslav

Ivic, the great Croatian coach, said in the early days of the war that he felt Yugoslav and thought that all this fighting was silly.

The Dynamo fans did feel Croat. Puhovski told me that when he was 12 years old his schoolteacher had asked the pupils what they were. Some had said Croat, and others Yugoslav. When two Algerian boys were asked, they said, "We're Croats." The teacher told them that this was absurd. Puhovski then led a protest for the Algerians' right to be Croatian, and was hauled up before the headmaster. "Why do you say that they are Croats?," the headmaster asked. Puhovski replied: "Firstly because they speak Croat, and secondly because they support Dynamo." To support Dynamo was to be a Croat.

When war broke out, many intellectuals also felt Croatian. But, Puhovski told me, "As you know, when a war starts it is not usually the intellectuals who are at the front line firing guns." The Bad Blue Boys went instead. On the Serb side, Arkan (real name Zeljko Raznjatovic), one of the most evil war criminals in Bosnia, was head of Red Star's fan club. He lives in a three-story bunker across the road from the Red Star ground, and he took many of the club's fans with him into Bosnia.

"The soccer fans were really influential in the fighting," Laura Silber, the *Financial Times* correspondent in Belgrade, told me. "It's like the Boy Scouts: if you all go in, it makes an influential force." Laura was getting ready for dinner with a Western ambassador: "Oh, he's so gross. He said to me, 'I don't have time to talk now—but,' " and she put on a Humphrey Bogart voice, " 'why don't you come to dinner?' "

Darko and Neno claim to be the leaders of the BBB. Sitting in Cafe Z, a clean bar full of pretty girls, they told me about the war. Darko, who bears shrapnel wounds from a grenade in Vukovar, tried rolling up his sleeve of his lumberjack shirt to show me the mark on his arm. But the sleeve would not go high enough, and it looked to the other people in Cafe Z as though he was undressing. Embarrassed, he moved up a seat to sit behind a wall, and there he dislodged his clothes enough to show me a discolored patch. On his other arm he displayed a Union Jack with the word "Dynamo" on it. In the 1980s Darko used to sit in the British Council building in Zagreb reading reports about English hooligans in the *Telegraph, The Times* and *Soccer Monthly*. He fell for Chelsea because their fans seemed to be involved in 90 percent of the trouble.

"Chelsea: good mates, good fighters," he told me. "I like the English supporter, because he likes his club very much. It's really the most important thing in the world for him." So the Bad Blue Boys had chosen an English name for themselves, and Darko and Neno were drinking Guinness. They spoke good English, and remembered more as the conversation went on: after about ten minutes they suddenly began using the word "fucking," as in "Vinny Jones is fucking mental."

Darko is now a war invalid, and gets a pension of £350 a month, which he considers lots of money. Prices in Croatia are about as high as in Britain. Some British volunteers had come to fight for Croatia in the war, Darko and Neno said. Most had ended up hanging around with Bad Blue Boys, who are natural groupies for tough Brits. The BBB had worn Dynamo badges on their uniforms, and Neno had slept in a house on the frontline which had a Dynamo flag hanging from the window. Convoys would hoot as they drove past.

"Many people died in this war with the Dynamo emblem on their sleeve," Darko said.

I asked whether he and Neno had lost many friends. They reflected. Five or six had died, they said, but the strange thing was that they had all been killed in car crashes. One friend, who had tried to cross Serb lines, who had been under siege in Vukovar, and who had spent nine months in a POW camp with Darko, had been killed in a crash with a car full of teenagers on his way to a party two days before Christmas.

Darko and Neno no longer go to watch Dynamo. Most of the BBB had stopped going after the Croatian president, Franjo Tudjman, rebaptised the club Croatia during the war. Crowds are now sometimes as low as 1,000, compared with 15,000 before the war. I asked Darko and Neno when they would start going to matches again. "When Dynamo will be the name of the club," Neno said. But I suspected that the truth was that at 27 they had grown out of the BBB. Now that they had fought a war, wandering around Zagreb looking for fans from the Croat provinces to beat up must have seemed a tame way of spending a Sunday afternoon.

The club's name change had cost President Tudjman dearly. Born 25 miles from Zagreb, in a village near the birthplace of his hero Marshall Tito, Tudjman had always been a sports nut. As a young general forty years ago he became president of Partisan Belgrade, the club of the Yugoslav army. Today his political opponents in Croatia often ask: "How can a person lead us who used to run Partisan?"

When Tito had tired of him, Tudjman had returned to Zagreb to work as a historian. He came to believe that Croats had been yearning for independence for 900 years, and he got it into his head he was the Croatian George Washington, the father of the nation. He became president, took to wearing military uniforms, fought a war against Serbia, and started changing the names of streets and soccer clubs. A father of the nation has to change things.

Tudjman had watched Dynamo since his return to Croatia, but as president he took a special interest. Once, a few days before Dynamo were due to play Auxerre in a crucial European match, the club met Primorac in the league. "Before kickoff Tudjman came into our changing room," claimed the Primorac vicechairman. "He said, 'Boys, no illusions. It's going to be 6–0, so pull your feet out of tackles.' Dynamo won 6–0." It is the kind of political support Manchester United would have appreciated before their European games.

Tudjman renamed Dynamo while the BBB were away at war. The first name he chose, HASK Gradjanski, sounded dull, and older people remembered that HASK and Gradjanski had been rival clubs: it was a bit like calling a team Manchester City Manchester United. So the club name was later changed again, to Croatia Zagreb.

Just before I arrived in Zagreb, Tudjman had been speaking at an election rally where he had spotted a Dynamo banner in the crowd. Losing his George Washingtonesque calm, he began berating the fans, whereupon they began chanting, "Dynamo not Croatia!." "If you want Dynamo, go to Serbia!" Tudjman responded. The exchange had not done wonders for his reputation, and a month later his party lost the local elections in Zagreb. All the other parties had pledged to help the club change its name back. "Changing the name was a stupid thing, and it was a very important mistake," Zvonko Makovic, a Croatian poet, told me, minutes before he crashed our car. I had to hitchhike back to Zagreb.

Tudjman lost Dynamo, but he still had the national team. This was more important, as he still had a job to do to make his people feel Croatian. He knew that a clever politician could make people feel anything; Tito had even made them feel Yugoslav. When Yugoslavia beat the USSR in the 1950s, and loudspeakers broadcast the match into the streets, Croats, fresh from massacring Serbs and Jews, began feeling proud of the new state. The feeling grew. On the night in 1980 that the news came of Tito's death, the Croatian crowd and all the players at a Hajduk Split match burst into tears. The game had to be abandoned, and the crying was shown on TV. But Professor Puhovski told me: "Now many of the players are saying that they weren't there, or that the TV pictures are bad, and so on." Everyone's a Croat now.

I went looking for Tomaslav Ivic at halftime of a minor match in Zagreb. Suddenly a small, neat man was hugging me. Unsure whether or not he was Ivic, I began by asking him, "So, what are you doing now?" It emerged that he was Ivic, that he was about to go off and coach the United Arab Emirates, and that he now felt completely Croatian. I told him about the magazine interview three years before in which he had said he could not understand the war. "No, no," he said. "That was not me."

People are malleable. To make all his people Croatian like Ivic, Tudjman wants the new Croatia to do great things. It can't go and conquer the world, because it has a smaller population than Denmark. But quite by chance, Croatia today has a pretty good generation of soccer players.

"It's not nice to say it, but those players can do more for Croatia than a soldier giving his life," I was told by Mark Viduka, an Australian Croat who plays at center-forward for Dynamo. Viduka, whose uncle and grandfather were killed in one night by the Yugoslav army, was unhappy in Croatia, fed up with bad weather and filling in forms. He had not planned to come to Dynamo at all, but Tudjman had telephoned him at home in Melbourne and asked him to. The president thinks that soccer equals prestige.

"It's the same with Miss World," Makovic had told me. "A Croatian girl is always in the top five—well, always since we became independent three years ago. This year Miss Croatia came second, even though in my view she is nothing special, and these things are very important. The Eurovision Song Festival too—these things are questions of prestige."

The Croatian players know this, and go on *ad tedium* about how much their country means to them. They even paid some of their own airfares to play for Croatia. Normal people only briefly get excited about having a new nation, and then get back to their everyday life of working and drinking. I asked Viduka if there had been people celebrating on the streets after Croatia qualified for the European Championships. "No," he said. But people who play for their country's soccer team, and are told by their president that they are helping him to build the new nation, stay patriotic.

Boban, the team captain, is from the south of Croatia, where people are notoriously patriotic, and he never stops talking about his country. However, on the day before Croatia vs. Italy, he admitted to the Italian paper *La Gazzetta dello Sport* that if the match were between Croatian and Italian literary classics instead of soccer players Italy would win hands down. "Dante, Petrarch, Leopardi . . . it wouldn't be a contest," he confessed. Boban should know. He told the *Gazzetta* that his first book had been *The Little Prince* by Antoine de Saint-Exupery, that he had "grown up" on Chekhov and Dostoevsky, that he "adored" Borges, but Marquez less so, and that Roberto Baggio should read Siddharta by Hermann Hesse. To Matarrese, the president of the Italian FA, Boban recommended Nietzsche.

I met Miroslav Blazevic, the national team manager, in the press lounge after a Dynamo game. He spoke good French and I spoke bad French. As far as I know, he told me: "On every occasion before a match I speak to the players of Croatia's problems, the suffering of all our patriots. Because in soccer motivation is very important." Yugoslavia, an unmotivated side, had never won anything, despite always having had some of the best players in Europe.

Was it true that Blazevic discussed tactics with Tudjman before a game? "I speak to him about soccer, because he is an expert on soccer." Or as he once told the president: "After you, I am the one who knows most about soccer."

Tudjman and the manager have a special friendship. Tudjman once even helped Blazevic become both owner and manager of Dynamo Zagreb. But then the name was changed, the club started doing badly, there was management infighting, and Tudjman helped oust Blazevic as owner.

Blazevic, in a Croatian newspaper, recalls a day around this time when Tudjman was playing cards with his ministers and his personal doctor after a game of tennis. (Tudjman wins most of his tennis matches these days.) Blazevic, as usual, was sitting on a small chair behind Tudjman watching the card game. No one was paying any attention to him, and Blazevic could see that they were all fed up with him. However, he stayed. "At that moment pride was born in me, so I sat in a rocking chair and watched TV. Everyone was tacitly asking me, 'What are you doing here?' "

Then, suddenly, Tudjman asked: "Where is Ciro?"—his pet name for Blazevic. "And suddenly," Blazevic recounts, "everyone smiled and started waving at me to sit next to them."

Now Blazevic and Tudjman are best friends again, despite Blazevic's brief embroilment in the Bernard Tapie bribery saga in France. When a Croatian newspaper recently pressed him on the affair, Blazevic began by arguing that he was honest. Then he switched tack, and asked: "Is there any soccer player in the world who has not received money in an illegal way?" And then he began to impress on the magazine how close he was to Tudjman. Before a recent game against Estonia, he said, Tudjman had predicted that Croatia would win 6–1. With 15 minutes to play the score indeed reached 6–1. Blazevic shouted to Boban, the captain: "Stop! Do not score anymore." Sadly, Davor Suker had made it 7–1.

Blazevic was very happy when I met him. He told me that hours before, England had agreed to play his team in a friendly at Wembley. This had eased the slight that the English had delivered by refusing to play Croatia in September 1995. That was just after Croatian troops had invaded the Krajina, the quarter of the country where Serbs lived, and had driven people from their homes and worse. The British Ambassador in Zagreb had to appear on Croatian television to say that the FA's decision to ban the game had had nothing to do with him. The Croats knew why the English refused to play: Britons and Serbs are best friends, and Terry Venables knew that England would lose against Croatia.

The day after Croatia drew against Italy, at a celebratory breakfast, Tudjman had still been talking about the banned match. "It would be very important for Croatia to play at Wembley," he is reported to have said. "But never beg anybody for anything. Let England invite us again!"

Playing in England means something special to Croats. People in Zagreb are keen to let you know that they are not part of the Balkans. They say that Serbia is a crude, Balkan state where people use the Cyrillic alphabet and gouge each other's eyes out and drink too much, while Croatia is a sophisticated, western country very like Sweden or Holland. "We don't belong anymore to this part of the world. We are in Europe," I was told by a man named Zajec, a Croat who had captained Yugoslavia in the 1980s.

In fact, of course, Croatia is a mix of "Europe" and the Balkans. The streets are clean and no one talks to anyone else in the trams, but cafes and nightclubs have signs saying "No guns please," the drinks list on menus is always several times longer than the list of dishes, and there is the little matter of the torture camps in which Croats held Bosnian Moslims. "The others had camps as well," counters Tudjman.

So, Croatia desperately wants to be accepted by the West, and there are few stronger symbols of Western Europe than Wembley. The stadium stands for the old, unchanging Europe. For Croatia, playing at Wembley is almost as if Tudjman were asked to address the House of Commons. To play at Wembley is to be accepted.

Darko and Neno were coming to the European Championships, to watch Croatia and stay with their friends at Chelsea and Sheffield United. They came in peace, they said, however, "If you say fuck off, sure thing I will kick you in the head."

CHAPTER 21

GLOBAL GAME, GLOBAL JiHAD

IN EARLY 1994, OSAMA bin Laden spent three months in London, where he visited supporters and bankers and went to watch Arsenal play four times. Before returning to Sudan a step ahead of being extradited to Saudi Arabia, he bought his sons gifts from the club's souvenir shop.

Bin Laden had been steeped in soccer for most of his life. In fact, it was the game that first drew him toward fundamentalism: as a teenager in the Saudi Arabian town of Jedda, Bin Laden was one of a group of boys persuaded by a Syrian gym teacher to stay after school in the afternoons, on the promise that they could play soccer. The Syrian then educated them in a violent brand of Islam, as Steve Coll reported in the *New Yorker* in December 2005.

Bin Laden's affection for the game did not stop him from getting involved in a plot to massacre the American and British teams at the World Cup of 1998; still, after his visit to London, he told friends he had never seen passion like that of soccer fans.

Possibly nowhere else does soccer have more importance today than in the Middle East and North Africa. To the region's terrorists, the game must seem the perfect entertainment: a traditionally masculine and sexless passion with a global reach, often contested between opposing tribes. The local dictators—a dying breed elsewhere in the world—use soccer for prestige. And to find dissent in these dictatorships, go to the stadium.

One reason soccer matters so much in this part of the world is that there are few other entertainments going. There's a joke told about various of the region's capitals, which has a foreign visitor getting into a taxi. "Listen," whispers the taxi driver, "do you want to go to a place where you can have some fun?" "Yes," says the foreigner. "And where you can get a drink?" "Yes," says the foreigner. "And where there are women?" "Yes!" says the foreigner. "There isn't one," says the driver.

For a young man in the Middle East, obliged to spend his leisure time hanging around with other young men, soccer is often the only recreation. That's why in Tripoli, the Libyan capital, games between the two biggest clubs draw crowds of 100,000—more than anywhere in Europe except occasionally at Barcelona or Real Madrid. All this passion hasn't made the region any good at soccer. If you inhibit most exchange with the West—if your best players don't join European clubs, or watch European soccer on TV, or play against European teams—bad soccer is the almost inevitable result. Yet the game does help us understand this secretive region. In societies like Libya, Iran, and previously in Saddam Hussein's Iraq, where there is no free press, no legal dissent, and hardly any foreign journalists, soccer can reveal the undercurrents.

Iraq. When the Finnish translator of this book visited Iraq as a journalist in 2002, several months before the U.S. invaded, he was surprised to find himself constantly engaged by Iraqi men in erudite debate about European soccer. Didn't he agree, for instance, that Luis Figo was not playing quite as well for Real Madrid as he had for Barcelona?

My friend discovered that Iraqis watched oodles of European soccer on both satellite and state television. Many of them walked around in the club stripes of Manchester United, Juventus, or Real Madrid, or at least pirated versions bought in Baghdad markets. He was delighted with the almost perfectly authentic-looking Arsenal strip he got for just $10.

Going to a match, he was surprised to find that the soccer was excellent too. This was partly because, as President Bush used to complain, the sanctions against Iraq were not watertight. The country had sent four athletes to the Olympics of 2000, while the national soccer team happily played in international competitions, in 2002 winning the West Asian Soccer Championship in Syria. It had prepared for that with a training camp in Italy.

Even while waiting for the Americans to invade, fans were preoccupied by Iraq's soccer league and the Mother of All Battles Cup. In fact, then probably more than ever: the soccer stadium was a good place briefly to forget that your relatives might soon be tortured in one of Saddam's gulags, or your country razed by American bombs. So trying to forget politics for a couple of hours, Iraqis went to cheer on the Police Club or the Air Force Club or the Anti-Aircraft Club.

Saddam's family liked sport. Each April, to celebrate Saddam's birthday, Baghdad hosted the Saddam Olympics. You won't have caught these on Fox Sports, but in their final incarnation in 2002, with Baghdad's Russian–Iraqi Friendship Society as sponsor, they attracted athletes from seventy-two countries. Perhaps inspired by this, Saddam's Iraq was bidding to host the 2012 Olympics. The plan was to build a 100,000-seat stadium in Baghdad that would meet all international standards, and include a sealed-off VIP area for Saddam and his entourage. Who knows whether London would be hosting the Games if Saddam had been free to lobby IOC members?

However, the president mostly left sport to his son Uday. A mix of playboy and torturer, paralyzed from the waist down in an assassination attempt in 1996, Uday has no equivalent in the sport of any other country. He ran Iraq's soccer federation, its Olympic Committee, and also a prison in the National Olympic Committee building, where athletes were tortured if they underperformed. Many Iraqi athletes quit sport out of fear. One member of the national soccer team in the Uday era reported being beaten on the soles of his feet, dragged on his bare back through gravel, and then put in a sewage tank so that his wounds would be infected. Other defectors told similar stories. Issam Thamer al-Diwan, a former Iraqi volleyball player who now lives in the U.S., told *Sports Illustrated* that he carried a list of fifty-two athletes he says were murdered by Saddam's family.

FIFA sent a committee to Iraq to investigate the claims of torture. The Iraqis produced players and coaches who swore blind it was all lies. FIFA swallowed this, and so Saddam's Iraq was allowed to play international soccer. American soldiers killed Uday and his brother Qusay in July 2003, after a tipster betrayed their hideout.

Libya. In Libya, Colonel Qaddafi used to be wary of sport. He devoted the last chapter of his Little Green Book, the Qaddafi answer to Mao's Little Red Book, to an attack on spectator sports. "It is stupid for crowds to enter a restaurant just to look at a person or a groups of persons eating," he wrote. "The same holds true of the crowds which fail to practise sport themselves because of their ignorance."

The colonel had reason to be wary. Libya is the epitome of the country where the only haven of free speech is the soccer stadium. "The last display of public discontent and resentment towards the [Libyan] government," reported the U.S. State Department in 1999, "occurred when a riot broke out over a penalty called at a soccer match in Tripoli on July 9, 1996. The rare instance of public unrest began when a contentious goal was scored by a team that Qaddafi's sons supported and the referee called the play in their favor."

Fans started chanting anti-Qaddafi slogans, whereupon the ruler's sons and their bodyguards began shooting (some say at each other). Spectators stampeded onto the streets, where they stoned cars and continued to chant against Qaddafi. The government later admitted that eight people had died, but others spoke of up to fifty deaths. The most extraordinary thing was that because all this occurred at a big soccer match, it was shown live on TV. For the first time Libyans could see that dissent existed. A Spanish woman who worked in Tripoli at the time told me that after that game, people suddenly began approaching her with complaints about the regime.

It was only later, though, that soccer in Libya acquired a political piquancy it possesses nowhere else. Around the turn of the millennium, the colonel's son Saidi decided he wanted to play for the national team. At the time he did not even play for a club—as he was chairman of the Libyan soccer association, that would have broken Libya's strict ethics codes—and so he hired a private Dutch trainer.

Saidi pumped much of Libya's oil money into soccer. Stadiums shot out of the sand like oil. On the advice of Saidi's friend and mentor Diego Maradona, Carlos Bilardo, who had coached Argentina to the World Cup of 1986, came to manage the national team. The disgraced Canadian sprinter Ben Johnson (apparently the world's worst soccer player) became the team's athletics coach.

Later, when Saidi did join a Libyan club, the odd hilarious video would emerge of opposing defenders running away from the ball to let him shoot. Meanwhile, the stadium during his team's matches became the one place where people could mock a symbol of the Qaddafis. When a donkey wearing a team shirt with the No. 10 was kicked onto the pitch during one game, everyone understood that it represented Al Saidi. He must have had some admirers, though: Saidiwas named Libyan soccer's MVP, and became captain of the national team.

Eventually, like so many great players, he moved to Italy's Serie A. He began at Perugia, where he appeared in one match, but was soon banned for taking drugs. (Perhaps he had been listening to Maradona and Ben Johnson.) Despite all this, Udinese was delighted to sign him next. As I write, Saidi and his entourage are occupying the finest hotel in Udine (which isn't saying much for someone used to spending his country's oil wealth). He has yet to appear in an Udinese game, but all of us who ever dreamed of being a pro know exactly why he is there.

It's thought that Saidi pops Udinese the odd few euros, in contravention of the tradition that a club pays its players. But the Italian club that gets most Libyan oil money is Juventus. In 2002

Saidi's father bought a stake in the great Turin club. Now the Qaddafis are paying $285 million over ten years to advertise Libya's oil company, Tamoil, on Juve's shirts. It's the biggest shirt deal in soccer, even though you wouldn't have thought an oil producer had much need to reach consumers. The sponsorship may just be Qaddafi megalomania. On the other hand, it may be more thoughtful than that: perhaps the Qaddafis, by entwining themselves with one of Italy's most popular institutions, hope to have the country's friendship next time Libya squabbles with the U.S.

Iran. The game may matter even more in Iran, where at times in recent years observers have spoken of "a soccer revolution." This began in 1997, when Iran beat Australia to qualify for the 1998 World Cup, and great crowds poured onto the streets. Thousands of women broke into the Azadi stadium to join the celebrations, with some removing their veils. (Few countries seem to have as passionate female soccer fans as Iran.) At street parties across the country, men and women danced and kissed, defying government warnings and clerical taboos. It was a popular explosion on a scale not seen even when Ayatollah Khomeini returned from exile in February 1979.

At the 1998 World Cup, I saw the Iran–USA game in Lyon. Beforehand, the newspapers had portrayed the match as a clash of two great enemies. The hardline conservative press in Iran had warned the Iranian players not to shake hands with the representatives of the Great Satan.

In fact, the American and Iranian players showed no great interest in each other. "None of the players is viewing it as anything other than an incredible opportunity to get three points against a team we should beat," Alexei Lalas, the goateed American defender, assured me when I visited the U.S. team's chateau before the game.

And indeed, at the match, the political clash was not between Iranians and Americans at all, but between Iranians and Iranians. Most of the spectators in the ground seemed to be Iranians in exile.

They all wore T-shirts showing the face of the female leader of Iran's *mujahedin*, an opposition group then based in Iraq. Every time the ball went into the stands, people would stand up holding forward their T-shirts for the world's cameras to see.

The only problem was that the cameras didn't show them. I was sitting in the press stand, with a television on my desk, and could see that whenever the ball went out of play, the surroundings were blacked out. Fifa, which could teach courses on media management to aspiring dictators, had apparently decided to censor anything political. And so the mujahedin's demonstration never reached the hundreds of millions watching on TV.

Yet that World Cup introduced many Iranians to soccer. Fandom began to replace cigarette smoking as the iconic image of Western youth culture. A British friend of mine, walking through the Iranian town Isfahan soon after the September 11 attacks, was approached by a student who bombarded him with questions: "You are from England? After Israel and America, you are our biggest enemy. Don't you think George Bush is the biggest terrorist of all for supporting Israel? Do you think Beckham should play on the right for Manchester United, or in the center?"

Trying to answer at least the last two questions, my friend said: "Sure. On the right?"

"What?" said the flabbergasted student. "And Paul Scholes in the center?"

That fall of 2001, as Iran looked as if it would qualify for the World Cup again, the street parties resumed. Initially the fans just seemed to be expressing nationalism, but in some towns the mood changed. Fans attacked state-owned banks and other public buildings, chanting, "Death to the Mullahs." There were chants in support of the exiled monarchy. Hundreds, perhaps thousands of people were arrested over several nights. Eventually Iran had only to beat tiny Bahrain to qualify for the World Cup. The tournament would have brought weeks of street parties and demonstrations. So when

Iran lost the game 3-1, rumors abounded in Tehran that the mullahs had pressured the players to lose, in what may be a unique case of a regime wanting its national team to fail. No one knows, but Iran's forwards appeared so unwilling to try to score that eventually the Iranian television commentator exclaimed, "Why doesn't someone shoot that ball?" A few thousand people, who believed the government had ordered Iran's defeat, subsequently clashed with police.

In November 2001, in a playoff against Ireland, Iran failed in its last attempt to reach the World Cup. Nicola Byrne, an Irish woman who was among the forty or so foreign women admitted to the Azadi stadium by special dispensation of the Iranian authorities, reported in London's *Observer*, "Under an enormous mural of the late Ayatollah Khomeini, Iranians ripped out and set fire to seats, tore down banners depicting images of the country's senior mullahs and trashed the windows of several hundred cars outside."

In 2005, when Iran did qualify for the World Cup, many of the team's victories sparked demonstrations. After the team beat Japan that March, six fans were reported to have been killed, the worst toll yet in Iranian soccer, possibly by police firing at demonstrators after the match.

A few Iranian women had been allowed to watch the game against Japan. The right of women to watch soccer became an issue in the presidential elections that June. Akbar Hashemi Rafsanjani, trying to woo young people, said he favored permitting it. But he lost the election to an even more conservative man, Mahmoud Ahmadinejad.

In fact, Iran's "soccer revolution," in each of its incarnations, has changed nothing. This illustrates a greater truth about soccer and politics: the game is a good way of studying what is going on in repressed societies, but it rarely changes these societies.

Terrorists have long been enchanted by soccer. To them it is often more than just a hobby. The two pursuits have certain similarities. Being a member of a soccer team is a form of male bonding not completely unlike being a member of an Islamic terrorist cell. In both groups, young men tend to develop a sense of "us against the world." It's no wonder that the Palestinian soccer team of the Jihad mosque in Hebron doubled as an incubator of suicide bombers: five of its players blew themselves up attacking Israeli targets.

But the main allure of soccer to terrorists is the game's global reach. Terrorism is a form of public relations. The aim is to spread the greatest fear with the least effort. To do that, terrorists seek out the most public places and events. That means sport. This is why the Palestinian group "Black September" kidnapped and killed eleven Israeli athletes at the Munich Olympics of 1972. Thanks to recent improvements in satellite technology, hundreds of millions of people watched the horror live on TV. Terrorists everywhere realized that sport could bring them a big audience.

Louis Mizell, a former special agent and intelligence officer with the state department, told me in 2005 that he had logged 171 terrorist attacks in sport since Munich. When anti-Castro murderers exploded a plane carrying the Cuban fencing team in 1976, they may not have been thinking chiefly about sport, but later terrorists were. Many atrocities are hardly remembered today: the twenty Philippine soldiers killed in a race in 1987, after terrorists posing as volunteers handed them poisoned water; or the Canadian killed by a booby-trapped softball bat at a tournament in Chile in 1990. Perhaps the worst atrocity was North Korea's explosion of a South Korean airliner in 1987, which killed all 115 passengers. "The whole plan was to destabilize the 1988 Olympics in Seoul," says Mizell, who worked on the case. But he adds: "The single sport targeted most is soccer, because it's the most popular sport in the world."

Most terrorists used to be parochial. But in recent years, a new breed has arisen that seeks a global audience. And just as they began to go global, so did soccer. Since the 1990s the game has been conquering the final frontiers: Americans, Japanese, Chinese, women. It has left almost all other sports behind. The World Cup, in particular, has been spread by satellite dishes to the farthest-flung places. Each successive World Cup final becomes the most watched television program in the history of the world.

The tournament was bound to attract terrorists eventually. On March 3, 1998, seven members of an Algerian terrorist group were arrested in a raid on a house in Belgium. On May 26, European police launched raids on dozens of suspects' homes. Nearly 100 people in seven countries were taken in for questioning. "It was a matter of urgency," said a French government spokesman later that day. "Now we can approach the World Cup more serenely."

Terrorism was then considered something of a yawn, and the episode was soon forgotten. European police never said much more about it. However, the plot against the World Cup is detailed in the curiously ignored book *Terror on the Pitch* by Adam Robinson, the pen name of a journalist based in the Middle East. Quoting letters detailing the plot sent by members of the Algerian Armed Islamic Group, Robinson says they meant to strike at the England–Tunisia game on June 15, 1998. Why England? Partly because the well-known young players Michael Owen and David Beckham were already in their squad, such an attack would make news.

The terrorists planned to infiltrate the Marseilles stadium, shoot some England players, blow up others, and throw grenades into the stands. Their colleagues were then to burst into the U.S. team's hotel and murder players. Others would crash a plane into the nuclear power station near the French town of Poitiers, causing meltdown. The result would have been a European September 11, only worse. It is possible to dismiss this as a terrorist wish list, but we now know that these people aren't dreamers.

Many Algerian terrorists had served in Al Qaeda. Bin Laden, writes Robinson, "had funded and helped organize the plan when it was presented to him, and agreed to offer additional funding and arms, in addition to the Algerians sending key personnel for expert training in Al Qaeda camps."

One bin Laden biographer, Yossef Bodansky, writes that the plan reactivated "dormant terrorist networks." He says one reason why Al Qaeda bombed the American embassies in Kenya and Tanzania in August 1998, killing 224 people, was "the failure of the primary operation, an attack on the soccer World Cup." The chief plotter against the World Cup, Omar Saiki, spent less than two years in jail, after which he requested political asylum in Britain.

After September 11, 2001, when the world was introduced to bin Laden, Arsenal fans coined a new chant:

He's hiding near Kabul
He loves the Arsenal
Osama
Oh oh oh oh

Soon after that, bin Laden showed that he and his followers still retained a soccer fan's view of the world. In December 2001, the U.S. Department of Defense released a videotape of him reminiscing about the September 11 attacks. On it, bin Laden recalls a follower telling him a year earlier: "I saw in a dream, we were playing a soccer game against the Americans. When our team showed up in the field, they were all pilots!" In the dream, the Al Qaeda pilots won the game.

On the same tape, another Al Qaeda member recounts watching a television broadcast of the attacks on the World Trade Center. "The scene was showing an Egyptian family sitting in their living room. They exploded with joy. Do you know when there is a soccer game and your team wins? It was the same expression of joy." The Manichean worldview of the terrorist had met the Manichean worldview of the soccer fan. This, as much as anything I had seen anywhere else, was soccer against the enemy.

WHERE ARE THEY NOW?

IT'S BEEN TWELVE YEARS since I finished my journey around the world to research this book. I will never do it again. Forty-eight hours in a Ukrainian train, weeks without hot water, and conversations in languages I don't speak—I have had enough. When the manuscript began rolling off the printer in my parents' house in London, at 2 A.M. on September 5, 1993, I felt as if I had had a baby.

What I remember most about the hundreds of people I met while writing the book is how nice almost all of them were. I was twenty-two to twenty-three years old (I celebrated my birthday with a falafel in Barcelona), shabbily dressed, staying in youth hostels, and claiming on no evidence to be an English journalist writing a book. Nevertheless, many gave hours of their time to answer my questions, and only a few seemed motivated by egomania. Unfortunately I have kept track of just a handful of them and their stories.

The Dutch have begun to feel ashamed of their anti-German outburst in 1988–1992. Lately they have come to accept that their wartime behavior was mostly gray and cowardly. The younger generation has stopped laying claim to the heroism of the handful of mostly dead resistance fighters. In January 2003 I published a book devoted largely to this subject: *Ajax, The Dutch, The War: Football in Europe During the Second World War.* As I predicted, Holland vs. Germany is not such a grudge match anymore.

I kept in touch with Helmut Klopfleisch for years. When he came to England for Euro 96, I bought him lunch. It was the least

I could do. In 1999 I went to a Hertha Berlin game with him. But he was then a sad man, in poor health, who had never recovered from his experiences in the GDR.

I have not been back to the Baltics again. But I have practically stalked Richard Möller Nielsen, whom I first met in Latvia. He appears three times in this book, and when I wrote an extra chapter on Finnish soccer for the Finnish edition of this book in 1999, he appeared in that again: Fate had arranged for him to be manager of Finland just when I arrived in the country. In January 2000 he and I landed in Israel at the same time, he to coach the national team, me to research the book about Ajax. We didn't meet. I'm sure it bothers him.

Andrius Kubilius is one of the few people in this book to achieve fame after meeting me. In 1999 he became Lithuanian prime minister. He only lasted a year, but that was pretty good for a Lithuanian prime minister. I still remember him fondly, for sitting down a nervous twenty-two-year-old chancer in torn clothes and answering his questions about soccer. Kubilius is now the leader of Lithuania's conservative opposition.

I returned to Moscow in 2002, and what a cold and depressing experience it was. The city center now has Starbucks and designer fashion stores and some wealthy people. But the hope I sensed in 1992 that things could get better, that Russia could become a happy country, had disappeared.

I think I'll skip Kiev for the next few decades. I worry that some Ukrainian mafioso has heard of the chapter I wrote and is angry. I am also worried that the Dynamo official who told me everything has been made to suffer for it. I changed his name, but any insider could recognize him easily. I have not heard a word of him since.

Paul Gascoigne is now battling with alcoholism, Margaret Thatcher with memory loss, and John Major—British prime minister for nearly seven years—has simply been forgotten. But every time Britain gets a new prime minister or England a new manager, I write an updated version of this chapter for a magazine.

Helenio Herrera died in 1997. Somebody told me that he and his wife separated shortly before his death. Last I heard, she was campaigning to get him buried in the English cemetery in Venice.

There has been little to celebrate in African football lately. To my regret, I was right to predict African football would get worse. Cameroon has been through a miserable thirteen years too. In October 2004, President Paul Biya won a new seven-year term in presidential elections that, according to Commonwealth observers, lacked credibility in key areas. The country remains extremely corrupt. I feel sorry for my friend Charles: a gifted young man in the wrong place. Every now and then I wonder what happened to the Cameroon *Post* journalists in their hideout. Nobody outside the country seems to care, and Cameroon continues to make news only through soccer, most recently when their midfielder Marc-Vivien Foé dropped dead on the pitch in Lyons in 2003.

When I saw Thabo Mbeki lining up patiently at the Botswana border I took it as a good omen. In 1999 he was elected successor to Nelson Mandela as a president of South Africa, becoming only the second man in this book to run a country after meeting me. The Pahad brothers are powers behind the throne. I met Essop again in February 2003, on the veranda of his lovely house in Johannesburg with a swimming pool and a tennis court, and again since. He is as charming as ever, minister in the presidency, and a member of South Africa's organizing committee for the World Cup of 2010. He insisted that I not identify the English team he was starting to like more and more.

Eric Wynalda's good half season in Saarbrücken proved to be the highlight of his career. In the 1994 World Cup he scored a beautiful free kick against Switzerland, but four years later he was as bad as the rest of the team. He is retired now—not that anyone outside the U.S. cares, nor many people inside either. However, Bora Milutinovic grew into something of a legend. As China's coach in 2002, he became the only man to lead five different teams at five World Cups in a row.

At Euro 96 I ran into Bobby Charlton again, and he didn't remember me. I got his autograph for a cousin. A couple of months later, at a reception in London, I spotted a familiar face: the diplomat who had introduced me to Charlton in 1993. He had forgotten me too. Maradona is now a talk-show host. Carlos Menem reluctantly stepped down as president and then almost got the job back in 2003, but by then Argentine voters had wised up.

In August 1999 I visited Brazil for the second time and interviewed Carlos Alberto Parreira again. He was no longer the manager of Brazil, but of Fluminense, then in the third division. In the posh neighborhood around the club's ground, we watched kids kick around on a playground, and when Parreira patted one of them on the head, the boy did not even look round.

Parreira had become a pariah in Brazil. Nobody seemed to be grateful to him for leading the country to the World Cup in 1994, because they played boring football. Parreira told me that, in retrospect, he should have given up coaching after winning the Cup. He could not achieve anything greater than that. Yet now (at the time of writing, anyway) he is about to manage Brazil at a World Cup again. Weird.

I returned to Glasgow in April 1999. The weather was still miserable, the city ugly and the mood rude. I suspect that if Glasgow were a pleasant place, Celtics and Rangers fans would be sweet and shiny people. I have had another couple of meetings with Mark Dingwall, who has grown older but stayed a fanatic. He has spent a lifetime in the stands shouting the same curses.

Maurice Johnston, once the Salman Rushdie of Scottish soccer, became coach of the New York Metrostars in November 2005. The club's president and general manager, Alexei Lalas, said: "The fact that he's a fellow redhead only made my decision easier. I've been saying for years that we don't have enough of the mutant gene in MLS."

Mark Viduka, whom I met at the start of his career, ended up having a fine one. At the time of writing he is thirty years old, playing for Middlesbrough in the English Premier League, and about to captain Australia in the World Cup. Zagreb is probably just a bad memory for him now, as it is for me.

President Tudjman died in December 1999. Croatia seems to be becoming a decent country again.

BiBLiOGRAPHY

General Works:
Lincoln Allison (ed.). *The Politics of Sport* (Manchester University Press, Manchester, 1986).
Peter Ball and Phil Shaw (eds.). *The Book of Soccer Quotations* (Stanley Paul, London, 1986).
Neil Blain, Raymond Boyle and Hugh O'Donnell. *Sport and National Identity in the European Media* (Leicester University Press, Leicester, 1993).
François Colin and Lex Muller. *Standaard gouden voetbalgids* (Standaard, Antwerp, 1982).
Ronald Frankenberg (ed.). *Cultural Aspects of Soccer, Sociological Review*, Vol. 39, August 1991 (Routledge, London, 1991).
Brian Glanville. *The Puffin Book of Soccer players* (Puffin Books, Harmondsworth, 1978).
Brian Glanville. *Champions of Europe* (Guinness, Enfield, 1991).
Philip Goodhart and Christopher Chataway. *War Without Weapons* (W.H. Allen, London, 1968).
A. Tomlinson and G. Whannel (eds.). *Off the Ball* (Pluto, London, 1986).

Russia:
Nikolai Starostin. *Futbol skvoz gody* (Sovetskaya Rossiya, Moscow, 1989).

Paul Gascoigne:
Robin McGiven. *Gazza! A Biography* (Penguin Books, London, 1990).

Bobby Robson:
Pete Davies. *All Played Out* (Heinemann, London, 1990).
Arnold Mühren and Jaap de Groot. *Alles over links* (SSP, Hoornaar, 1989).
Nico Scheepmaker. *Cruijff, Hendrik Johannes, fenomeen, 1947–1984* (Van Holkema & Warendorf/Unieboek, Weesp, 1984).

Holland vs. Germany:
Lútsen B. Jansen. *Bekend en onbemind: Het beeld van Duitsland en Duitsers onder jongeren van vijftien tot negentien jaar* (Clingendael Institute, The Hague, 1993).
Theun de Winter (ed.). *Nederland-Duitsland: voetbalpoëzie* (Gerard Timmer Productions, Amsterdam, 1989).

Old Firm:

Raymond Boyle. *Faithful Through and Through: A Survey of Celtic F.C.'s Most Committed Supporters* (National Identity Research Unit, Glasgow, 1991).

Jimmy Johnstone and J. McCann. *Jinky . . . Now and Then. The Jimmy Johnstone Story* (Edinburgh, 1987).

Archie McPherson. *Action Replays* (Chapmans, London, 1992).

Bill Murray. *The Old Firm* (John Donald, Edinburgh, 1984).

Bill Murray. *Glasgow Giants: A Hundred Years of the Old Firm* (Mainstream, 1988).

South Africa:

Robert Archer and Antoine Bouillon. *The South African Game: Sport and Racism* (Zed Press, London, 1982).

Argentina:

Joseph L. Arbena. "Generals and Goles: Assessing the Connection Between the Military and Soccer in Argentina," in the *International Journal of the History of Sport*, Vol. 7, No. 1, May 1990.

Eduardo P. Archetti. "In Search of National Identity: Argentinian Soccer and Europe," paper presented at the conference *"Le soccer et l'Europe,"* European University Institute, Florence, May 1990.

Eduardo P. Archetti. "Masculinity and Soccer: The Formation of National Identity in Argentina," paper presented at the conference "Soccer: Identity and Culture," University of Aberdeen, April 1992.

Eduardo P. Archetti. "Argentine Soccer: A Ritual of Violence?," in the *International Journal of the History of Sport*, Vol. 9, No. 2, August 1992.

Eduardo P. Archetti and Amílcar Romero. "Death and Violence in Argentinian Soccer," unpublished paper, January 1993.

Osvaldo Bayer. *Fútbol argentino* (Editorial Sudamericana, Buenos Aires, 1990).

Carlos Ferreira. *A mi juego . . .* (Ediciones La Campana, Buenos Aires, 1983).

Amílcar G. Romero. *Deporte, violencia y política (crónica negra 1958–1983)* (Biblioteca Política Argentina, Buenos Aires, 1985).

John Simpson and Jana Bennett. *The Disappeared: Voices from a Secret War* (Robson Books, London, 1985).

Brazil:

Janet Lever. *Soccer Madness* (University of Chicago Press, Chicago, 1984).

I also drew heavily on the following magazines: *France Soccer, Follow, Follow, Not the View, Shedzine, Voetbal International, Vrij Nederland, When Saturday Comes* and *World Soccer.*